The Mitchell Beazley Nature Library

Wild Flowers

Peter D. Moore Ph.D.

Mitchell Beazley

Nomenclature

The common names of wild flowers vary widely and are often misleading, but the scientific (Latin) name is determined by strict international rules. Every plant has a double name: the first is the genus name, the second the species (specific) name. Thus Lords and ladies or Cuckoo pint is always given the Latin name *Arum maculatum*. Each genus contains one or more species; several related genera are grouped into a family—*Arum* is in the family Araceae. A species may be divided into subspecies showing a small variation and have a third name: e.g. the bog orchid is *Orchis laxiflora* subsp *palustris*. This book follows the Latin names used in the standard work *Flora Europaea* (see p. 192).

Abbreviations

alt	alternate	hrlss	hairless	seg	segment
ann	annual	Ht	height	sev	several
bi	biennial	inc	including	sh	shoot
br	branch	indiv	individual	sim	similar
c.	about	infl	inflorescence	sol	solitary
cm	centimetre	lf(y)	leaf(y)	sp(p)	species (plural)
col	colour	lflt	leaflet	spl	sepal
D	distribution	lvs	leaves	stk(d)	stalk(ed)
decid	deciduous	m	metre	stm	stamen
diam	diameter	mm	millimetre	str	structure
esp	especially	mts	mountains	subsp	subspecies
fl	flower	nr	near	succ	succulent
Fl	flowering season	opp	opposite	unstkd	unstalked
fr	fruit	per	perennial	uprt	upright
frag	fragrant	pr(d)	pair(ed)	v	very
gp	group	ptl	petal	veg	vegetative
hr(y)	hair(y)	rt	root	yr	year

♂ male ♀ female 1–12 months of the year January–December

Distribution (D) **throughout Europe**

Arct	Arctic	NE	Northeastern (E Baltic–Finland)
C	Central (E France–Poland)	NW	Northwestern (Britain–Scandinavia)
Carp	Carpathians	Nwy	Norway
Dk	Denmark	S	Southern (France–S Germany)
E	Eastern (E Germany–E Baltic)	SE	Southeastern (S Germany–Czechoslovakia)
EC	East Central (E Germany–Poland)	SW	Southwestern (France–SW Britain)
Eng	England	Swed	Sweden
Eur	Europe	T	Throughout
Fenno-scand	Fennoscandinavia (Scandinavia–Finland	UK	United Kingdom
Fin	Finland	W	Western (Britain–France–W Scandinavia)
GB	Great Britain		
Med	Mediterranean		
N	Northern (N Britain–Denmark–Fennoscandinavia)		

Editor Ruth Binney **Executive Editor** Susannah Read
Designer Derek St Romaine **Art Editor** Douglas Wilson
Production Julian Deeming

Illustrators Jac Jones/The Garden Studio; Josephine Martin/The Garden Studio; Nina Roberts/The Garden Studio; Kathleen Smith; Gill Tomblin

First published in 1980 as
The Mitchell Beazley Pocket Guide to Wild Flowers
This edition published 1983

Edited and designed by
Mitchell Beazley Publishers Limited
87–89 Shaftesbury Avenue, London W1V 7AD

ISBN 0 85533 497 5

Typeset by Tradespools Ltd, Frome
Colour reproduction by Photoprint Plates
Printed and bound in Hong Kong by Mandarin Offset International Ltd

Contents

Habitat symbols 4
Glossary 4
Plant key 6
The plants 12
Index 182
Further reading 192

Introduction

The sheer beauty of wild flowers needs no emphasis, yet their enjoyment can be greatly enhanced when spiced with more understanding of their construction and relations to one another. Fundamental to this fuller knowledge is correct identification and it is here that we seek to meet the naturalist's needs.

One valuable feature of plants is their immobility—but this also makes them vulnerable for they are easily destroyed by careless misuse. This book is designed so that it can easily be carried into the field for on-the-spot identification, making it unnecessary to collect specimens and so deplete the countryside of its natural heritage. The serious field botanist will also need a hand lens (× 10 is the ideal magnification) and a notebook. Sometimes it may be necessary to remove a single flower (but *only* if the plant is widespread) to look at it in detail by cutting a section through it, so take a pocket scalpel with you.

Over 1,000 European wild flower species are illustrated in this book, and others are mentioned in the text. The selection of plants has been based on their frequency and ease of identification; some have been omitted because their special features are too complex. Geographically the book covers N Europe, south to the Massif Central in France and east to the Soviet Union. The many lovely plants exclusive to the Alps and the Mediterranean are not here as they are too numerous to deal with fully.

How to use this book

The best way to begin identifying a wild flower is to keep this book closed and examine the plant! It may be tempting to flick through the pictures but this is not the most effective and not necessarily the quickest way to achieve accurate identification.

Start with the whole plant. What size is it? Is it erect, creeping or tussock-forming? How are its leaves arranged? What shape and size are they? Are they stalked or hairy? Are the stem leaves different from those at the base? Are the flowers arranged singly or in groups? Now look more closely at the flower and examine a single one in detail (the explanations on pages 4–6 show plant parts and the ways they can be arranged). How many sepals and petals has it? Are they joined or completely free from one another? Are the sepals hairy? What colour are the petals? How many stamens are there? Are they attached to the petals or to the base of the flower? Now examine the carpels. This may be more difficult for they are often fused in a group—if so, are their styles and stigmas free? It may be helpful to cut a section across the ovary to count the number of cells inside, but let common sense be your guide. Finally note the type of habitat in which the plant is growing, e.g. heathland, roadside or grassland, and any obvious environmental features such as damp or chalky soil.

With all this information you should now be able to tackle the key to plant families on pages 6–11; then turn to the pages dealing with the family to which the plant belongs and check against the pictures and descriptions of key features of each species. Do not rely on the illustrations alone; always check that the plant also matches with its "word picture".

Alongside the Latin and English common names of each plant are symbols showing the habitat in which it is most likely to be growing. These are explained on the next page. Because plant heights are very variable an average figure is given; the same is true for some plant parts. Unless stated, the measurement refers to the length of the part concerned. To save space abbreviations have been used (see opposite). Technical terms have been kept to a minimum but those used are explained on pp. 4–5.

Habitat symbols

Woods, forests, grassland

- Coniferous woods
- Deciduous woods
- Grassland, meadows
- Chalk and limestone grassland

Mountain, moorland

- Mountain grassland
- Mountain rocks, scree
- Heath, moorland

Freshwater

- Marsh and fens
- Bogs
- Aquatic
- Banks, edges
- Salt marsh

Disturbed ground

- Wasteland, arable
- Hedges, scrub
- Roadsides
- Walls

Maritime

- Sand dunes
- Shingle
- Cliffs
- Near sea
- Sea

Soils

- Damp soil
- Acid soil
- Chalky soil
- Sandy soil

Glossary

Above towards the top of a plant or plant part; upper surface of a leaf
Achene one-seeded dry fruit that does not split
Alternate (alt) leaves growing singly at nodes on either side of a stem
Anther pollen-producing organ, top part of a stamen
Axil the angle between a stem and a leaf or bract
Axillary growing in an axil
Basal nearest the ground
Below towards the base of a plant or plant part; lower surface of a leaf
Biennial (bi) plant taking more than one but less than two years to complete its life cycle
Bifid, bifurcating forked into two
Bloom powdery or waxy covering
Bract leaf-like structure with a flower in its axil or, in Compositae (daisy family), in a whorl round flower head
Bracteole a secondary bract usually on the flower stalk or, in Umbelliferae (carrot family) bract-like structure at the base of a secondary umbel
Bulbil small bulb found in leaf axils or among flowers
Capsule dry fruit that splits open when ripe
Carpel single female unit of a flower consisting of the stigma, style and ovary (see p 6)
Cell seed-containing cavity in an ovary, best seen by cutting ovary horizontally
Compound in several parts, as a leaf divided into leaflets
Corm swollen underground stem
Elliptic oval and narrowed at the ends
Emergent part of an aquatic plant growing above water
Entire not divided—without teeth or lobes
Epicalyx extra sepal ring outside true sepals
Equal the same length
Floret one of the small flowers in a composite (e.g. daisy); disc florets are tubular, ray florets strap-shaped
Follicle dry fruit that splits down one side only
Glaucous blue-grey in colour, covered with a bloom
Head compact mass of flowers or florets
Helmet hooded upper lobe of an orchid flower
Herb plant normally without woody tissue
Inferior an ovary placed below other plant parts
Inflorescence (infl) grouping of individual flowers
Keel lower petals of a leguminous flower (e.g. pea) or a sharp ridge on a plant part (see p 6)

Alternate · Axil · Bracteole · Bract · Elliptic · Compound · Leaflet · Ligule · Ray floret · Inferior

Lance-shaped in the shape of a spear
Lateral placed at the side
Leaflet (lflt) leaf-like structure, part of a compound leaf
Ligulate possessing a tongue-like projection (ligule)
Linear long and narrow with parallel sides
Lip lobe of a flower in which petals are fused
Lobed divided into (usually round) segments
Midrib central vein of a leaf
Node site on a stem at which a leaf or leaves arise
Nut woody, single-seeded fruit
Obovate egg-shaped (ovate) but wider towards the tip
Ochreae sheathing leaf bases in Polygonaceae (docks)
Opposite (opp) two leaves at a node on opposite sides of a stem and in the same plane
Ovary flower part containing structures that develop into seeds. Part of one or several fused carpels (see p 6)
Ovoid egg-shaped
Palmate divided as the palm and fingers of a hand
Pappus simple or feathery hairs in fruit and flowers of the Compositae (daisy family)
Parasite plant dependent on other plants as a food source, normally with no green pigment. Partial or semi-parasites may have green pigments
Perennial (per) plant surviving for more than two years
Pinnate leaf divided into leaflets arranged on opposite sides of the midrib; 2-pinnate: each leaflet is further subdivided in a pinnate way; 3-pinnate: 3 levels of subdivision
Radially symmetrical symmetrical about more than one axis passing through the centre
Reflexed bent backwards
Rhizome creeping underground stem bearing roots, leafy and flowering shoots. An organ of propagation
Rootstock underground stem from which new plant parts arise
Runner long slim prostrate shoot, rooting to form a new plant at its tip or elsewhere along its length
Scale thin flap, often a modified leaf
Scape flower stem growing directly from the base of a plant as in Primulaceae (primroses), lacking leaves
Sepals (spls) outer ring of flower parts outside the petals
Serrate with a toothed edge
Sessile without a stalk
Simple not divided or lobed
Solitary (sol) flower not associated with other flowers in a head or inflorescence
Spadix elongated club-like flower head
Spathe leaf-like bract or sheath enclosing a flower head
Spathulate spoon-shaped (narrow at the base)
Spike long unbranched flower heads bearing unstalked flowers, the youngest flowers at the tip
Spur hollow projection from a petal or sepal
Stamen (stm) male organ of a flower made up of anthers each borne on a stalk or filament (see p 6)
Standard upright rear petal as in a pea flower (see p 6)
Stigma tip of the style on which pollen is deposited
Stipule leaf-like or scale-like outgrowth at the base of a leaf stalk; usually in pairs
Stolon shoot growing from a plant above or below ground; gives rise to a new plant at its tip
Style elongated structure joining the stigma and ovary
Superior ovary with other flower parts attached beneath
Tendril coiled organ on stem or leaf, used for climbing
Terminal at the apex of a plant or plant part
Trifoliate with three leaflets
Tuber swollen underground stem or root
Umbel flower head with flower stalks arising from one point and spread out like umbrella spokes. Smaller (secondary) umbels often arise from main umbel stalks
Whorl 3 or more leaves radiating from a single point
Wing expanded ridge, e.g., on a stem or fruit; one of the side petals on leguminous (pea family) (see p 6)

Lance-shaped
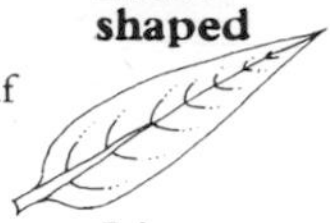

Linear
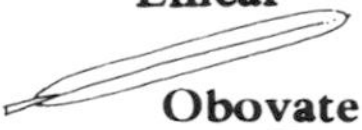

Obovate
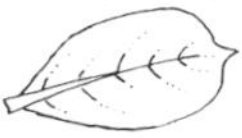

Opposite
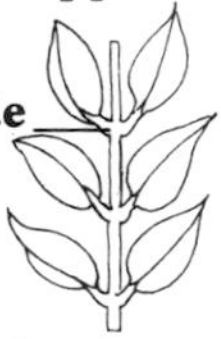
Node

Ovoid
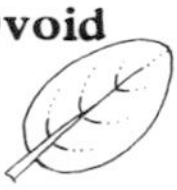

Palmate
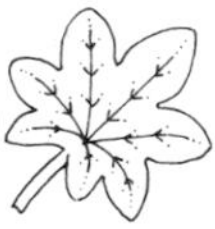

2-pinnate
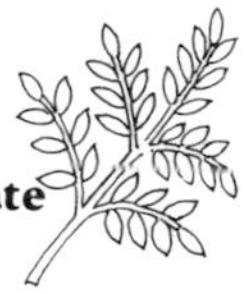

Serrate
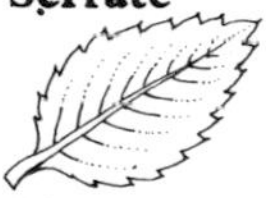

Simple
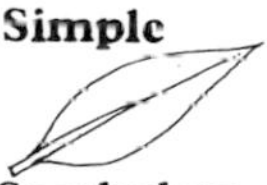

Spathulate
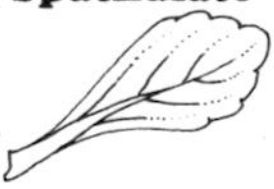

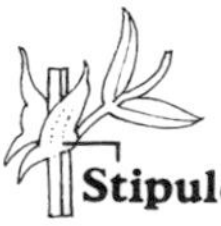
Stipule

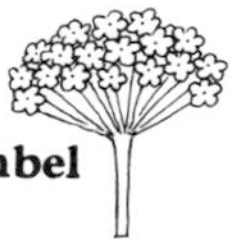
Umbel

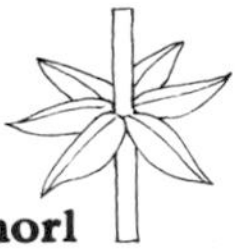
Whorl

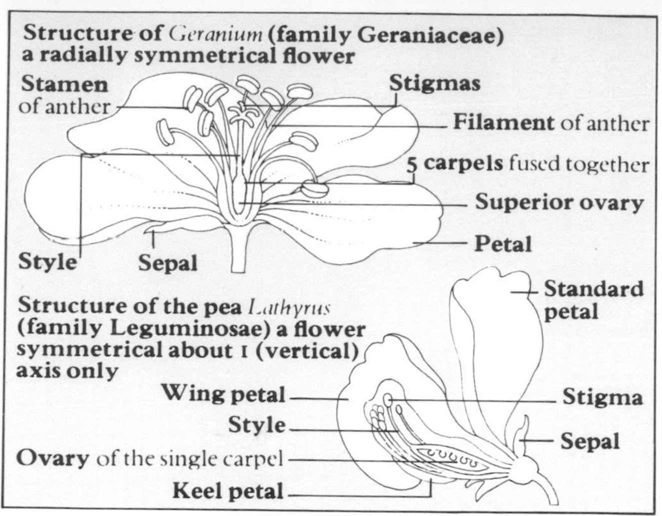

Plant key

Work the key by asking questions; each offers 2 (rarely 3) choices between which you should choose on the basis of your observations (see p. 3). The plant shown here is a test example; it is an erect herb about 50 cm tall with yellow flowers found growing in wet grassland.

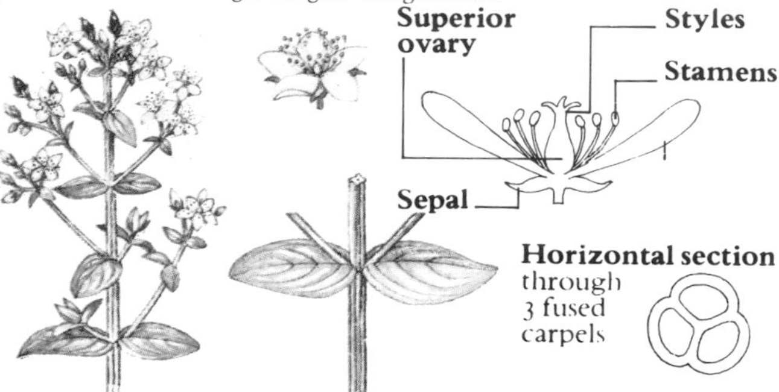

The first decision to make from the key is between options **1a** and **1b**, i.e., whether the plant is green or not. The plant is green so go to **2**; it is terrestrial so you proceed to **4**. Now you are asked about the flowers. They are obvious and coloured so you are sent to **5**; there are exactly 5 petals so you choose **5a** and are directed to **6** where you must choose option **6a**. This leads to **7**. Now a careful check is needed to see if the 5 petals are joined in a tube (even if only near the base). The plant has free (unjoined) petals so you go on to **8** which concerns the shape of the flower. Because the plant has more than one plane of symmetry (i.e., is radially symmetrical), unlike a pea flower, for example, you arrive at **GROUP H**.

GROUP H (p.9) begins with 3 options, all demanding detailed examination of the ovary. In this plant the flower parts (petals, sepals and stamens) are attached below the ovary so the ovary is superior. There is a single ovary with 3 styles projecting so this suggests 3 fused carpels. A horizontal section cut through the ovary confirms this so you choose **1b** and move to **6**. The plant has many—certainly far more than 10—stamens so go to **7**. Leaves are in opposite pairs, stipules are absent, so the choice is **7b** which leads to **9**. As already shown there are 3 free styles, suggesting that **9b** is the correct choice. A careful look at the stamens shows them to be joined in groups near their bases, which confirms that the plant is a member of the **Guttiferae** or **St John's wort family (pp. 76–77).**

Turning to these pages, you will see that members of the Guttiferae vary in such features as growth habit, flower size, hairiness and stem character. Our plant is hairless and has square stems, which confirms it as *Hypericum tetrapterum*, the Square-stemmed St John's wort.

Key to plant groups

		Proceed to
1a	Plants with no green parts	**Group A** (below)
1b	Plants green	2
2a	Growing in water	3
2b	Growing on land	4
3a	Floating aquatics, rooted in mud	**Group B** (below)
3b	Aquatics, rooted in mud	**Group C** (below)
4a	Individual flowers inconspicuous, may be in clusters, e.g., catkins, colour green or brown	**Group D** (p. 8)
4b	Flowers obvious, coloured	5
5a	5 or more petals or petal-like parts	6
5b	Fewer than 5 petals	10
6a	5 petals	7
6b	6 or more petals	**Group L** (p. 11)
7a	Petals free (not joined together)	8
7b	Petals joined together	9
8a	Flowers radially symmetrical	**Group H** (p. 9)
8b	Flowers symmetrical about 1 axis only	**Group J** (p. 10)
9a	Flowers radially symmetrical	**Group I** (p. 10)
9b	Flowers symmetrical about 1 axis only, hooded, lipped or spurred	**Group K** (p.11)
10a	0, 2 or 3 petals or petal-like parts	**Group E** (p. 8)
10b	4 petals	11
11a	Petals free	**Group F** (p. 8)
11b	Petals joined at least at base	**Group G** (p. 9)

Group A Plants with no green pigment

1a	Plant erect	2
1b	Plant twining around another species	**Convolvulaceae p. 105**
2a	Flowers radially symmetrical drooping	**Pyrolaceae p. 92**
2b	Flowers not radially symmetrical	3
3a	Flowers 2-lipped, tubular below	**Orobanchaceae p. 128**
3b	6 free petal-like structures, prominent lower lip	**Orchidaceae p. 170**

Group B Floating aquatics, not rooted in mud

1a	Plant small (less than 1 cm), disc-like or lobed	**Lemnaceae p. 181**
1b	Plant larger than 1 cm, not disc-like	2
2a	Leaves finely divided, has small bladders	**Lentibulariaceae (*Utricularia*) p. 129**
2b	Leaves not divided	3
3a	Flowers with 4 petals	**Trapaceae p. 80**
3b	Flowers with 3 petals	**Hydrocharitaceae p. 157**

Group C Aquatic plants, rooted in mud

1a	Plant erect, tall, emerging from water	2
1b	Plant not erect, usually immersed or floating	7
2a	Flowers conspicuous, individual flowers greater than 1 cm	**Butomaceae p. 157** **Alismataceae p. 156**
2b	Individual flowers small, inconspicuous, but may be in dense, obvious clusters	3
3a	Leaves whorled	**Hippuridaceae p. 83**
3b	Leaves not whorled	4
4a	Inflorescence surrounded by a sheath (spathe)	**Araceae (*Calla*) p. 180**
4b	Inflorescence without encircling sheath	5
5a	Inflorescence cylindrical	6
5b	Inflorescence globular, fruits pointed	**Sparganiaceae p. 181**
6a	Plant sweet-smelling, inflorescence to one side	**Araceae (*Acorus*) p. 180**
6b	Plant not scented, inflorescence terminal	**Typhaceae p. 181**
7a	Flowers conspicuous, white or yellow	8
7b	Flowers inconspicuous, but may be in dense spikes, green or brown	10
8a	Petals free	**Nymphaceae p. 27**
8b	Petals united	9

Group C continued

9a	Flowers radially symmetrical, white	**Menyanthaceae p. 102**
9b	Flowers symmetrical about only 1 axis, yellow	**Lentibulariaceae (*Utricularia*) p. 129**
10a	Leaves whorled	**Ceratophyllaceae p. 28** **Haloragaceae p. 83** **Najadaceae p. 159**
10b	Lower leaves in opposite pairs	**Callitrichaceae p. 109** **Najadaceae p. 159** **Potamogetonaceae (*Groenlandia*) p. 158**
10c	Lower leaves alternate	**Zosteraceae p. 158** **Potamogetonaceae p. 158** **Ruppiaceae p. 159**

Group D Terrestrial plants. Flowers inconspicuous, green or brown, but often arranged in prominent clusters

1a	Flowers in catkin-like structures	2
1b	Flowers not in catkins	3
2a	Erect or creeping shrubs	**Salicaceae p. 12** **Myricaceae p. 12**
2b	Erect herbs or climbers	**Urticaceae p. 13** **Cannabaceae p. 13**
3a	Plant parasitic on trees	**Loranthaceae p. 14**
3b	Plant not parasitic on trees	4
4a	Leaves compound	5
4b	Leaves simple	8
4c	Leaves absent, stems cylindrical, succulent	**Chenopodiaceae (*Salicornia*) p. 19**
5a	Flowers in dense heads	6
5b	Flowers not in dense heads	7
6a	Flowers in heads of 5, flowers at right angles to each other	**Adoxaceae p. 131**
6b	More than 5 flowers per head	**Rosaceae p. 50**
7a	No petals, 4 stamens	**Rosaceae (*Alchemilla*) p. 54 (*Aphanes*) p. 55**
7b	4–5 petals, many stamens	**Ranunculaceae (*Thalictrum*) p. 34**
8a	Inflorescence a dense spike with sheath (spathe)	**Araceae p. 180**
8b	Not so	9
9a	Milky juice, flowers in umbels	**Euphorbiaceae p. 71**
9b	No milky juice present, flowers not arranged in umbels	10
10a	Opposite or whorled leaves	11
10b	Alternate leaves	14
11a	Low, creeping stems	12
11b	Plant erect	13
12a	5 sepals and petals	**Caryophyllaceae p. 20**
12b	4 sepals	**Saxifragaceae (*Chrysosplenium*) p. 49**
13a	Stinging hairs, 4 stamens	**Urticaceae p. 13**
13b	No stinging hairs, many stamens	**Euphorbiaceae (*Mercurialis*) p. 72**
14a	Leaves with sheaths around base	**Polygonaceae p. 15**
14b	No sheaths at leaf bases	15
15a	Flowers in dense, narrow spikes, leaves linear, not fleshy	**Plantaginaceae p. 130** **Ranunculaceae (*Myosurus*) p. 34**
15b	Flowers not in narrow spikes, often fleshy and/or mealy	**Chenopodiaceae p. 18**

Group E Terrestrial plants. Flowers conspicuous, 0, 2 or 3 petals

1a	Petals absent, flowers in dense, reddish heads	**Rosaceae (*Sanguisorba*) p. 55**
1b	Petals present, flowers not in dense heads	2
2a	2 petals	**Onagraceae (*Circaea*) p. 81**
2b	3 petals	3
3a	Petals joined in a tube	**Aristolochiaceae p. 14**
3b	Petals free	**Alismataceae p. 156**

Group F Terrestrial plants. Flowers conspicuous, 4 petals or petal-like parts, not joined together at base nor in a tube

1a	Leaves undivided	2
1b	Leaves divided into segments	7
2a	More than 8 stamens	**Resedaceae p. 44**
2b	Less than 8 stamens	3
3a	4 sepals	4
3b	2 sepals, soon falling	**Papaveraceae p. 35**
4a	Ovary inferior	5
4b	Ovary superior	6
5a	Flowers with large, whitish, petal-like bracts	**Cornaceae p. 83**
5b	Flowers with true petals	**Onagraceae p. 80**
6a	Ovary 1-celled	**Caryophyllaceae p. 20**
6b	Ovary 2-celled	**Cruciferae p. 36**
6c	Ovary 5- or 6-celled	**Linaceae (*Radiola*) p. 70**
7a	More than 8 stamens, leaves palmate-lobed	**Rosaceae (*Potentilla erecta*) p. 52**
7b	Usually 6 stamens, leaves not palmate	**Cruciferae p. 36**

Group G Terrestrial plants. Flowers conspicuous, 4 petals or petal-like parts, joined together at their base, or in a tube

1a	Flowers radially symmetrical	2
1b	Flowers not radially symmetrical	6
2a	Leaves in whorls	3
2b	Leaves not in whorls	4
3a	4 or 5 stamens	**Rubiaceae p. 103**
3b	8 stamens	**Ericaceae p. 93**
4a	Leaves opposite, 5 stamens	**Gentianaceae p. 99**
4b	Leaves alternate, more than 5 stamens	5
5a	Sepals petal-like, no true petals	**Thymelaeaceae p. 76**
5b	Green sepals and coloured petals present	**Ericaceae p. 93**
6a	Flowers in dense heads, whorled bracts beneath	**Dipsacaceae p. 133**
6b	Flowers not in dense heads	7
7a	2 stamens, ovary 1-celled	**Papaveraceae (*Fumaria*) p. 36**
7b	4 stamens, ovary 2-celled	**Scrophulariaceae p. 118**

Group H Terrestrial plants. Flowers conspicuous, 5 petals or petal-like parts, not joined together

1a	Ovary superior, carpels free	2
1b	Ovary superior, carpels fused	6
1c	Ovary inferior	21
2a	More than 10 stamens	3
2b	10 or fewer stamens	4
3a	Stipules present	**Rosaceae p. 50**
3b	Stipules absent	**Ranunculaceae p. 28**
4a	Succulent (fleshy) leaves	**Crassulaceae p. 46**
4b	Leaves not succulent	5
5a	Leaves divided into lobes	**Rutaceae p. 73, Rosaceae (*Sibbaldia*) p. 53**
5b	Leaves not divided into lobes	**Polygonaceae p. 15, Ranunculaceae (*Myosurus*) p. 34**
6a	More than 10 stamens	7
6b	10 or fewer stamens	10
7a	Leaves alternate, stipules present	8
7b	Leaves opposite, no stipules	9
8a	Leaves palmate, stamens fused in a ring	**Malvaceae p. 75**
8b	Leaves not palmately lobed, stamens free	**Rosaceae p. 50**
9a	Single style, stamens free	**Cistaceae p. 79**
9b	Several styles, stamens in bundles	**Guttiferae p. 76**
10a	2 sepals	**Portulacaceae p. 20**
10b	More than 2 sepals	11
11a	Leaves opposite or whorled	12
11b	Leaves alternate or in a basal rosette	14
12a	Leaves simple, unlobed	13
12b	Leaves palmately or pinnately lobed	**Geraniaceae p. 68**
13a	Ovary 1-celled	**Caryophyllaceae p. 20, Frankeniaceae p. 82**

Group H continued

13b	Ovary 4–5 celled	**Linaceae p. 70**
14a	Leaves with sticky glands, insectivorous	**Droseraceae p. 45**
14b	Not so	15
15a	Leaves with 3 lobes	**Oxalidaceae p. 67**
15b	Not so	16
16a	5 stigmas	17
16b	Fewer than 5 stigmas	19
17a	Leaves entire (not lobed)	18
17b	Leaves pinnate or palmately lobed	**Geraniaceae p. 68**
18a	Many stem leaves present	**Linaceae p. 70**
18b	Leaves confined to basal rosette	**Plumbaginaceae p. 99**
19a	1 style	**Pyrolaceae p. 92**
19b	2–4 styles	20
20a	5 stamens alternating with feathery structures	**Parnassiaceae p. 50**
20b	10 stamens	**Saxifragaceae p. 48**
21a	More than 5 stamens	22
21b	5 stamens, flowers in umbels	23
22a	More than 10 stamens	**Rosaceae p. 50**
22b	10 stamens	**Saxifragaceae p. 48**
23a	Herbs	**Umbelliferae p. 84**
23b	Woody climber	**Araliaceae p. 84**

Group I Terrestrial plants. Flowers conspicuous, 5 petals joined together, radially symmetrical

1a	Ovary superior	2
1b	Ovary inferior	12
2a	10 stamens	3
2b	5 stamens	4
3a	Woody plants, usually evergreen	**Ericaceae p. 93**
3b	Succulent, round-leaved herb	**Crassulaceae (*Umbilicus*) p. 47**
4a	Stamens opposite the petals	5
4b	Stamens alternating with the petals	6
5a	Single stigma and style	**Primulaceae p. 96**
5b	5 stigmas	**Plumbaginaceae p. 99**
6a	Leaves opposite	7
6b	Leaves alternate	8
7a	2 free carpels with a single style	**Apocynaceae p. 102**
7b	Single ovary with 2 styles or 1 style, 2 stigmas	**Gentianaceae p. 99**
7c	Single ovary and style, 3-lobed stigma	**Diapensiaceae p. 91**
8a	Ovary strongly 4-lobed	**Boraginaceae p. 106**
8b	Not so	9
9a	Flowers in a terminal inflorescence	10
9b	Flowers axillary or in axillary clusters	11
10a	Leaves simple	**Scrophulariaceae p. 118**
10b	Leaves pinnate	**Polemoniaceae p. 105**
11a	Sepals free	**Convolvulaceae p. 105**
11b	Sepals united in a tube	**Solanaceae p. 117**
12a	8–10 stamens	**Ericaceae p. 93**
12b	5 or fewer stamens	13
13a	Flowers in dense heads	14
13b	Flowers not in dense heads	16
14a	Stamens completely free	15
14b	Stamens united by their anthers into a tube	**Compositae p. 137**
15a	5 stamens, alternate leaves	**Campanulaceae p. 134**
15b	2 or 4 stamens, opposite leaves	**Dipsacaceae p. 133**
16a	Leaves opposite	17
16b	Leaves alternate	19
17a	Creeping with flowers in pairs	**Caprifoliaceae (*Linnaea*) p. 132**
17b	Erect, with small flowers in clusters	18
18a	Milky sap, ovary with 2 carpels, 2-celled	**Asclepiadaceae p. 102**
18b	No milky sap, single-celled ovary	**Valerianaceae p. 132**
19a	Twining climber	**Cucurbitaceae p. 82**
19b	Not climbing	**Campanulaceae p. 134, Primulaceae (*Samolus*) p. 98**

Group J Terrestrial plants. Flowers conspicuous, 5 free petals, but flowers symmetrical about only 1 axis

1a	More than 8 stamens	2
1b	8 or fewer stamens	3
2a	10 stamens, no spur to flower	**Leguminosae p. 56**
2b	Many stamens, flowers spurred	**Ranunculaceae p. 28**
3a	5 stamens, flowers spurred	**Violaceae p. 78**
3b	8 stamens, flowers not spurred	**Polygalaceae p. 73**

Group K Terrestrial plants. Flowers conspicuous, 5 joined petals, flowers hooded, lipped or spurred, symmetrical about 1 axis

1a	Flowers in dense heads	2
1b	Flowers not in dense heads	3
2a	Leaves opposite	**Dipsacaceae p. 133**
2b	Leaves alternate	**Globulariaceae p. 128**
3a	Flowers spurred	4
3b	Flowers not spurred	5
4a	Sticky, insectivorous leaves in rosette	**Lentibulariaceae p. 129**
4b	Leaves not sticky, present on fleshy stem	**Balsaminaceae p. 74**
5a	Stamens joined in a tube by their anthers	**Campanulaceae (*Lobelia*) p. 136**
5b	Stamens free	6
6a	Woody, twining climber, 5 stamens	**Caprifoliaceae p. 132**
6b	Not a climber, 2 or 4 stamens	7
7a	Ovary 2-celled	**Scrophulariaceae p. 118**
7b	Ovary 4-celled	**Labiatae p. 110, Verbenaceae p. 109**

Group L Terrestrial plants. Flowers conspicuous, 6 or more petals or petal-like parts

1a	Petals free	2
1b	Petals joined together	13
2a	More than 12 stamens	3
2b	12 or fewer stamens	4
3a	Stipules present, clear area round ovary	**Rosaceae p. 50**
3b	Stipules absent, no clear area round ovary	**Ranunculaceae p. 28**
4a	Ovary superior	5
4b	Ovary inferior	11
5a	3 stamens (may be joined together)	6
5b	More than 3 stamens	7
6a	Leaves linear, flowers stalked in leaf axils	**Empetraceae p. 95**
6b	Leaves broad, pointed, stiff, flowers stalked in centre of leaf-like structure	**Liliaceae (*Ruscus*) p. 166**
7a	Leaves with sticky glands (insectivorous) all in basal rosette	**Droseraceae p. 45**
7b	Leaves without sticky glands	8
8a	Leaves cylindrical, succulent	**Crassulaceae p. 46**
8b	Leaves not succulent	9
9a	2 whorls of 3 petal-like parts, no green sepals	**Liliaceae p. 159**
9b	Single whorl of petals, sepals green	10
10a	Flowers pink or red	**Lythraceae p. 82**
10b	Flowers yellow/green or white	**Resedaceae p. 44**
11a	Flowers radially symmetrical	12
11b	Flowers symmetrical about only one axis	**Orchidaceae p. 170**
12a	6 stamens	**Amaryllidaceae p. 167**
12b	3 stamens	**Iridaceae p. 168**
13a	Climber with heart-shaped leaves	**Dioscoreaceae p. 169**
13b	Not a climber	14
14a	No obvious sepals or sepals petal-like	15
14b	Green, leafy sepals present	18
15a	Flowers in dense heads, surrounded by whorls of bracts	**Compositae p. 137**
15b	Flowers not so arranged	16
16a	Ovary superior	**Liliaceae p. 159**
16b	Ovary inferior	17
17a	6 stamens	**Amaryllidaceae p. 167**
17b	3 stamens	**Iridaceae p. 168**
18a	Stamens opposite petal lobes	**Primulaceae p. 96**
18b	Stamens alternating with petal lobes	**Gentianaceae p. 99**

Willow family Salicaceae

Deciduous trees and shrubs with simple leaves that often have outgrowths (stipules) at their base. Male and female flowers without sepals or petals are in catkins on separate plants.

Dwarf willow

Salix herbacea

Creeping willow

S. repens

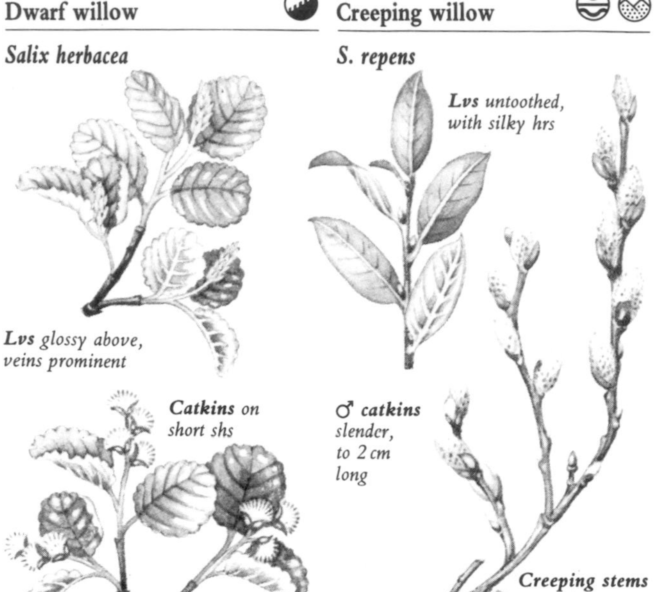

Prostrate shrub. Shoots rise only 2–3 cm above soil surface. Lvs to 2 cm, rounded, edges toothed *D:* Fennoscand, Carpathians; *Fl:* 4–5

Perennial. Creeping stems and uprt shs to 1.5 m. Lvs to 4.5 cm and longer than broad appear before catkins. *D:* N to S. Scand; *Fl:* 4–5

Bog myrtle family Myricaceae

Trees and shrubs with aromatic leaves which have no stipules. The flowers have no sepals or petals and are in catkins.

Sweet gale

Myrica gale

Shrub. Male and female catkins on separate plants appear on tips of side shoots before the leaves, which are narrow, downy below and 2–5 cm long. *Ht:* 60–150 cm; *D:* N and W to S. Scand; *Fl:* 4–5

Hemp family Cannabaceae

Herbs with lobed leaves which have stipules. Male and female flowers are on separate plants. Stalked male and female flowers have parts in fives. The female flowers are unstalked.

Hop

Humulus lupulus

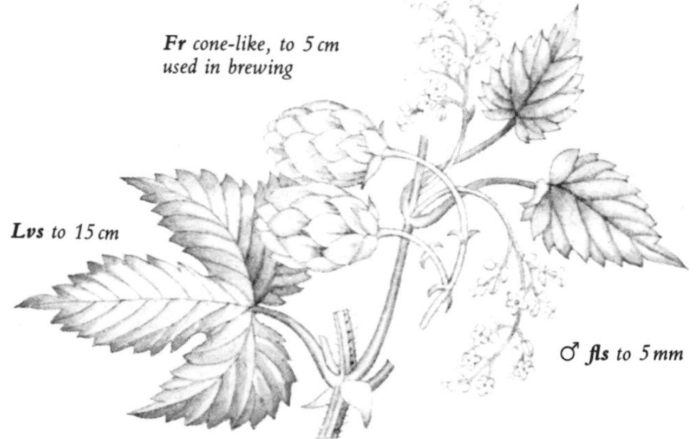

Woody climber. The square stem is 3–6 m long and twists clockwise. Leaves placed opposite each other have 3–5 lobes and serrate edges. Stem and leaves are roughly hairy. *D:* T; *Fl:* 7–8

Nettle family Urticaceae

Herbs or shrubs, often with stinging hairs. Male and female flowers are in separate catkin-like structures. Flower parts are arranged in fours or fives; the male flowers have 4 or 5 stamens.

Stinging nettle

Urtica dioica

Annual nettle

U. urens

Pellitory of the wall

Parietaria diffusa

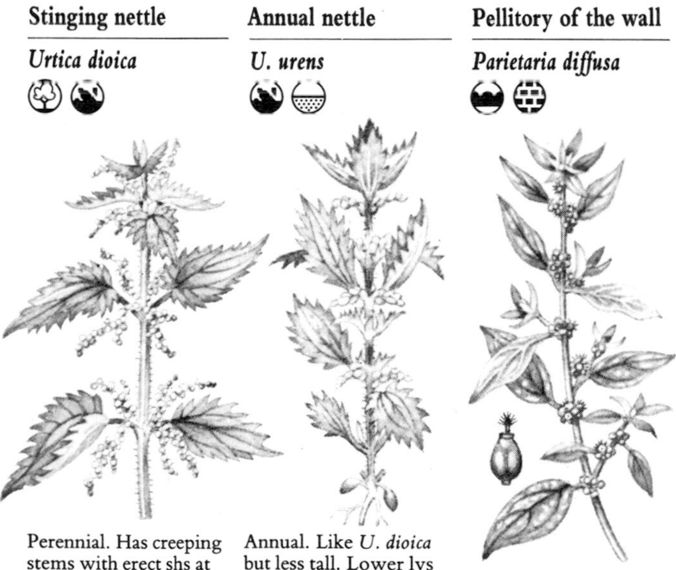

Stinging nettle: Perennial. Has creeping stems with erect shs at intervals. Stem and lvs have stinging hrs. All lvs have blades longer than stks. *Ht:* to 1.5 m; *D:* T; *Fl:* 6–8

Annual nettle: Annual. Like *U. dioica* but less tall. Lower lvs have stks longer than blades. Each plant has both ♂ and ♀ fls on lfy branches. *Ht:* 45 cm; *D:* T; *Fl:* 6–9

Pellitory of the wall: Erect per covered in non-stinging hrs. ♂ fls borne on stem sides, ♀ fls on stem tips. *Ht:* to 1 m; *D:* T; *Fl:* 6–10

Mistletoe family Loranthaceae

Woody plants with undivided leaves. They are parasitic on trees but also have green tissues that can function normally. The fruit is a one-seeded berry.

Mistletoe 

Viscum album

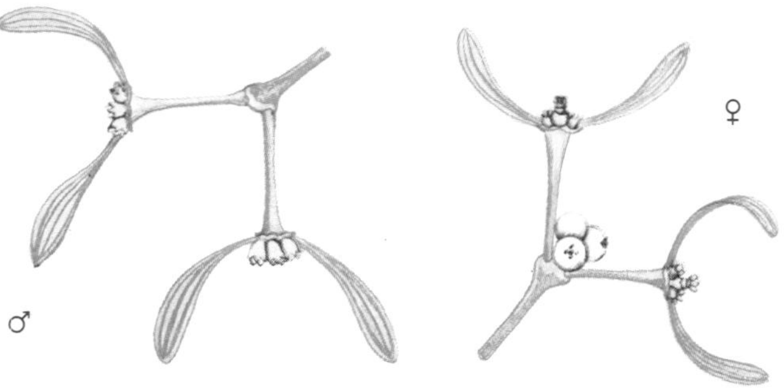

Woody evergreen to 1 m growing on tree branches, especially apple. Stklss ♂ and ♀ fls on separate plants. Leaves 2–8 cm long are opposite each other in pairs. Reputedly aphrodisiac. *D:* T (not N or E); *Fl:* 2–4

Birthwort family Aristolochiaceae

Herbs or woody climbers with leaves placed alternately on their stems. The flower-parts are three-lobed and arranged in a single whorl. The fruit is a capsule.

Asarabacca 

Asarum europaeum

Low-growing per with thick creeping rhizome. Leaves kidney-shaped. Fls sol, brownish, hry on outside. *Ht:* to 5 cm; *D:* T to S Fennoscand; *Fl:* 5–8

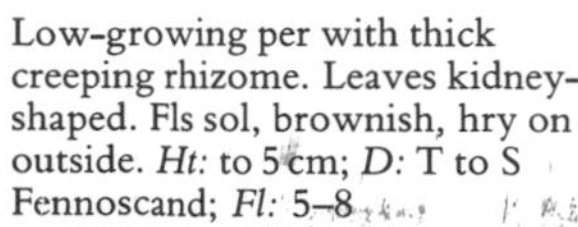

Birthwort 

Aristolochia clematitis

Perennial to 80 cm, distinctive smell. Has creeping rhizome and erect shs on which fls are borne. Fls to 3 cm, swollen at base. Lvs heart-shaped. *D:* C, S; *Fl:* 6–9

Dock family Polygonaceae

Herbs or shrubs with alternate leaves and sheathing stipules called ochreae. The flower parts, in threes or sixes, persist round the hard, often triangular fruit.

Common sorrel

Rumex acetosa

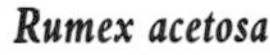

Erect, hrlss to 1 m. Lvs to 10 cm, downward-pointed lobes at base, upper lvs clasping; fr round. *D:* T; *Fl:* 5–6

Sheep's sorrel

R. acetosella

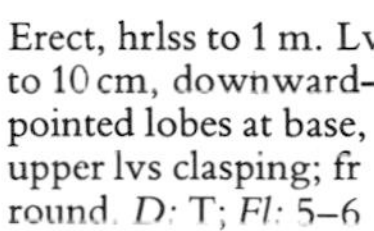

Erect per to 30 cm. Lvs to 4 cm, basal lobes spreading. Top lvs do not clasp stem. *D:* T; *Fl:* 5–8

Fiddle dock

R. pulcher

Flowers on spread brs that may tangle in fr. Fl parts toothed, fruit 3-warted. *Ht:* 40 cm; *D:* S, W; *Fl:* 7–8

Broad-leaved dock

R. obtusifolius

Erect per. Lvs broad, to 25 cm, hry below; fl parts toothed, fr 1-warted. *Ht:* 70 cm; *D:* T; *Fl:* 6–10

Golden dock

R. maritimus

Perennial to 50 cm in fr. Persistent, fine-toothed fl parts; fr 3-warted, long stkd. *D:* T (not far N); *Fl:* 6–9

Clustered dock

R. conglomeratus

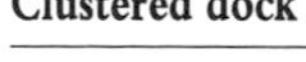

Upright, brs spread; lf blade longer than stk; ptls untoothed, fr 3-warted. *Ht:* 55 cm; *D:* T (not far N); *Fl:* 7–8

Wood dock

R. sanguineus

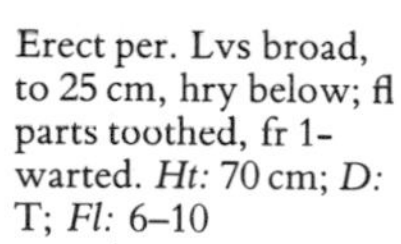

Erect per to 1 m. Brs make acute angles with stem. Fl parts not toothed, 1 wart on fr. *D:* T; *Fl:* 6–8

Curled dock

Rumex crispus

Erect per. Lvs long, narrow, curled and crisp at the edges. Infl dense, little branched. Fruit has 3 warts and an edge without obvious teeth. *Ht:* 1 m; *D:* T; *Fl:* 7–9

Marsh dock

R. palustris

Upright ann or bi. 3-warted fr has short, thick stk. Fl parts around fr blunt-tipped with rigid teeth. Plant becomes yellow-brown in fruit. *Ht:* to 1 m; *D:* S; C; *Fl:* 6–9

Water dock

R. hydrolapathum

Robust per. Leaves to 1 m. Fruit 3-warted, 6–8 mm long, with triangular segments and a few short teeth. *Ht:* to 2 m; *D:* T (not far N); *Fl:* 7–9

Scottish dock

R. aquaticus

Robust per. Leaves triangular, tapering from base. Lf stks as long as blades. Frs untoothed, unwarted, borne on slender stalks. *Ht:* to 2 m; *D:* C, N, E; *Fl:* 7–8

Shore dock

R. rupestris

Erect per. Like *R. conglomeratus* (p 15) but brs almost vertical. Lvs blue-green. Fruit: 3-warted with untoothed margins. *Ht:* to 70 cm; *D:* W; *Fl:* 6–8

Mountain sorrel

Oxyria digyna

Hairless per. Lvs kidney-shaped. Fl and fr stks slender. Outer fl parts spread or bent back. Fruit is broad-winged. *Ht:* 25 cm; *D:* N, C, S; *Fl:* 7–8

Redshank

Polygonum persicaria

Hairless, branched per. Lvs lance-shaped, often with black blotch. Fl parts lack glands. Fr ridged. *Ht:* to 80 cm; *D:* T; *Fl:* 6–10

Bistort

P. bistorta

Hairless. Lvs narrow abruptly at base to winged stks. Infl dense, to 1.5 cm across. *Ht:* to 50 cm; *D:* C, N (not Scand); *Fl:* 6–8

Alpine bistort

P. viviparum

Creeping, some shoots upright. Lvs taper at base and tip. Fl head often has bulbils at base. *Ht:* to 40 cm; *D:* N, S; *Fl:* 6–8

Amphibious bistort

P. amphibium

Hairless, varies in form. On mud to 75 cm high, in water has floating lvs more tapered at their base. Fl has 5 protruding stamens. *D:* T; *Fl:* 7–9

Knotgrass

P. aviculare

Main stem lvs longer than branch leaves. Flowers single or in small clusters. *Ht:* to 1 m; *D:* T; *Fl:* 7–10

Pale persicaria

P. lapathifolium

Erect shs often hairy. Lvs to 20 cm may have central blotch. Yellow glands on pale fl parts. Infl dense. *Ht:* to 1 m; *D:* T; *Fl:* 6–10

Water pepper

P. hydropiper

Flowers in slim nodding head have yellow glands. Plant has a burning taste. *Ht:* to 75 cm; *D:* T (not N); *Fl:* 7–9

Buckwheat

Fagopyrum esculentum

Leaves broad, heart-shaped. Fr 2–3 times length of fl parts. Once widely cultivated. *Ht:* to 60 cm; *D:* T (not Fennoscand); *Fl:* 7–8

Goosefoot family Chenopodiaceae

Herbs or shrubs, often with fleshy stems and leaves. Plants look silvery or mealy. Leaves borne alternately have no stipules. The small, simple, greenish flowers have 3–5 lobes.

Nettle-leaved goosefoot

C. murale

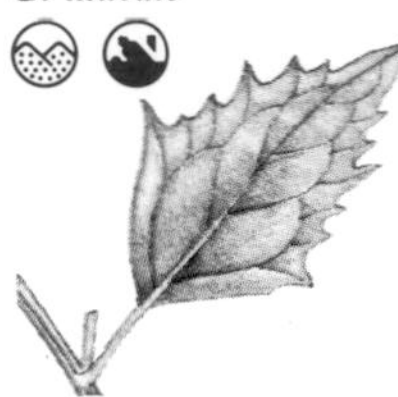

Angular lvs with coarse, sharp teeth. Infl much branched. *Ht:* to 70 cm; *D:* T; *Fl:* 7–10

Red goosefoot

C. rubrum

Shining, reddish. Lvs angular with blunt teeth. Flower head dense. *Ht:* 50 cm; *D:* T; *Fl:* 7–9

Stinking goosefoot

C. vulvaria

Leaves toothless, mealy, with pointed tips. Plant smells of bad fish. *Ht:* 25 cm; *D:* T; *Fl:* 7–9

Many-seeded goosefoot

C. polyspermum

Leaves oval, toothless to 8 cm, not mealy. Stem 4-angled. *Ht:* to 1 m; *D:* T; *Fl:* 7–10

Fat hen

Chenopodium album

Variable ann. Stems erect, often red-tinged. Lvs dark green or mealy, angular, narrower in infl. Flower parts keeled. Ancient food plant replaced by spinach. *Ht:* to 1 m; *D:* T; *Fl:* 7–10

Common orache

Atriplex patula

Lf stks *1 cm long*

Erect, branched, mealy ann. Upper lvs linear, lower have spreading basal lobes. Lfy structures present around fr. *Ht:* to 90 cm; *D:* T; *Fl:* 9–10

Grass-leaved orache

Atriplex littoralis

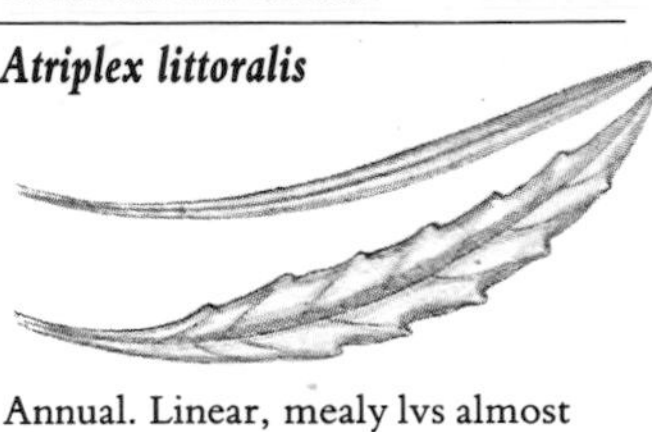

Annual. Linear, mealy lvs almost toothless. Rough lfy parts round fr. *Ht:* 70 cm; *D:* C, W, S; *Fl:* 7–8

Spear-leaved orache

A. hastata

Lower lvs triangular, mealy below; brs more uprt than *A. patula*. *Ht:* 80 cm; *D:* T; *Fl:* 8–9

Sea purslane

Halimione portulacoides

***Lvs** untoothed, mealy, elliptical*

Perennial shrub. Infl dense at sh tips. Fr not stkd. *Ht:* to 1 m; *D:* N to Dk; *Fl:* 7–9

Annual seablite

Sueda maritima

Succulent, hrlss ann. Lvs to 4 cm, narrow, pointed. *Ht:* to 50 cm; *D:* T; *Fl:* 8–10

Prickly saltwort

Salsola kali

Prostrate ann. Leaves unstkd, with spine at tip. *Ht:* to 60 cm; *D:* T; *Fl:* 7–9

Glasswort

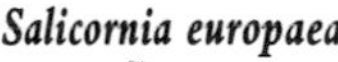

Salicornia europaea

Succulent ann. Stems and brs segmented, succ. Lvs tiny scales. Edible. *Ht:* 20 cm; *D:* T; *Fl:* 8–9

Sea beet

Beta maritima

Succulent, sprawling, often reddish. Basal lvs hrlss, not toothed, in a rosette. Infl dense, fls green. *Ht:* 1 m; *D:* N to S. Scand; *Fl:* 7–9

Purslane family Portulacaceae

Herbs, usually hairless, Flowers have 4–6 petals and two sepals distinguishing them from members of the pink family.

Blinks  

Montia fontana

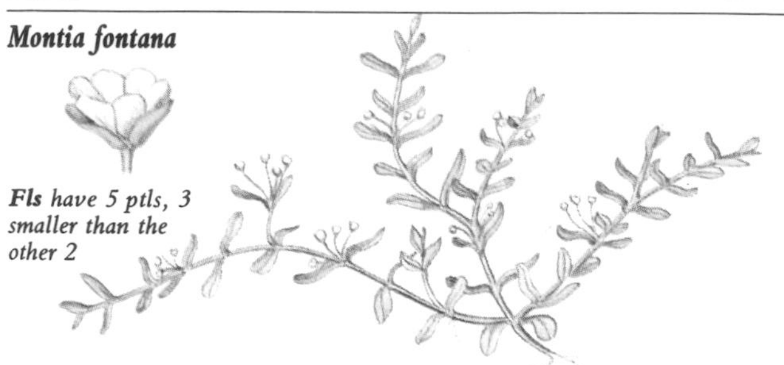

Weak, straggling much-branched herb. Lvs opposite, egg-shaped. Fls in clusters. Spherical fr contains black seeds. *Ht:* to 50 cm; *D:* T; *Fl:* 5–10

Pink family Caryophyllaceae

Herbs with opposite leaves that have no lobes or teeth. Flowers with 4–5 unjoined petals and sepals are in clusters at shoot tips. Petals are often lobed at their tips.

Field mouse-ear 

Cerastium arvense

Perennial herb. Brs prostrate to 30 cm. Unstkd, hry lvs to 2 cm. Fls in loose groups. Ptls 2 × length of spls. *D:* T (not far N); *Fl:* 4–8

Sticky mouse-ear 

C. glomeratum

Annual. Shs uprt. Stem lvs and spls hry. Ptls and spls equal in length. *Ht:* 25 cm; *D:* T (not NE); *Fl:* 4–9

Common mouse-ear  

C. fontanum

Creeping hry per. Fl clusters spread out in fr. Ptls and spls equal length. *Ht:* 40 cm; *D:* T; *Fl:* 4–9

Alpine mouse-ear

C. alpinum

Prostrate per. Dense soft hrs on lvs. Ptls 2 × spls. *Ht:* 10 cm; *D:* N, S; *Fl:* 6–8

Sea mouse-ear

C. diffusum

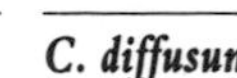

Much branched ann. Lvs and shs dark green and covered with hrs. Fls to 6 mm with 4 ptls shorter than the 4 spls. *Ht:* 20 cm; *D:* S, W, C, N to Swed; *Fl:* 5–7

Thyme-leaved sandwort

Arenaria serpyllifolia

Leaves hry, pointed, to only 6 mm. Fls 7 mm, ptls notched, shorter than spls. *Ht:* 20 cm; *D:* T; *Fl:* 6–8

Three-nerved sandwort

Moehringia trinervia

Weak ann. Lvs with 3 parallel veins. Fl to 6 mm, ptls shorter than spls. *Ht:* 25 cm; *D:* T; *Fl:* 5–6

Fringed sandwort

Arenaria ciliata

Prostrate hry per. Fls to 1 cm, 3 hry ridges on spls. *Ht:* 6 cm; *D:* T (local); *Fl:* 6–7

Mossy sandwort

Moehringia muscosa

Prostrate hrlss per; 4 ptls 1.5 × length of spls. Fr 4-toothed. *Ht:* 20 cm; *D:* C, S; *Fl:* 6–8

Sea sandwort

Honkenya peploides

Prostrate, succ. Fls to 1 cm among lvs, ♂ and ♀ fls separate. *Ht:* 15 cm; *D:* NW; *Fl:* 5–8

Spring sandwort

Minuartia verna

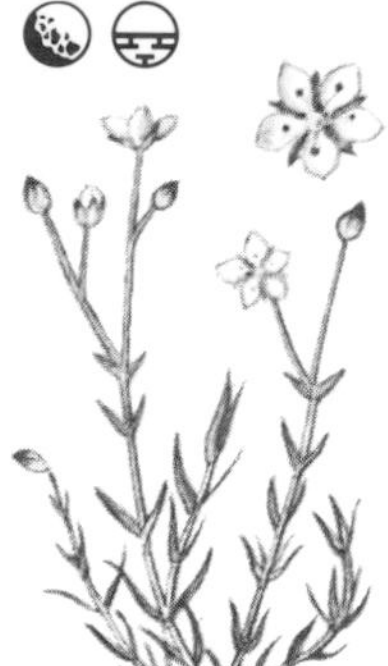

Tufted per. Lvs and spls strongly 3-veined, lf tips pointed. Ptls just longer than spls. *Ht:* 10 cm; *D:* S, W, C; *Fl:* 5–9

Coral necklace

Illecebrum verticillatum

Creeping, hrlss. Lvs have oval stipules. Ptls longer than succ spls. *Ht:* 15 cm; *D:* W, C; *Fl:* 7–9

Lesser sea spurrey

Spergularia marina

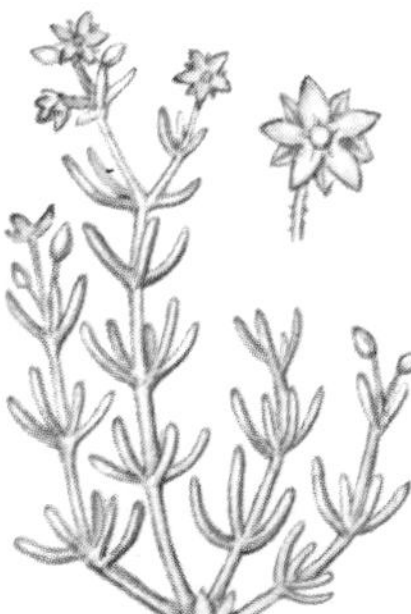

Creeping brs to 20 cm. Lvs succ, pointed. Blunt ptls shorter than spls, less than 8 stms. *D:* T; *Fl:* 6–8

Mossy cyphel

M. sedoides

Densely tufted per. Makes cushions to 25 cm across by 8 cm high. Lvs succ. Fls to 5 mm diam with 5 spls, no ptls. *D:* Scotland, S, E; *Fl:* 6–8

Corn spurrey

Spergula arvensis

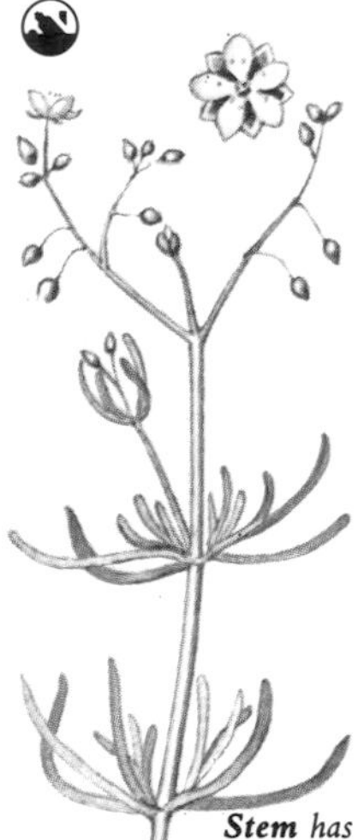

Annual. Spreading brs from base. Lvs succ, grooved below. *Ht:* 25 cm; *D:* T; *Fl:* 6–8

Sea pearlwort

Sagina maritima

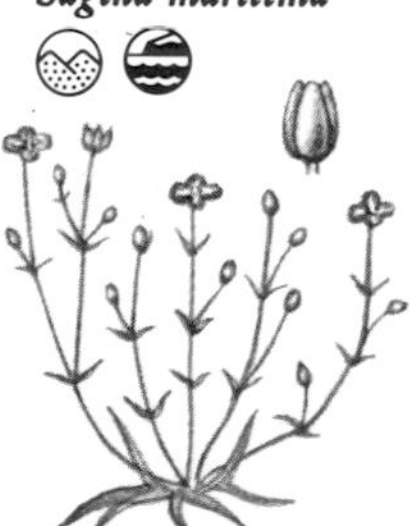

Leaves spineless. Fls on main stem only have 4 spls, no ptls. Many sim spp. *Ht:* 15 cm; *D:* N to S Fin; *Fl:* 5–9

Four-leaved allseed

Polycarpon tetraphyllum

Hairless v branched; lvs oval, upper in opposite prs. Fls have 5 hooked spls. *Ht:* 10 cm; *D:* S, W; *Fl:* 6–7

Knotted pearlwort

S. nodosa

Delicate tufted per. Lvs spined, *c.* 1.5 cm at base, shorter above. Ptls 2 × spl length. *Ht:* 10 cm; *D:* T; *Fl:* 7–9

Smooth rupturewort

Herniaria glabra

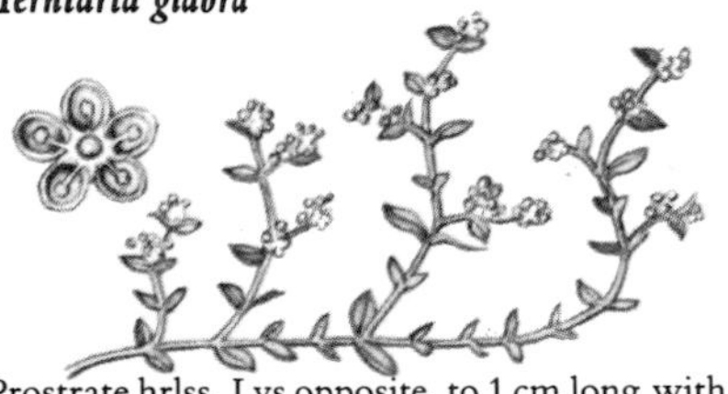

Prostrate hrlss. Lvs opposite, to 1 cm long with stipules. Fls in dense clusters each 2 mm diam, 5 tiny ptls. *Ht:* 15 cm; *D:* T (not far N); *Fl:* 7

Marsh stitchwort

S. palustris

Creeping perennial. Untoothed lvs. Bracts have green stripe. Ptls v deeply cleft. *Ht:* 40 cm; *D:* N, C; *Fl:* 5–7

Greater stitchwort

S. holostea

Stems brittle, uprt, 4-angled. Lvs rough. Fls to 3 cm, ptls cut to half length, 10 stms, 3 styles. *Ht:* 45 cm; *D:* T (not far N); *Fl:* 4–6

Lesser stitchwort

S. graminea

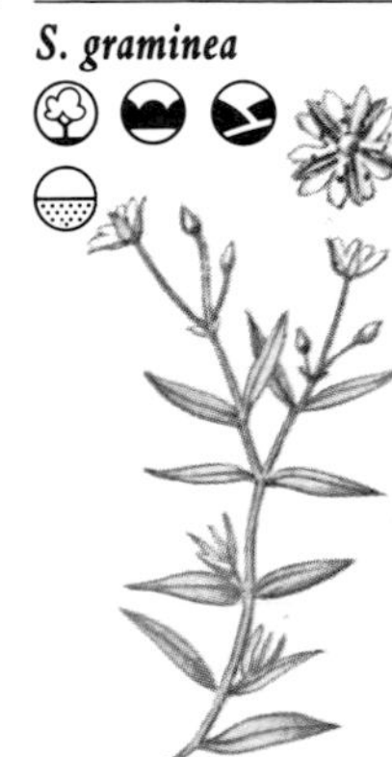

Leaves toothless, hry at base. Colourless bracts. Fls to 1.2 cm, ptls and spls equal. *Ht:* 50 cm; *D:* T; *Fl:* 5–8

Upright chickweed

Moenchia erecta

Perennial. Erect stem to 12 cm. Lvs hairless, longest below. Fls to 8 mm, spls longer than ptls. *D:* W, C, N to Eng; *Fl:* 5–6

Common chickweed

Stellaria media

Weak ann. Stems have 1 line of hrs between lf pairs. Ptls cleft. Fr 6-lobed. *Ht:* to 40 cm; *D:* T; *Fl:* 1–12

Water chickweed

Myosoton aquaticum

Weak, spreading per. Shs to 1 m, hry above. Upper lvs unstkd; fls to 1.5 cm, lobed ptls 1.5 × spls. *D:* T (not far N); *Fl:* 7–8

White campion

Silene alba

Shoots erect, hry. Lvs hry to 10 cm, upper lvs unstkd. Fl to 3 cm, spls a tube. Separate ♂ and ♀ plants. *Ht:* 60 cm; *D:* T; *Fl:* 5–9

Bladder campion

S. vulgaris

Branched per. Upper lvs unstkd, blue-green. Infl much branched with inflated spl tube and colourless bracts. Fl to 1.8 cm. *Ht:* 60 cm; *D:* T; *Fl:* 6–8

Red campion

S. dioica

Like *S. alba*. Stems hry. Winged stks on basal lvs. Teeth on fr curled back. *Ht:* 60 cm; *D:* T; *Fl:* 5–6

White sticky catchfly

S. viscosa

Plant covered in dense, sticky hrs. Infl looks whorled. Ptls lobed. *Ht:* to 60 cm; *D:* C, E; *Fl:* 6–7

Northern catchfly

S. wahlbergella

Unbranched per, less than 30 cm. Ptls just outside swollen spl tube. *D:* Arct; *Fl:* 6–8

Sand catchfly

S. conica

Very sticky, hry ann. Fl to 5 mm, spl tube hry, conical. *Ht:* 25 cm; *D:* C, S; *Fl:* 5–6

Forked catchfly

S. dichotoma

Stems hry. Branched infl, 5–10 fls per br. Spl tube hry. *Ht:* 60 cm; *D:* E; *Fl:* 5–8

Spanish catchfly

S. otites

Sticky hrs on stem. Basal lvs spathulate. Many 4 mm fls in infl, spl tube hrlss. ♂ and ♀ separate. *Ht:* 55 cm; *D:* C, S, E; *Fl:* 6–9

Nottingham catchfly

S. nutans

Perennial. Erect shoots have sticky hrs above. Lvs hry, basal lvs long-stkd. Ptls narrow, v cut, lobes inrolled. *Ht:* 60 cm; *D:* T; *Fl:* 5–7

Sea campion

S. maritima

Cushion-forming. Lvs stiff. Fls 2.5 cm, 4 per infl. Bracts lf-like. Fr 6-toothed. *Ht:* 15 cm; *D:* W; *Fl:* 6–8

Rock catchfly

S. rupestris

Short per. Lvs narrow. Infl spread, fls long-stkd, ptls notched but not deeply lobed. *Ht:* 15 cm; *D:* Fennoscand, W, C; *Fl:* 6–9

Moss campion

S. acaulis

Cushion-forming. Lvs v narrow in rosettes. Fls single to 1.2 cm. Spl tube often reddish, wider at mouth. *Ht:* 8 cm; *D:* Arct, C, W; *Fl:* 7–8

Creeping gypsophila

Gypsophila repens

Creeping hrlss per. Up to 30 fls in infl, fl stks 2 × length of spl tube, 2 styles. *Ht:* 20 cm; *D:* C; *Fl:* 6–9

Annual gypsophila

G. muralis

Very branched ann, hrlss above. Infl loose, fls to 4 mm, ptls 2 × spl length. *Ht:* 20 cm; *D:* C, E; *Fl:* 6–10

Tunic flower

Petrorhagia saxifraga

Hairless ann, narrow lvs. Spl tube 5-toothed, 5-veined. Spls half ptl length. *Ht:* to 45 cm; *D:* C, S; *Fl:* 6–8

Cheddar pink

D. gratianopolitanus

Tussocky. Prostrate non-flowering shs. Fl shs uprt, hrlss. Fls sol, 4–6 scales. *Ht:* 15 cm; *D:* W, C; *Fl:* 6–7

Maiden pink

D. deltoides

Tufted, roughly hry. Fls have 2–4 scales half spl length. *Ht:* 30 cm; *D:* T; *Fl:* 6–9

Soapwort

Saponaria officinalis

Hairless lvs to 10 cm. Infl dense, no scales below spls. *Ht:* 60 cm; *D:* T (not N); *Fl:* 7–9

Large pink

Dianthus superbus

Fl *to 6 cm*

Branched. Lvs linear. Ptls very cut, 2–4 scales round spls. *Ht:* 70 cm; *D:* C, N; *Fl:* 6–9

Carthusian pink

D. carthusianorum

Erect, hrlss per. Lvs long, pointed. Fls well clustered. Scales half spl length. *Ht:* 40 cm; *D:* S, W, C; *Fl:* 5–8

Corn cockle

Agrostemma githago

Unbranched stem and fl stks have white hrs. Spls long, pointed. *Ht:* to 1 m; *D:* S; *Fl:* 6–8

Deptford pink

D. armeria

Fl *to 1.3 cm*

Leaves on stem linear, hry. Fls grouped; 2 hry scales as long as spl tube. *Ht:* 45 cm; *D:* T (rare in N); *Fl:* 7–8

Jersey pink

D. gallicus

Tufted, lvs blunt. Ptl tips shredded; 4 small scales; fragrant. *Ht:* 35 cm; *D:* W; *Fl:* 6–8

Ragged Robin

Lychnis flos-cuculi

Tall, branched per. Lvs rough, basal lvs stkd. Spls in ribbed tube. *Ht:* 60 cm; *D:* T; *Fl:* 5–6

Alpine catchfly

L. alpina

Leaves in basal rosette. Dense infl of *c.* 20 fls, ptls 2-lobed. *Ht:* 10 cm; *D:* N, S; *Fl:* 6–7

Sticky catchfly 

L. viscaria

Flower of Jove 

L. flos-jovis

Sticky hrs on upper stem. Infl of 3–6 short-stkd fls; ptls notched, spl tube long. *Ht:* 60 cm; *D:* T; *Fl:* 5–6

Branched per. Long-stkd fls in flat-topped infl. Ptls to 1 cm, deeply 2-lobed. *Ht:* 60 cm; *D:* C; *Fl:* 6–8

Water lily family Nymphaceae

Perennial aquatics with submerged rhizomes and floating leaves. Single flowers have 3–6 sepals and three or more petals.

White water lily 

Nymphaea alba

Circular floating lvs to 30 cm across deeply cleft at attachment to lf stk. Fls to 20 cm across have 4 spls and many ptls. *D:* T; *Fl:* 7–8

Yellow water lily 

Nuphar lutea

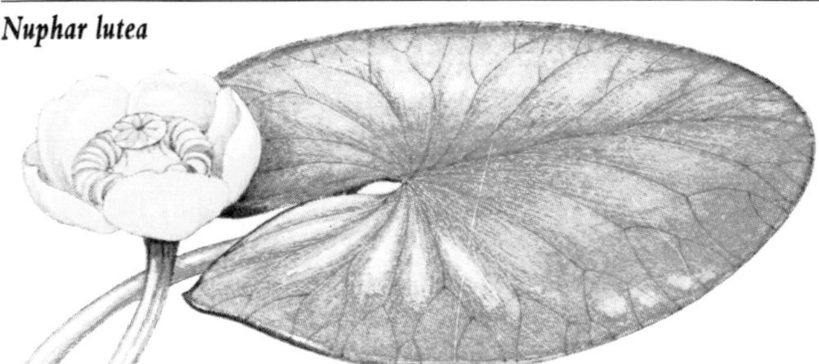

Floating lvs oval, to 40 cm across, cleft at base. Fls to 6 cm, raised above water, have 5–6 spls and many ptls a third of spl length. *D:* T; *Fl:* 7–8

Hornwort family Ceratophyllaceae

Submerged perennial aquatics with whorled leaves split into narrow lobes. Solitary, inconspicuous male and female flowers are borne in the leaf nodes on separate plants.

Rigid hornwort

Ceratophyllum demersum

***Lvs** to 2 cm*

Stiff waterweed, some stems to 1 m long. Lvs serrate, divided once or twice. Fr oval, to 4 mm, 2 spines at base but hard to see. *D:* T; *Fl:* 7–9

Buttercup family Ranunculaceae

Herbs, woody plants and climbers often poisonous and usually with spirally arranged leaves without stipules. The flowers vary widely but have many stamens and tend to attract insects.

Meadow buttercup

Ranunculus acris

***Lvs** on stem deeply cut*

Erect per. Stem branched, hry. Basal lvs not cut. Fls to 2.5 cm on hry, unridged stks. Spls hry, uprt. *Ht:* to 1 m; *D:* T; *Fl:* 6–7

Large white buttercup

R. platanifolius

Tall per to 1.3 m, hry below. Lvs have 5–7 palmate lobes not deeply cut. Fls to 2 cm, ptls small, fl stks 4–5 × lf length. *D:* C, S; *Fl:* 5–8

Goldilocks buttercup

R. auricomus

Hairy per. Upper lvs 3-lobed. Up to 5 ptls of uneven size. *Ht:* 30 cm; *D:* T; *Fl:* 4–5

Celery-leaved buttercup

R. sceleratus

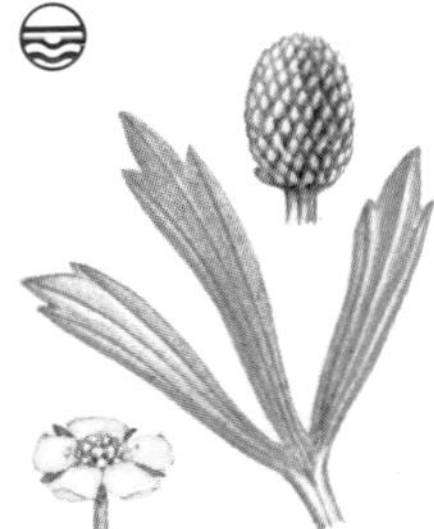

Robust ann. Stems hollow, furrowed. Ptls small. To 100 or more frs per head. *Ht:* 45 cm; *D:* T; *Fl:* 7–9

Corn buttercup

R. arvensis

Branched. Upper lvs 3-lobed. Fl stks hry, fr spined. *Ht:* 80 cm; *D:* S, W, C; *Fl:* 6–7

Bulbous buttercup

R. bulbosus

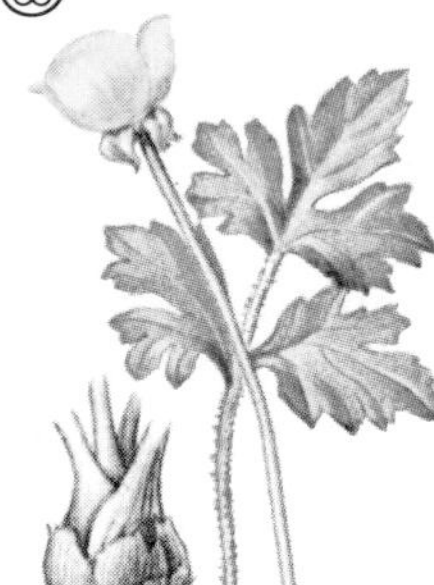

Bulbous swelling at sh base. Spls bent back, hry below. *Ht:* 35 cm; *D:* T; *Fl:* 5–6

Glacial buttercup

R. glacialis

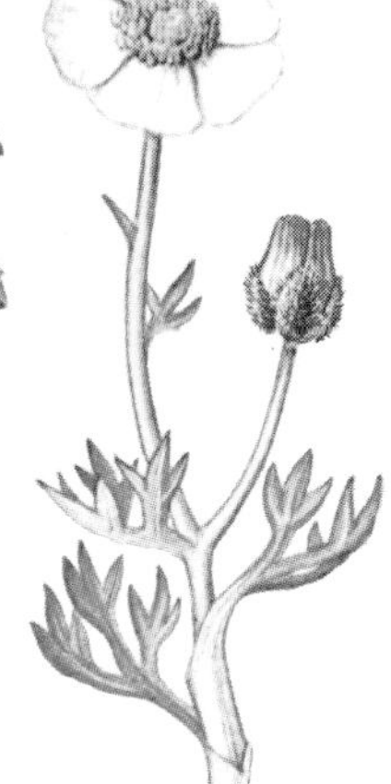

Perennial. Lvs and stem hrlss. Lvs fleshy, 3-lobed. Fls sol, spls hry, uprt. *Ht:* 15 cm; *D:* N, C; *Fl:* 6–8

Lesser celandine

R. ficaria

Has many rt tubers and may be bulbils in axils. Fls sol, 8–12 ptls. *Ht:* 20 cm; *D:* T; *Fl:* 3–5

Lesser spearwort

R. flammula

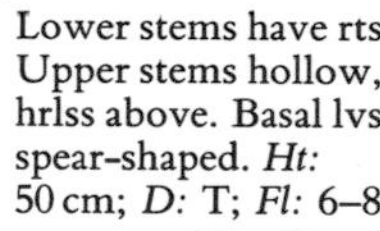

Lower stems have rts. Upper stems hollow, hrlss above. Basal lvs spear-shaped. *Ht:* 50 cm; *D:* T; *Fl:* 6–8

Greater spearwort

R. lingua

Branched per. Uprt, near-hrlss, hollow stems to 1.2 m rise from creeping base. Stem lvs unstkd. Fl 4 cm. *D:* T; *Fl:* 6–9

Creeping buttercup

R. repens

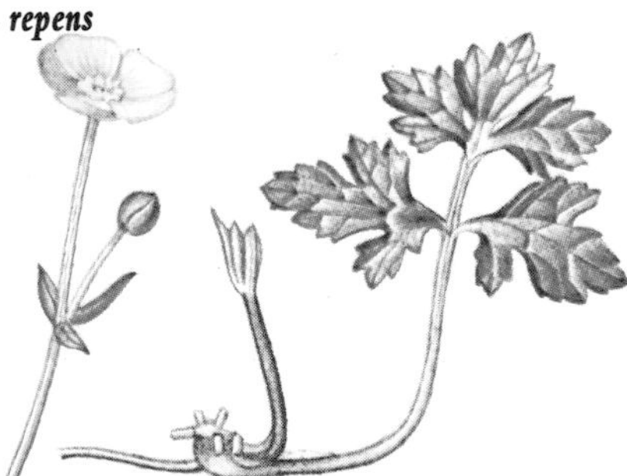

Erect per to 60 cm. Creeping runners root at nodes. Basal lvs 3-lobed, middle lobe stkd. Fl stks ridged, hry. Spls uprt or spread. *D:* T; *Fl:* 5–8

Water crowfoot 

Ranunculus aquatilis

Branched, hrlss. Fine-cut underwater lvs in many planes. Fls 3 cm, 15 + long stamens. *D:* T; *Fl:* 5–8

Ivy-leaved crowfoot  

R. hederaceus

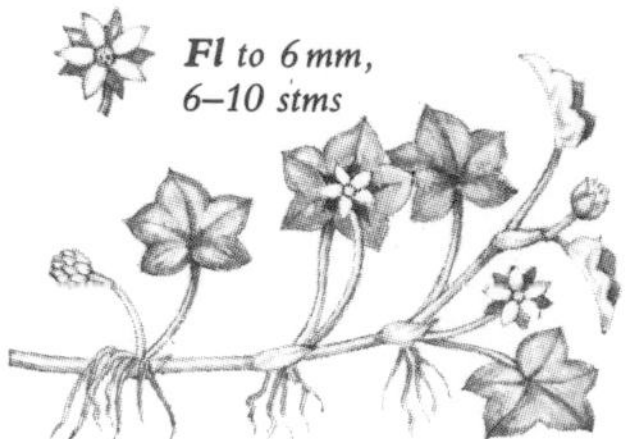

Branched per. Creeping stems to 40 cm. Lvs opp, stkd, 3–5 lobed. No submerged lvs. *D:* T; *Fl:* 6–9

River water crowfoot

R. fluitans

Robust waterweed with deeply divided submerged lvs to 30 cm with a few long segments. Stems to 6 m. Usually no floating lvs. *D:* W, C; *Fl:* 6–8

Wood anemone 

Anemone nemorosa

Perennial. Lvs borne on creeping rhizome and fl stems. Fls to 4 cm, sol. *Ht:* 20 cm; *D:* T; *Fl:* 3–5

Yellow anemone 

A. ranunculoides

Stem lvs on v short stks. One or more fls per fl stk. Fls 2 cm diam, 5 ptls. *Ht:* 20 cm; *D:* T; *Fl:* 3–5

Blue anemone

A. apennina

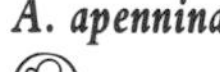

Dark rhizome. Lvs hry below. Fls sol, 10–15 ptls. *Ht:* 20 cm; *D:* S; *Fl:* 3–4

Narcissus-flowered anemone

A. narcissiflora

Robust, hry. Basal lvs stkd, stem lvs unstkd. Fls to 3 cm on 4 cm stks. *Ht:* 30 cm; *D:* T; *Fl:* 6–7

Palmate anemone

A. palmata

Stem hry. Basal leaves shallow-lobed. Fls 3 cm, 10–15 ptls. *Ht:* 20 cm; *D:* SW; *Fl:* 2–6

Snowdrop windflower

A. sylvestris

Fl *to 7 cm,*

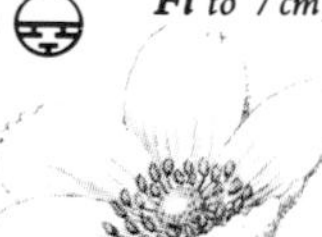

Hairy, has rt buds. Basal lvs long-stalked, lobed; fl sol. *Ht:* 35 cm; *D:* C, E; *Fl:* 2–6

Marsh marigold

Caltha palustris

Hairless. Lvs round or kidney-shaped, fine teeth; no true ptls. *Ht:* 20 cm; *D:* T; *Fl:* 3–7

Forking larkspur

Consolida regalis

Fl *long-spurred*

Annual. Brs spread, hry. Few fls in infl, fr single, hrlss. *Ht:* 40 cm; *D:* S, W, C, E; *Fl:* 6–7

Eastern larkspur

C. orientalis

Sticky hrs on shoots. Many fls in infl. Spur short. Fr hry, beaked. *Ht:* 70 cm; *D:* S; *Fl:* 6–7

Alpine larkspur

Delphinium elatum

Stem hrlss above. Upper lvs short-stkd; 3 hrlss frs per fl. *Ht:* to 2 m; *D:* C, S; *Fl:* 6–8

Columbine

Aquilega vulgaris

Leaves long-stkd, hrlss, lflts stkd. Spurs knobbed. *Ht:* 70 cm; *D:* W, C; *Fl:* 5–6

Monkshood

Aconitum napellus

Leaves deeply lobed. Wide hoods on fls; 3 frs per fl. *Ht:* 70 cm; *D:* W C; *Fl:* 5–6

Love-in-a-mist

Nigella damascena

Finely cut lvs, some under fls. Ptls clawed. Fr 5-membered. *Ht:* 20 cm; *D:* S; *Fl:* 6–7

Globe flower  

Trollius europaeus

Erect hrlss per. Basal lvs stkd, stem lvs unstkd. Fls consist of spls and nectaries. *Ht:* 40 cm; *D:* T (not far N); *Fl:* 6–8

Small pasque flower  

P. pratensis

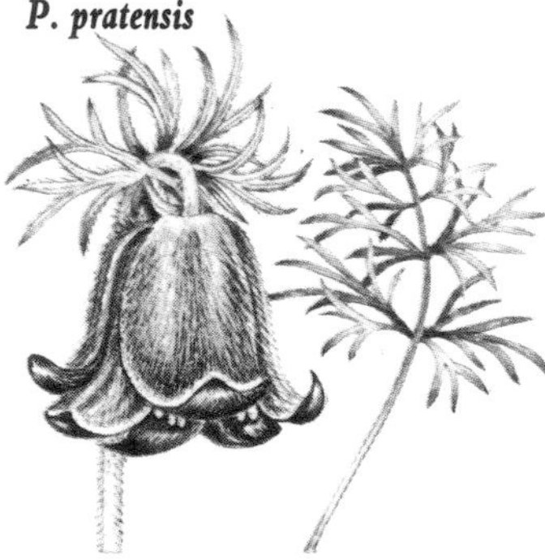

Small per to 10 cm but to 45 cm in fr. Lvs hry, v cut. Fls to 4 cm, ptls under 1.5 times stamen length. *D:* C, E; *Fl:* 5

Winter aconite

Eranthis hyemalis

Hairless per. Lvs palmately 3–5 lobed, arise after fls. Spls 6, ptl-like, 30 stamens, 6 carpels, fls to 3 cm. *Ht:* 10 cm; *D:* C, S, W; *Fl:* 1–3

Pasque flower  

Pulsatilla vulgaris

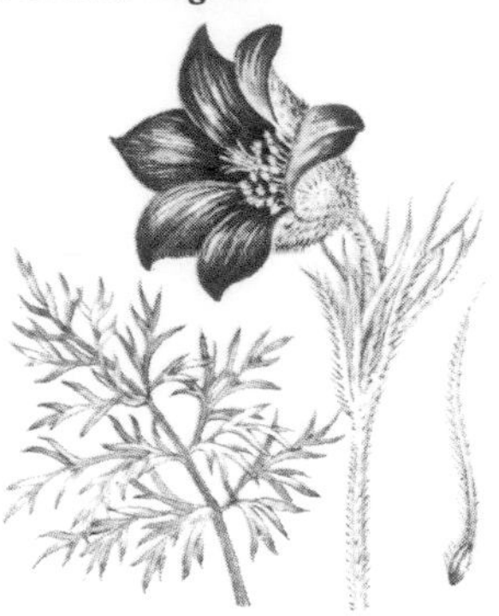

Has rosette of long-stkd, hry, v cut lvs. Fls sol, 8 cm; ptls hry to 3 × stamen length. *Ht:* 20 cm; *D:* NW; *Fl:* 4–5

Pale pasque flower 

P. vernalis

Perennial to 15 cm but to 35 cm in fr. Basal lvs evergreen. Fls to 6 cm nodding at first, then erect. *D:* C, N; *Fl:* 4–6

Alpine pasque flower  

P. alpina

Stems to 45 cm with long-stkd, hry doubly cut basal lvs. Stem lvs stkd unlike other spp. Fls to 6 cm, erect. *D:* C, S; *Fl:* 5–7

Stinking hellebore  

Helleborus foetidus

Strong-smelling per to 80 cm. Basal lvs evergreen, topmost lvs small, undivided. Fls 3 cm, many per sh, never wide open. *D:* S, W; *Fl:* 3–4

Christmas rose  

H. niger

Perennial. Basal lvs evergreen, stem lvs rounded, not divided. Fls to 10 cm, 2–3 per shoot, usually 7 carpels. *Ht:* 20 cm; *D:* E, S; *Fl:* 1–4

Summer pheasant's eye

Adonis aestivalis

Erect ann. Lvs v cut. Fls 2 cm, 5 spls cling to spread ptls. *Ht:* 25 cm; *D:* T (not N); *Fl:* 6–8

Green hellebore  

H. viridis

Erect per to 40 cm. Lvs long-stkd, hrlss, serrate, palmately divided. Fls to 5 cm, wide-spread ptls and 3 carpels. *D:* W, C; *Fl:* 3–4

Pheasant's eye

A. annua

Upright ann. Lvs hrlss, v cut. Fls to 2 cm, spls do not touch ptls. *Ht:* 25 cm; *D:* S; *Fl:* 6–8

Yellow pheasant's eye 

A. vernalis

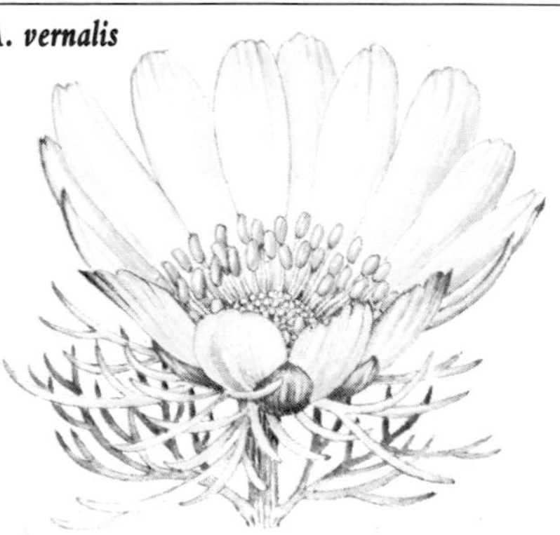

Erect per to 40 cm, base scaly. Stem lvs unstkd, cut twice. Ptls 2 × spl length. *D:* E, S, C; *Fl:* 4–5

Peony

Paeonia officinalis

Woody stemmed perennial. Lower lvs hrlss above, cut into 17–30 segments. Fl to 1.3 cm, fr has 2–3 hry follicles. *Ht:* 50 cm; *D:* S; *Fl:* 5–6

Hepatica

Hepatica nobilis

Lvs and fls arise direct from short stock. Lvs 3-lobed, purplish below. Fl 2 cm, 3 bracts. *Ht:* 10 cm; *D:* T (not far N); *Fl:* 3–5

Baneberry

Actaea spicata

Strong smelling. Lvs pinnate. Infl dense, long stamens, fruit a berry. *Ht:* 40 cm; *D:* T; *Fl:* 5–6

Lesser meadow rue

Thalictrum minus

Tufted perennial. Lvs pinnate, 3–4 × divided, lflts as broad as long. Inf loose, drooping stamens, fr uprt. *Ht:* 85 cm; *D:* T; *Fl:* 6–8

Common meadow rue

T. flavum

Leaves cut 2–3 ×, lower stkd; lflts longer than broad. Infl dense, stms erect. *Ht:* 75 cm; *D:* T; *Fl:* 7–8

Alpine meadow rue

T. alpinum

Slender per to 15 cm. Lvs 2 × cut mostly arise from a rhizome. Stamens hanging, yellow and purple stks. *D:* N, C; *Fl:* 6–7

Mousetail

Myosurus minimus

Hairless ann. Narrow undivided lvs in basal rosette. Fls small, in a spike, 5–10 stamens. *Ht:* 9 cm; *D:* T; *Fl:* 6–7

Traveller's joy

Clematis vitalba

Woody climbing per, stems to 30 m. Lvs have 5 coarsely toothed lflts. Fls to 2 cm, 4 hry ptls, long feathery styles on fr. *D:* T (not N); *Fl:* 7–8

Poppy family Papaveraceae

Herbs with deeply divided leaves. True poppies have a milky juice in all parts but the fumitories (now part of the family) do not. Flowers have 4 petals and two or many stamens.

Common poppy

Papaver rhoeas

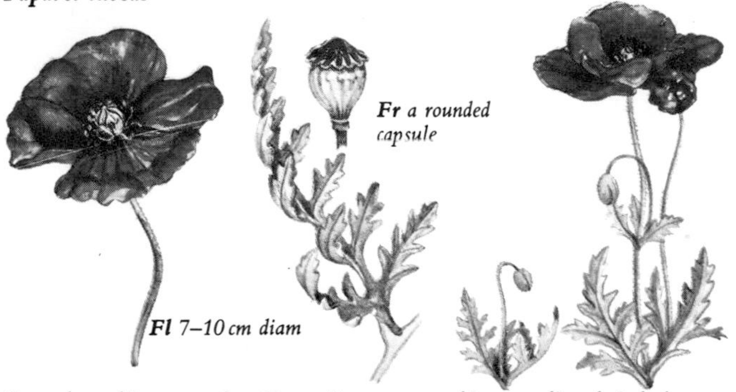

Erect, branching annual to 60 cm. Stems covered in spreading, bristly hrs. Lvs compound, pinnately divided, large central lobe. *D:* T; *Fl:* 6–8

Arctic poppy

P. radicatum

Tufted per, juice yellow. Lf bases persist as a sheath. Fl to 5 cm, fr a bristly elliptic-ovoid capsule. *Ht:* 15 cm; *D:* NW; *Fl:* 7

Long-headed poppy

P. dubium

Erect branched ann, flat hrs above. Fr to 2.5 cm, 2 × as long as wide. *Ht:* 40 cm; *D:* T; *Fl:* 6–7

Prickly poppy

P. argemone

Upright ann to 45 cm, flat hrs on stems. Lf tips v pointed. Fl to 6 cm; fr ridged, bristly to 2.5 cm. *D:* S; *Fl:* 6–7

Welsh poppy

Meconopsis cambrica

Tufted, hrlss stems to 60 cm. Basal lvs long-stkd. Fls to 8 cm, 2 hry spls, 4 ptls; fr oval, 4–6 valves. *D:* W; *Fl:* 6–8

Yellow horned poppy

Glaucium flavum

Branched, glaucous, to 90 cm, basal lvs hry. Fls short-stkd, fr to 30 cm. *D:* W; *Fl:* 6–9

Red horned poppy

G. corniculatum

Branched ann to 30 cm. Bristly spreading hrs on stems and lvs. Fls to 5 cm, short-stkd; fr to 22 cm. *D:* S; *Fl:* 6–7

Greater celandine

Chelidonium majus

Stems fragile to 90 cm, scattered hrs. Orange sap. Fls to 2 cm, fr to 5 cm. *D:* T; *Fl:* 5–8

Bulbous corydalis

Corydalis solida

Erect to 20 cm. Lobed bracts below fls. *D:* T (not far N); *Fl:* 4–5. *C. bulbosa* sim but bracts unlobed

Climbing corydalis

C. claviculata

Scrambling, lvs end in tendril. Ptl tube short-spurred, 6 fls in infl. *Ht:* 50 cm; *D:* W; *Fl:* 6–9

Yellow corydalis

C. lutea

***Infl** of 6–10 fls*

Branched, no tendrils. Ptl tube short-spurred to 1.8 cm. *Ht:* to 30 cm; *D:* W, C; *Fl:* 5–8

Common fumitory

Fumaria officinalis

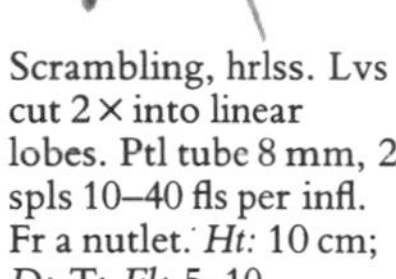

Scrambling, hrlss. Lvs cut 2× into linear lobes. Ptl tube 8 mm, 2 spls 10–40 fls per infl. Fr a nutlet. *Ht:* 10 cm; *D:* T; *Fl:* 5–10

Cabbage family Cruciferae

Annuals and perennials with spirally arranged leaves. The flowers have 4 sepals, 4 unjoined petals, 6 stamens and one stigma. The fruit opens by two valves. Many are weeds.

Wallflower

Cheiranthus cheiri

Erect branched perennial to 60 cm. Stems woody and ridged. Basal lvs 5–10 cm long, undivided and covered with forked hairs. Flowers to 2.5 cm diam, ptls twice sepal length. Fruit 3–7 cm long. *D:* W, S, C; *Fl:* 4–6

Shepherd's purse

Capsella bursa-pastoris

Fl c. *2.5 mm*

Stem lvs clasping with pointed lobes. Ptls 2 × spl length, fr 9 mm. *Ht:* 25 cm; *D:* T; *Fl:* 1–12

Hairy rocket

Erucastrum gallicum

Erect ann to 60 cm, hrs point down. Lobed lvs, bracts at infl base. Fls 8 mm, slender beak on fr. *D:* SW, C; *Fl:* 5–9

Annual wall rocket

Diplotaxis muralis

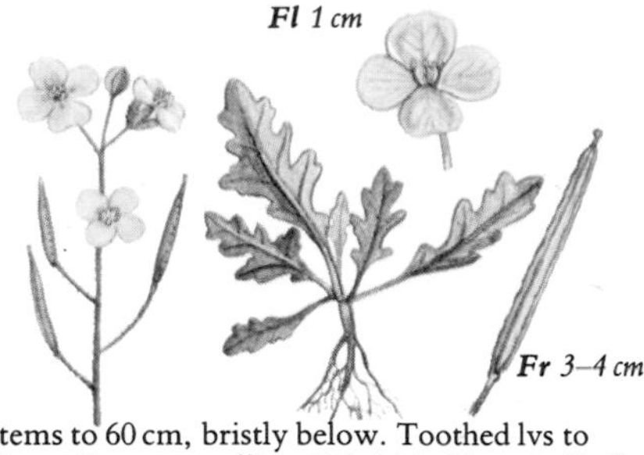

Stems to 60 cm, bristly below. Toothed lvs to 10 cm. Strong-smelling. Ptls 2 × spl length. *D:* S, C; *Fl:* 6–9

Small alison

Alyssum alyssoides

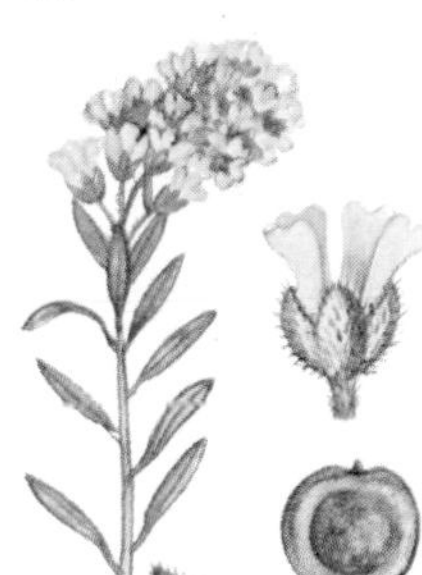

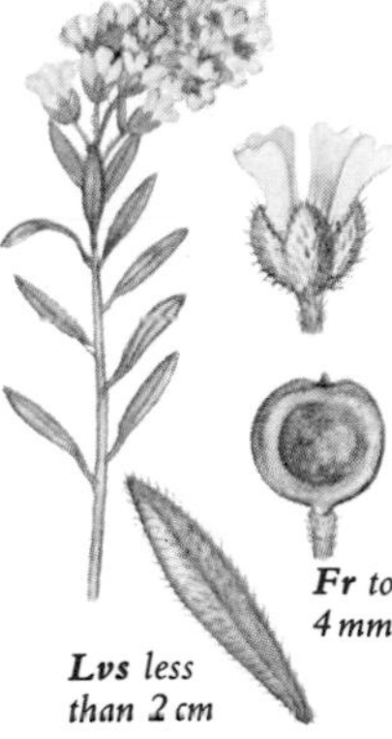

Erect ann, star-shaped hrs on shs. Fls 3 mm, spls persist in fr. *Ht:* 15 cm; *D:* T; *Fl:* 5–6

London rocket

Sisymbrium irio

Fr to 5 cm

Lower lvs stkd, lobed, stem lvs stkd. No bracts. Fls 4 mm. *Ht:* 40 cm; *D:* T (not far N); *Fl:* 6–8

Hedge mustard

Sisymbrium officinale

Stiffly erect ann to 90 cm. Downward-pointing hrs on stems, basal lvs in rosette, deeply lobed, no bracts. Fr narrow, erect. *D:* T; *Fl:* 6–8

Field pepperwort

Lepidium campestre

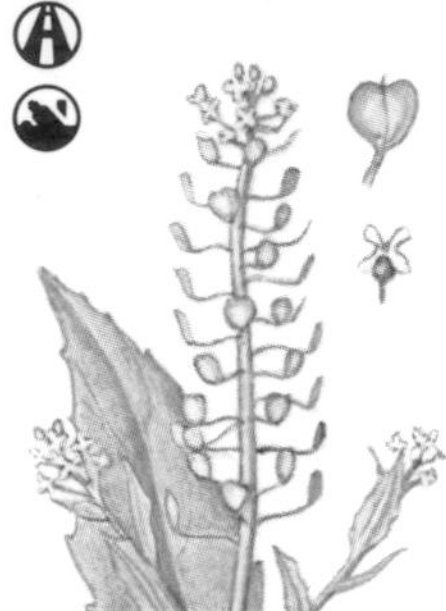

Has short, spreading hrs. Lvs unlobed. Fr notched at tip, spotted white. *Ht:* 40 cm; *D:* T; *Fl:* 5–8

Dittander

L. latifolium

Branched, hrlss. Basal lvs serrate. Spls white-edged, fr unnotched. *Ht:* 1 m; *D:* T (not N); *Fl:* 6–7

Flixweed

Descurainia sophia

Erect with star-shaped hrs. Fls 3 mm, fr 2 cm, strong midrib. *Ht:* 60 cm; *D:* T; *Fl:* 6–8

Sea kale

Crambe maritima

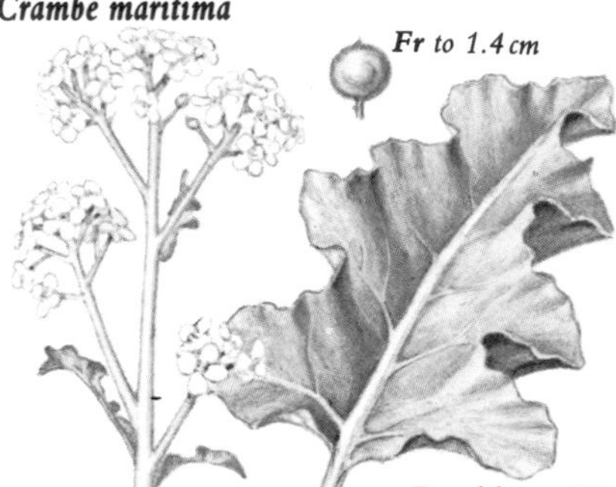

Erect per to 60 cm. Basal lvs long-stkd, glaucous. Ptls have green claws, fr 1-seeded. *D:* T; *Fl:* 6–8

Sea rocket

Cakile maritima

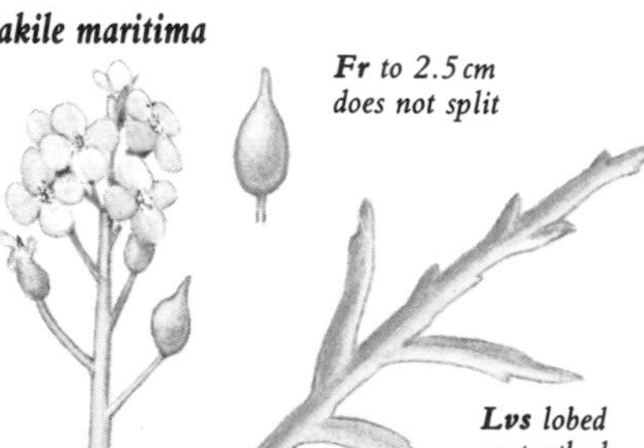

Often prostrate succ to 45 cm. Infl dense, fr in 2 sections, 1 seed in each. *D:* T (not far N); *Fl:* 6–8

Sea stock

Matthiola sinuata

Branched hrs on stems, sticky hrs on stem lvs. Basal lvs wavy. Fls *c.* 2.5 cm, fr 10 cm. *Ht:* 40 cm; *D:* W, S; *Fl:* 6–8

Hoary whitlow grass  

Draba incana

Basal lvs serrate with star-shaped hrs. Fls 5 mm, ptls just notched. *Ht:* 30 cm; *D:* N, mts in C, W; *Fl:* 6–8

Yellow whitlow grass 

D. aizoides

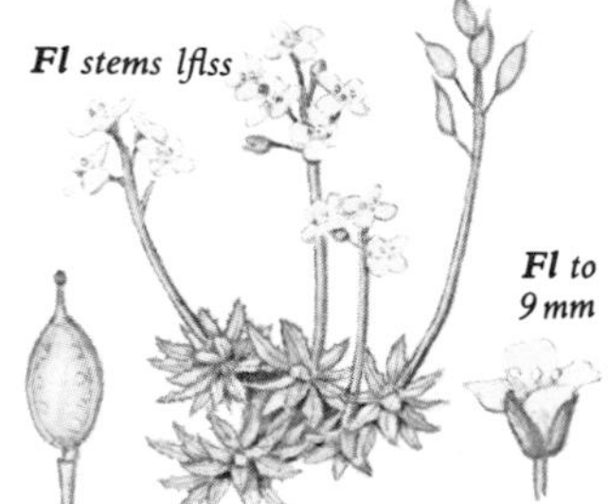

Hairless per. Tufted rosette of stiff, linear lvs, keeled, white spine at tip. Fr 1 cm. *Ht:* 7 cm; *D:* C, S; *Fl:* 3–5

Alpine whitlow grass 

D. alpina

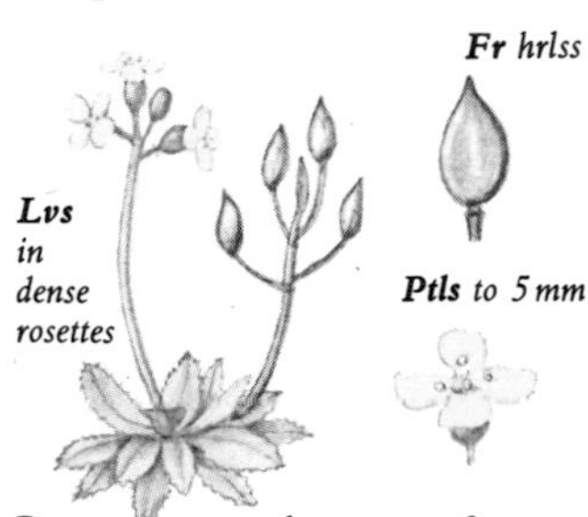

Represents complex group of spp. All have star-shaped hrs on leaves. *Ht:* 15 cm; *D:* Arct; *Fl:* 7–8

Common whitlow grass 

Erophila verna

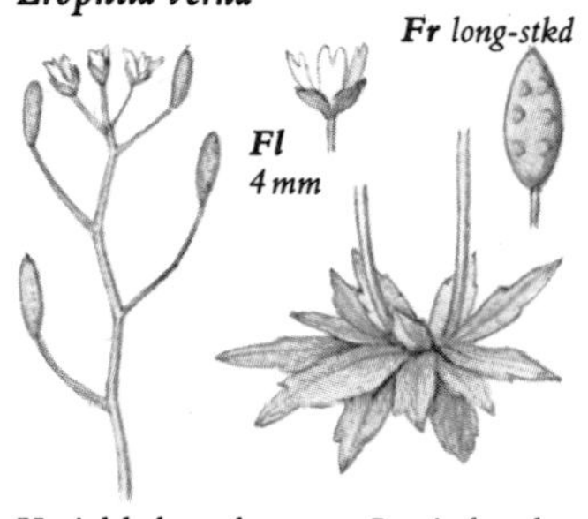

Variable low, hry ann. Lvs in basal rosette. Ptls v deeply cut, fr elliptic, hrlss. *Ht:* to 20 cm; *D:* T; *Fl:* 3–5

Common scurvy grass

Cochlearia officinalis

Basal lvs long-stkd. Upper lvs clasping. Fr 5 mm. *Ht:* 35 cm; *D:* NW; *Fl:* 5–8

English scurvy grass

C. anglica

Basal lvs taper to stk. Fls to 1.4 cm, fr oval, flattened, 1 cm. *Ht:* 25 cm; *D:* NW; *Fl:* 4–7

Alpine scurvy grass

C. pyrenaica

Very like *C. officinalis* and possibly the same sp as *C. alpina*. Lvs not succ. Fr tapers into stk and tip. *Ht:* 25 cm; *D:* C, W; *Fl:* 5–8

Tower cress

Arabis turrita

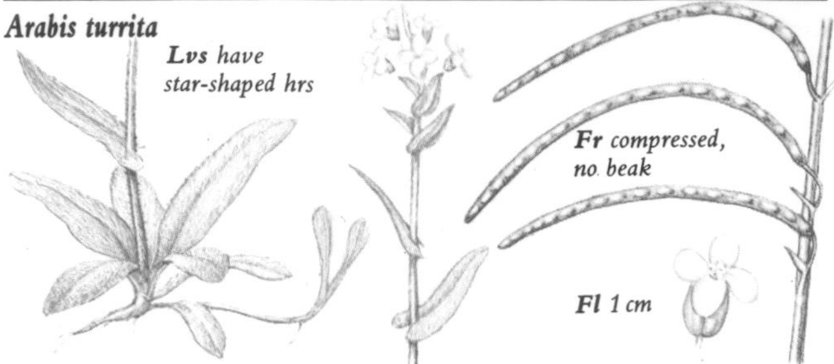

Biennial or per, horizontal at base with veg rosettes. Hry erect fl shs to 70 cm. Basal lvs serrate, narrow to stk, stem lvs oblong. *D:* C, S; *Fl:* 5–8

Hairy rock cress

A. hirsuta

Stems to 60 cm from rosette of obovate stkd lvs, hrs star-shaped; fr 4 cm. *D:* T; *Fl:* 6–8

Alpine rock cress

A. alpina

Creeping, erect fl shs to 40 cm. Basal lvs serrate, stkd. Fr 4 cm, spreading. *D:* N, W, S; *Fl:* 6–8

Great yellowcress

Rorippa amphibia

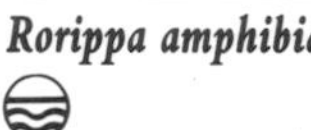

Hollow hrlss stems to 1.2 m. Ptls 2 × length of spls, fr long-stkd. *D:* T (not far N); *Fl:* 6–8

Marsh yellowcress

R. islandica

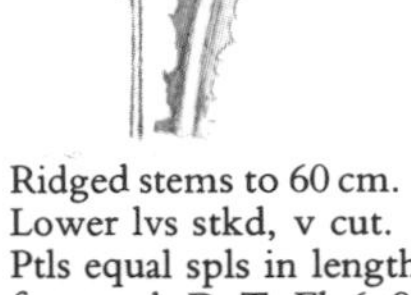

Ridged stems to 60 cm. Lower lvs stkd, v cut. Ptls equal spls in length, fr curved. *D:* T; *Fl:* 6–9

Thale cress

Arabidopsis thaliana

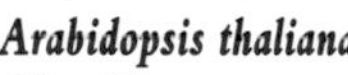

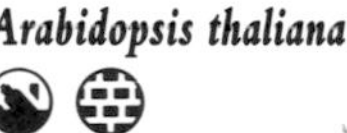

Erect shs to 50 cm, hry below; stem lvs unstkd. Fr 1.5 cm, erect on spread stks. *D:* (not far N); *Fl:* 4–5 (and 9–10)

Swine cress

Coronopus squamatus

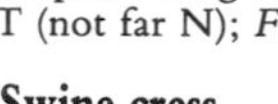

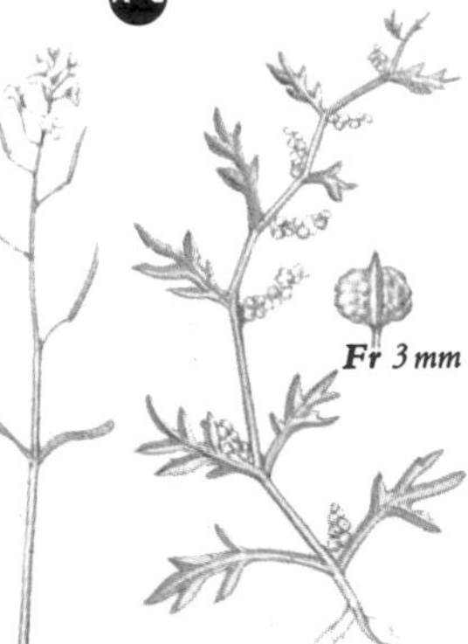

Prostrate lfy shs 20 cm. Lvs pinnately lobed. Infl unstkd, mostly opp lvs; fr short-stkd. *D:* W, C, S; *Fl:* 6–9

Watercress

Nasturtium officinale

Lvs pinnate

Hollow hrlss shs creep and float. Fr has 2 rows of seeds. *Ht:* 40 cm; *D:* T (not N); *Fl:* 5–10

Common wintercress

Barbarea vulgaris

Erect, hrlss, branched to 90 cm. Basal lvs stkd in rosette. Fr erect, 4-angled. *D:* T; *Fl:* 5–8

Cuckoo flower

Cardamine pratense

Erect per to 60 cm. Top lflt kidney-shaped. Fls long-stkd, ptls 3 × spl length, valves of fr curl up. *D:* T, *Fl:* 4–6

Coralroot bittercress

C. bulbifera

Has bulbils in stem lf axils. Shs to 70 cm. Ptls 1.5 cm, 3 × spl length. *D:* T (not far N); *Fl:* 4–6

Wavy bittercress

C. flexuosa

***Lvs** pinnate, basal lvs stkd*

Stems to 50 cm may be hry; ptls same length as spls, 6 stamens. Fr hardly extends above fls. *D:* W; *Fl:* 4–9

Hairy bittercress

C. hirsuta

Stems hrlss. Fls have 4 stamens; fr grows above fls. *Ht:* 20 cm; *D:* T (not far N); *Fl:* 4–7

Large bittercress

C. amara

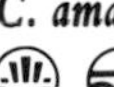
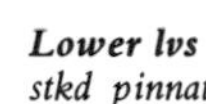

***Lower lvs** stkd pinnate*

Creeping; erect shs to 60 cm. Fr 3 cm, long persistent style. *D:* T (not far N); *Fl:* 4–6

Field pennycress 

Thlaspi arvense

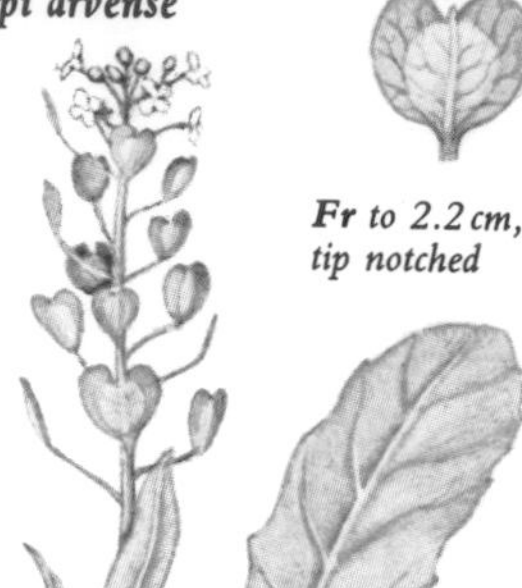

Erect, stems to 60 cm. Basal lvs broad, taper to stk. Fl 5 mm, fr broad-winged. *D:* T; *Fl:* 5–7

Wild radish 

Raphanus raphanistrum

Bristly, basal lvs have large top lobe. Ptls veined. Long-beaked fr splits crosswise. *Ht:* 40 cm; *D:* T; *Fl:* 5–9

Sea radish  

R. maritimus

Bristly hrs above. Ptls *c.* 2 cm, not veined. Fr short-beaked, does not split. *D:* W, N to GB; *Fl:* 6–8

Hoary cress    

Cardaria draba

Creeping. Uprt lfy shs to 90 cm. Basal lvs stkd, upper lvs clasping. Fr does not split. *D:* T; *Fl:* 5–6

Horse radish  

Armoracia rusticana

Robust hrlss. Rts fleshy, edible. Basal lvs 40 cm, wavy-edged. Infl v branched. *Ht:* 1 m; *D:* T; *Fl:* 5–6

Charlock 

Sinapis arvensis

Stems to 80 cm with bristly hrs. Basal lvs lobed, upper lvs serrate, unlobed. Fr smooth. *D:* T; *Fl:* 5–7

White mustard

Sinapis alba

Like *S. arvensis* (p 42) but all lvs pinnately lobed. Fr beaked. *Ht:* 60 cm; *D:* T; *Fl:* 6–8

Wild cabbage

Brassica oleracea

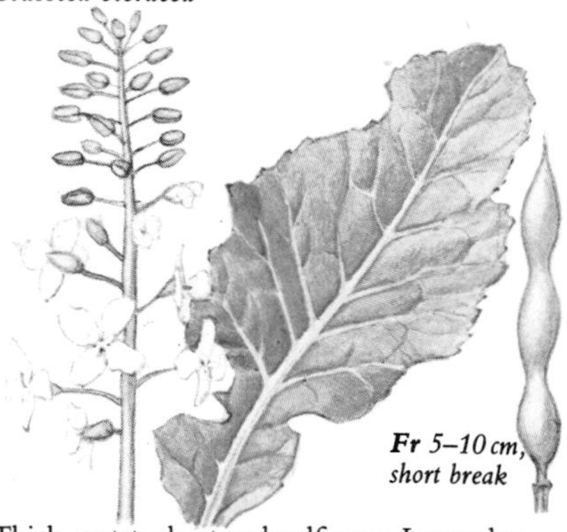

Thick rootstock, stem has lf scars. Lower lvs large, few basal lobes, upper lvs stkd, oblong. Ptls 2 cm. *Ht:* to 3 m; *D:* W, N to GB; *Fl:* 5–8

Black mustard

Brassica nigra

Annual to 1 m, bristly below. No thick rootstock, all lvs stkd. Ridged fr held near stem. *D:* T; *Fl:* 6–9

Buckler mustard

Biscutella laevigata

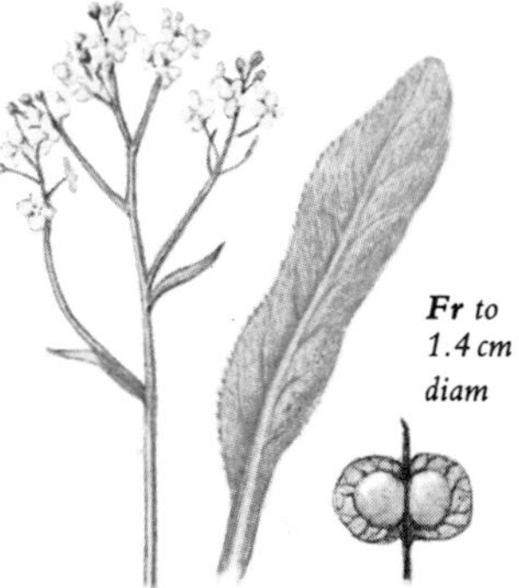

Basal rosette of unlobed, possibly wavy lvs. Fr of 2 fused discs. *Ht:* 30 cm; *D:* C, S; *Fl:* 5–8

Garlic mustard

Alliaria petiolata

Roots and lvs smell of garlic. Stem hry. Fr 4-angled. *Ht:* 1 m; *D:* T (not far N); *Fl:* 4–6

Ball mustard

Neslia paniculata

Annual to 80 cm with star-shaped hrs. Fr wrinkled, does not split. *D:* C, E; *Fl:* 6–9

Treacle mustard

Erysimum cheiranthoides

Leafy stem to 90 cm, hrs branched. Basal lvs die when infl formed; fr 4-angled. *D:* T; *Fl:* 6–8

Perennial honesty  

Lunaria rediviva

Erect to 1.4 m. Top lvs stkd (unlike *L. annua*). Infl at apex, fr oval. *D:* T (not far N); *Fl:* 4–6

Woad 

Isatis tinctoria

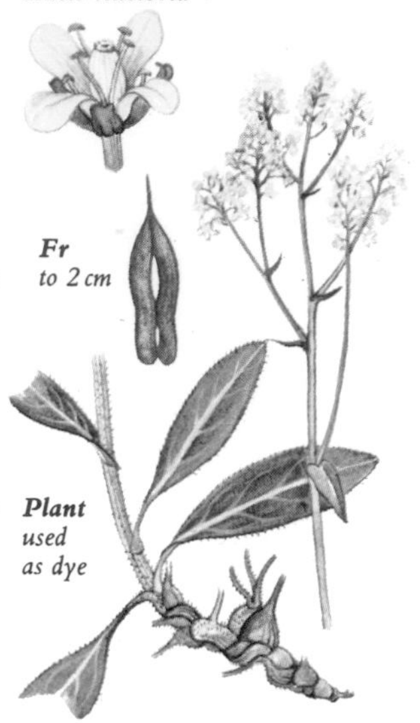

Hairless, several basal rosettes, stem lvs arrow-shaped, hanging fr. *Ht:* 1 m; *D:* T (not N); *Fl:* 7–8

Mignonette family Resedaceae

Herbs with simple or divided spirally arranged leaves. Flowers have 4–7 unfused petals and sepals, many stamens and 3–6 carpels fusing into a one-celled capsule.

Wild mignonette  

Reseda lutea

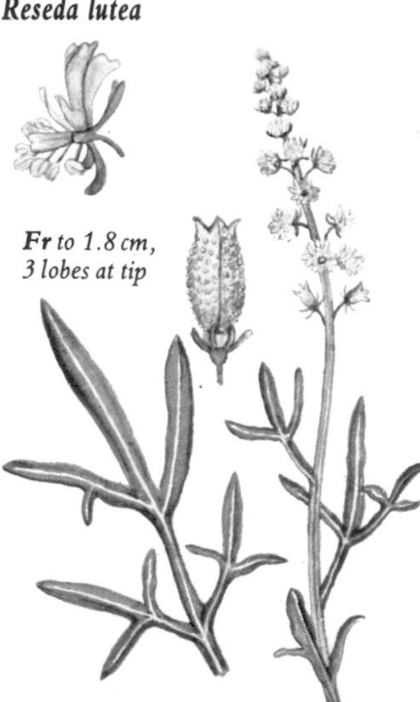

Branched, erect, hrlss to 75 cm. Basal lvs in rosette, pinnate stem lvs. Fl 6 mm, 6 ptls and spls, fr erect. *D:* S, W, C; *Fl:* 6–8

Upright mignonette 

R. alba

Leaves deeply cut into narrow pinnate lobes. Fls 9 mm, 5 ptls, fr oblong, 4 lobes at tip. *Ht:* 75 cm; *D:* S, C, NW; *Fl:* 6–8

Rampion mignonette 

Reseda phyteuma

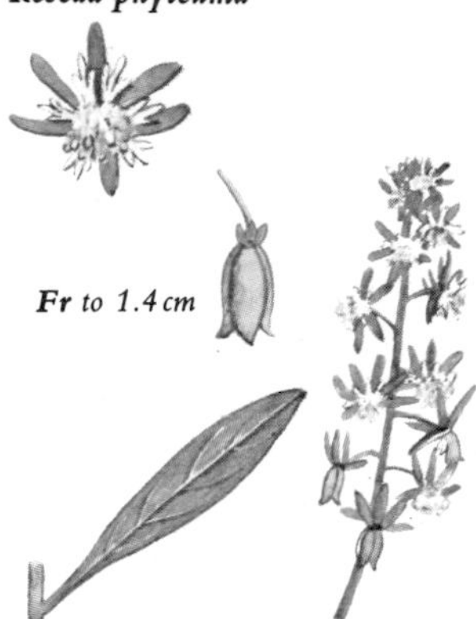

Branched to 30 cm. Lvs unlobed or in prs, blunt lobes above; 6 ptls, fr drooping, 3-lobed. *D:* S; *Fl:* 6–8

Weld   

R. luteola

Erect, hrlss to 1.5 m, little or not branched. Lf rosette in 1st yr, fl sh in 2nd. *D:* S, W, C; *Fl:* 6–8

Sundew family Droseraceae

Perennial herbs. The leaves have sticky hairs for trapping insects and are curled in bud. Flowers have 4–8 petals.

Common sundew    

Drosera rotundifolia

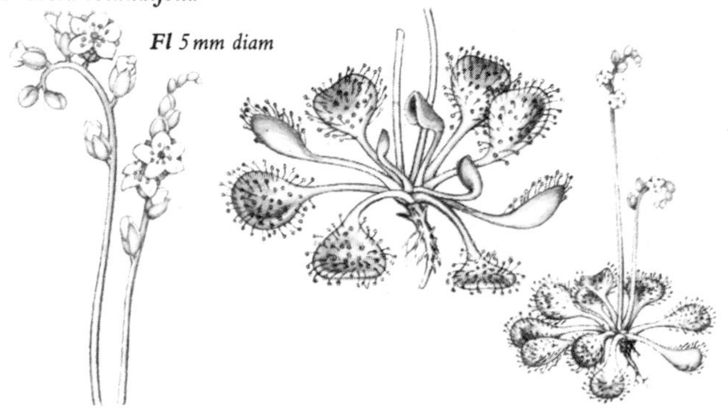

Perennial with low rosettes of leaves each 1 cm across with a long hry stk and circular blade. Erect fl shs to 25 cm and more than 2 × lf length from rosette centre. Fr pointed. *D:* T; *Fl:* 6–8

Great sundew 

D. anglica *Lf* blades to 3 cm

Erect lvs narrow to hrlss stks. Fl sh 2 × lf length from rosette centre; fr round. *D:* N, C; *Fl:* 7–8

Oblong-leaved sundew  

D. intermedia

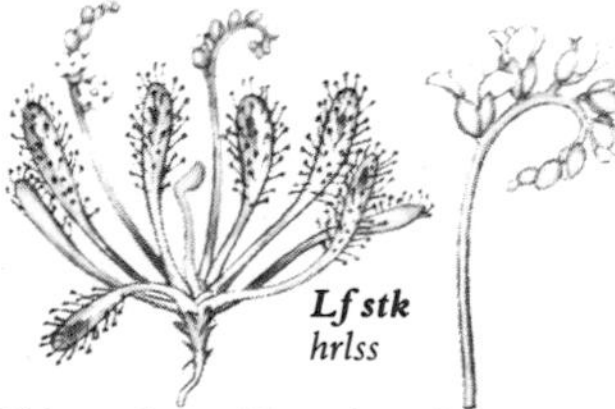

Oblong lvs *c.* 10 cm just shorter than fl sh arising under rosette, fr pointed *D:* N, W, C; *Fl:* 7–8

Stonecrop family Crassulaceae

Usually succulent herbs with undivided leaves. The flowers generally have 5 sepals and petals but may be more. The stamens are equal to or double the petals in number and there are as many unjoined carpels as petals.

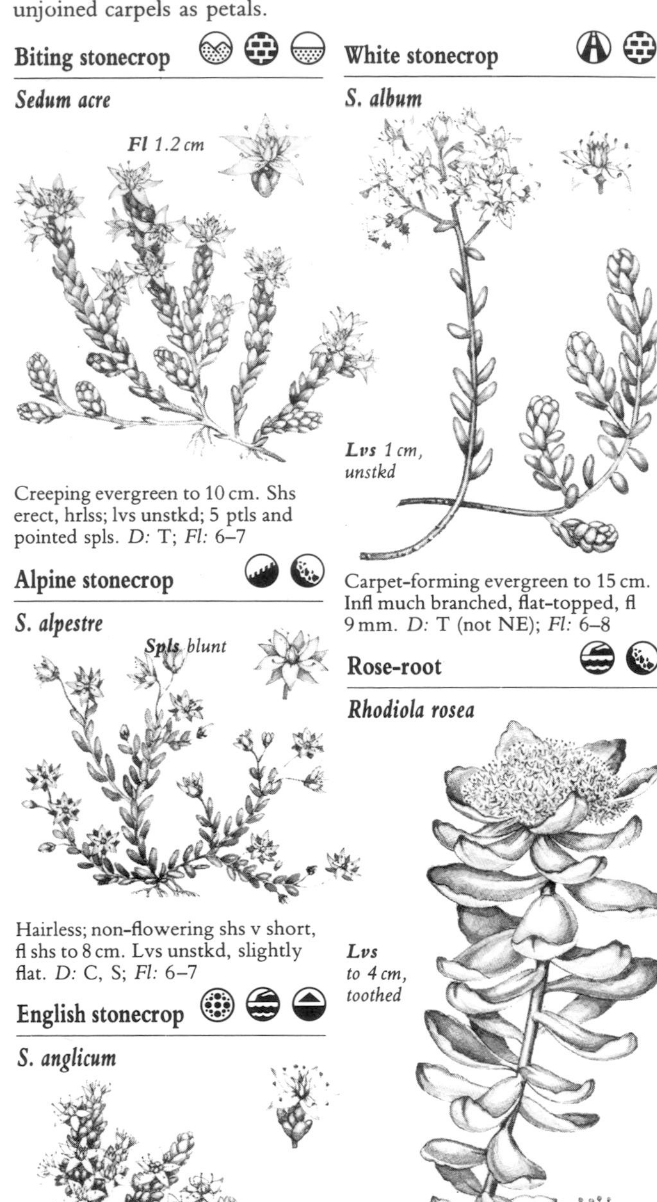

Biting stonecrop

Sedum acre

Creeping evergreen to 10 cm. Shs erect, hrlss; lvs unstkd; 5 ptls and pointed spls. *D:* T; *Fl:* 6–7

Alpine stonecrop

S. alpestre

Hairless; non-flowering shs v short, fl shs to 8 cm. Lvs unstkd, slightly flat. *D:* C, S; *Fl:* 6–7

English stonecrop

S. anglicum

Patch-forming, hrlss. Lvs globular, alternate. Fl stks short. *Ht:* 4 cm; *D:* W, N to Swed; *Fl:* 6–9

White stonecrop

S. album

Carpet-forming evergreen to 15 cm. Infl much branched, flat-topped, fl 9 mm. *D:* T (not NE); *Fl:* 6–8

Rose-root

Rhodiola rosea

Robust, erect, glaucous per; short stock bears lf scars. Lvs flat, round. ♂ and ♀ separate. *Ht:* 22 cm; *D:* N, mts in C; *Fl:* 5–8

Rock stonecrop  

S. forsteranum

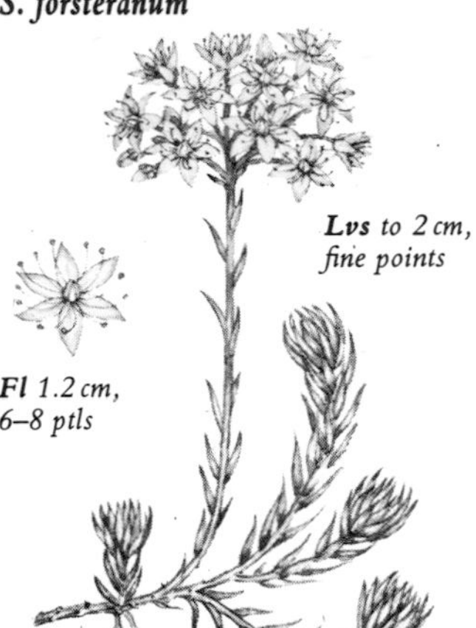

Creeping, glaucous. Old lvs stay on stems, new ones arise at tips. *Ht:* 22 cm; *D:* W; *Fl:* 6–7

Navelwort  

Umbilicus rupestris

Hairless, usually unbranched. Lf blade circular, central stk; fl tubular. *Ht:* 30 cm; *D:* S, W; *Fl:* 6–8

Mossy stonecrop 

Crassula tillaea

Dwarf, hrlss. Shs creeping, often reddish. Lvs and fls dense, 3 ptls and spls. *Ht:* 4 cm; *D:* S, W; *Fl:* 6–7

Reflexed stonecrop  

S. reflexum

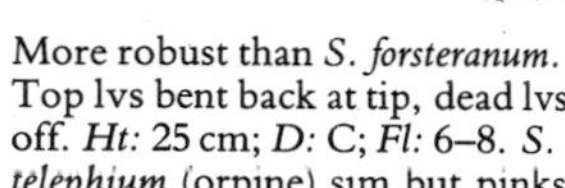

More robust than *S. forsteranum*. Top lvs bent back at tip, dead lvs fall off. *Ht:* 25 cm; *D:* C; *Fl:* 6–8. *S. telephium* (orpine) sim but pinks fls

Hen-and-chickens houseleek  

Jovibarba sobolifera

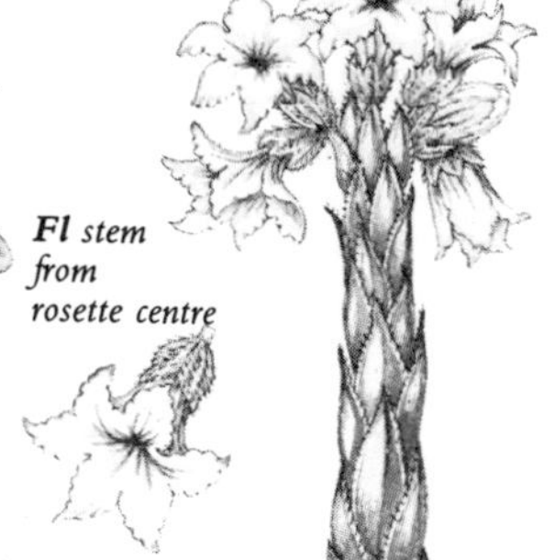

Dense lf rosette, basal plantlets joined by stolons; 6 hr-fringed ptls. *Ht:* 25 cm; *D:* C, E; *Fl:* 7–8

Saxifrage family Saxifragaceae

Herbs with alternate leaves. The symmetrical flowers usually have 5 petals and sepals, 5 or 10 stamens and two carpels which are joined at their base.

Meadow saxifrage

Saxifraga granulata

Mossy saxifrage

S. hypnoides

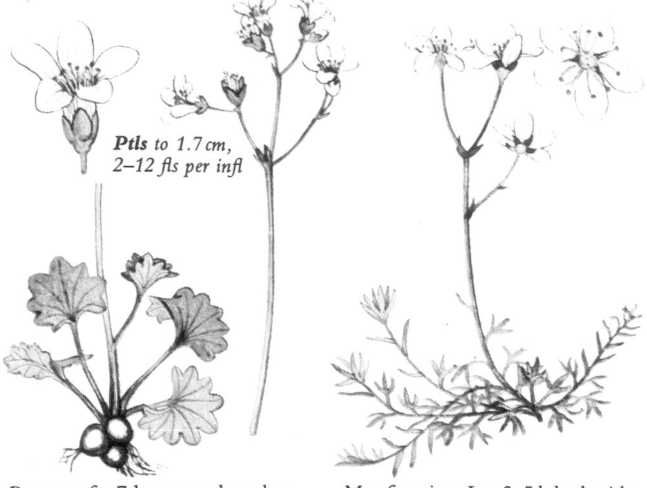

Rosette of *c.* 7 lvs, some long hrs; bulbils in lf axils. Fls have 10 stamens as all *Saxifraga* spp. *Ht:* 35 cm; *D:* N, C; *Fl:* 4–6

Mat-forming. Lvs 3–5 lobed with sharp points, narrow to stk; stem hrlss. Fl shs fine to 20 cm, ptls to 1 cm. *D:* NW; *Fl:* 5–7

Rue-leaved saxifrage

S. tridactylites

Upright to 15 cm, sticky hrs all over. Lvs 3–5 lobed, dense at base. Fls sol or in gps on long stks, ptls to 3 mm long. *D:* T (not far N); *Fl:* 4–6

Arctic saxifrage

S. nivalis

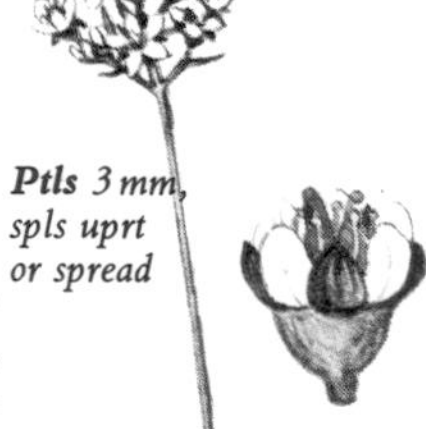

Leaves to 2 cm, oval or spathulate, serrate, purple below in basal rosette. Infl dense, 3–12 fls, fl sh to 15 cm. *D:* N; *Fl:* 7–8

Drooping saxifrage

S. cernua

Basal lvs 3–5 lobed in rosette, top lvs unstkd, bulbils in axils. Fl shs unbranched, fl sol on bulbil gp. *Ht:* 10 cm; *D:* N, Alps; *Fl:* 7

Purple saxifrage

S. oppositifolia

Perennial with long, prostrate branches. Erect shs only 1–2 cm tall. Dense lvs in 4 ranks. Fls sol on erect shs. *D:* N, S; *Fl:* 3–5

Yellow saxifrage

S. aizoides

Perennial. Vegetative and flowering shs to 20 cm tall. Lvs linear, unstkd, dense. Fl shs hry, infl of 1–10 fls with lfy bracts, spls spread, ptls to 7 mm long. *D:* N, mts in S; *Fl:* 6–9

Starry saxifrage

S. stellaris

Basal lvs as *S. nivalis* (p 48) but green, few long hrs. Over 12 fls in infl, spls reflexed. *Ht:* 10 cm; *D:* T; *Fl:* 6–8

Opposite-leaved golden saxifrage

Chrysosplenium oppositifolium

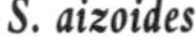

Prostrate rooting stems to 15 cm. Basal lvs round, narrow abruptly to short stk. *D:* T (not far N); *Fl:* 4–7

Alternate-leaved golden saxifrage

C. alternifolium

Very like *C. oppositifolium* but creeping shs lflss, basal lvs have notch at attachment to v long lf stk. *D:* T (not far N); *Fl:* 4–7

Grass of Parnassus family Parnassiaceae

Perennial herbs with undivided, alternate leaves. Terminal, solitary flowers have 5 sepals and petals, 5 true stamens plus 5 infertile structures and 4 fused carpels.

Grass of Parnassus 

Parnassia palustris

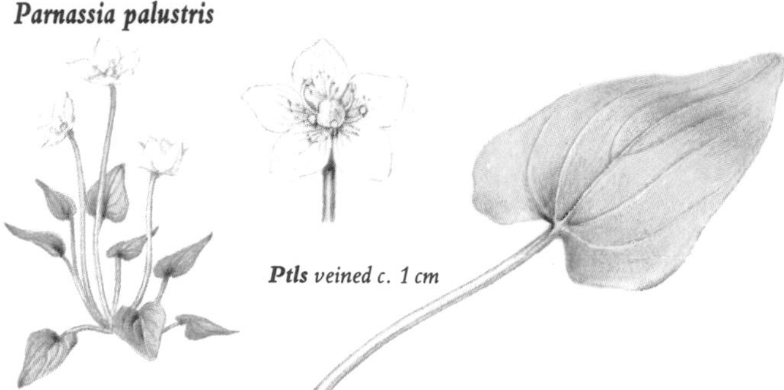

Hairless herb to 30 cm. Lvs heart-shaped, untoothed to 3 cm, stks longer than blades. Fl stks vertical, single lf near base. *D:* T; *Fl:* 7–10

Rose family Rosaceae

Herbs, shrubs and trees with alternate leaves having stipules. The flowers have 5 petals and sepals (and sometimes an epicalyx), more than 5 stamens and from one to many carpels. The flower stalk is often involved in fruit formation.

Dog rose

Rosa canina

***Stems** arched*

***Prickles** curved*

Leaflets hrlss or hry below. Fl stks 1 cm, spls fall before fr ripe, stigmas unfused, fr hrlss. *Ht:* 2.5 m; *D:* T (not far N); *Fl:* 6–7

Field rose

R. arvensis

***Prickle** tips hooked*

Scrambles to 2 m. Lflts usually hrlss. Fl shs to 4 cm, short spls soon fall, single style as long as stamens. *D:* C, S, W; *Fl:* 6–7

Burnet rose

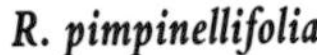

R. pimpinellifolia

Bush to 1 m. Straight prickles and stiff hrs on stems; 3–5 lflt prs. *D:* T (not Scand); *Fl:* 5–7

Downy rose

R. tomentosa

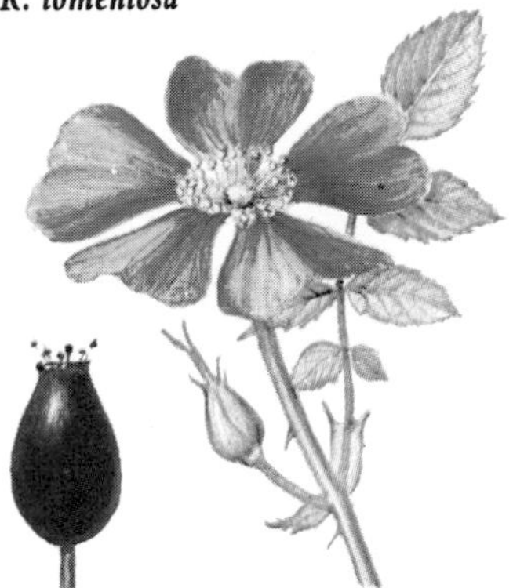

Prickles just curved; lvs have downy hrs; fl shs sticky, hry; spls fall. *Ht:* 1.5 m; *D:* T (not far N); *Fl:* 6–7

Alpine rose

R. pendulina

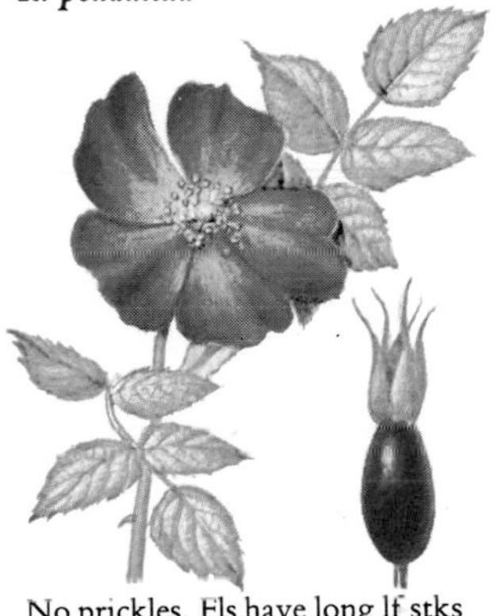

No prickles. Fls have long lf stks round shs, fl shs bend back in fr. *Ht:* 2 m; *D:* S mts, C; *Fl:* 6–7

Wild rose

R. stylosa

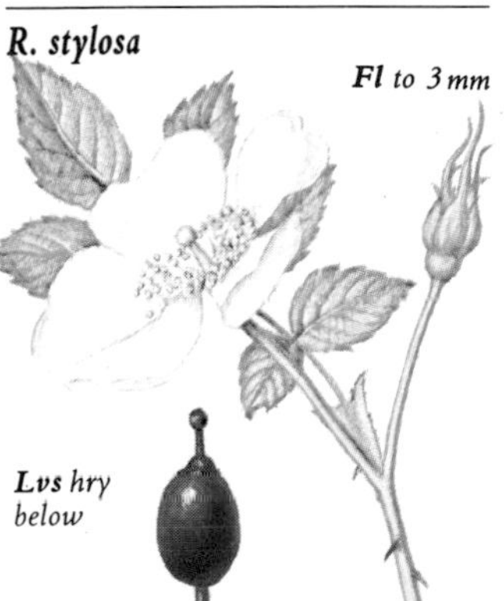

Arched shs 3 m, prickles hooked. Sticky hrs on fl shs; styles fused, separate in fr. *D:* W, S; *Fl:* 6–7

Sweet briar

R. rubiginosa

Stems uprt, hooked prickles vary in size; lflts have glands below. *Ht:* 1.5 m; *D:* T (not far N); *Fl:* 6–7

Provence rose

R. gallica

Patch-forming. Lflts glaucous, round. Fls to 9 cm, frag, styles hry. *Ht:* 65 cm; *D:* C, S; *Fl:* 5–6

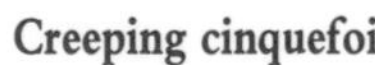

Creeping cinquefoil

Potentilla reptans

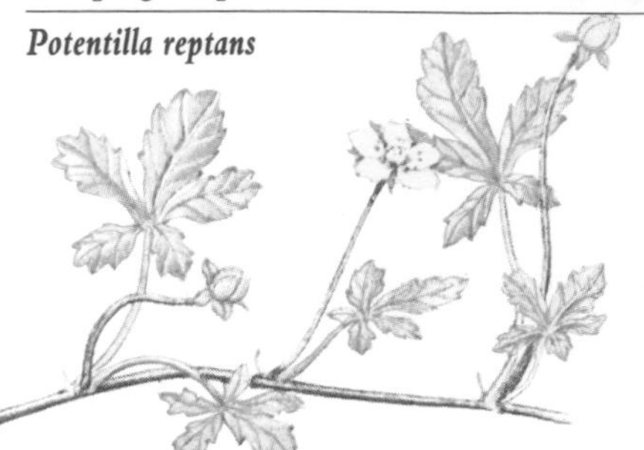

Prostrate, rts at nodes. Erect fl shs to 30 cm. Stipules untoothed. Fl has epicalyx as in all spp of *Potentilla*. *D:* T (not far N); *Fl:* 6–9

Shrubby cinquefoil

P. fruticosa

Ptls *to 1.2 cm*

Lvs *untoothed*

Shrub; lvs pinnate, 5-lobed. Fls in terminal infl. *Ht:* to 1 m; *D:* NW, mts in S; *Fl:* 6–7·

Hoary cinquefoil

P. argentea

Lower lvs *5-lobed, v hry below*

Upright fl shs often hry. Fls to 1.5 cm, spls hry. *Ht:* 40 cm; *D:* N, Alps; *Fl:* 6–9

Marsh cinquefoil

P. palustris

Spls *pointed*

Has creeping rhizome. Lvs serrate, 5 or 7 lflts, spls purple. *Ht:* 35 cm; *D:* T; *Fl:* 5–7

Norwegian cinquefoil

P. norvegica

Leaves serrate, hry; fl shs erect, clustered fls, 5 hry spls. *Ht:* 40 cm; *D:* N, C, E; *Fl:* 6–9

Silverweed

P. anserina

Creeping stolons to 1 m; 10 lflt prs, silky white hrs. Fls long-stkd, sol. *D:* T; *Fl:* 6–8

Tormentil

P. erecta

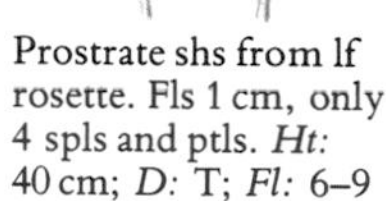

Prostrate shs from lf rosette. Fls 1 cm, only 4 spls and ptls. *Ht:* 40 cm; *D:* T; *Fl:* 6–9

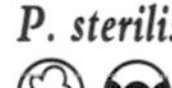

Barren strawberry

P. sterilis

Fl *to 1.5 cm*

Softly hry to 15 cm, spread stolons, lvs not glossy, ptls far apart. *D:* W, S, C; *Fl:* 2–5

Alpine cinquefoil

Potentilla crantzii

Lower lvs 5-lobed, hry, especially below; fl shs in lf axils, spls hry. *Ht:* 20 cm; *D:* N, S; *Fl:* 6–7

Hautbois strawberry

Fragaria moschata

Robust spread hrs on fl shs, fls 2 cm. Achenes on fr, but none near base. *Ht:* 30 cm; *D:* C, W; *Fl:* 4–7

Sibbaldia

Sibbaldia procumbens

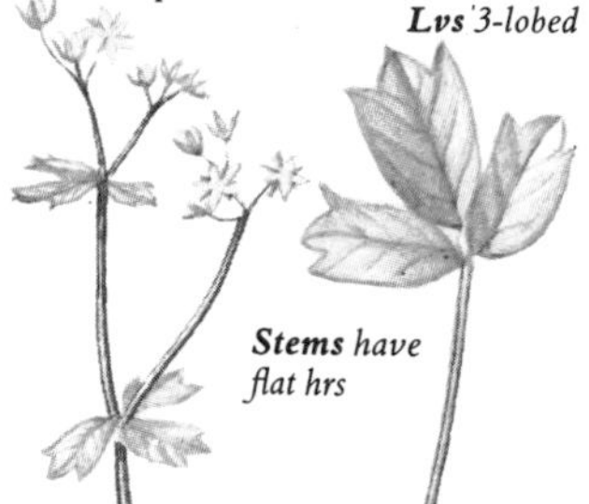

Tussocky. Infl dense, fls 5 mm, spls pointed, ptls v small or absent. *Ht:* 2 cm; *D:* N, S; *Fl:* 7–8

Wild strawberry

F. vesca

Like *Potentilla sterilis* (p 52) but no gaps between ptls; achenes all over fr. *Ht:* 20 cm; *D:* T; *Fl:* 4–7

Stone bramble

Rubus saxatilis

Prostrate, uprt fl shs 35 cm; lvs 3-lobed (unlike *R. chamaemorus*). *D:* T; *Fl:* 6–8

Arctic bramble

R. arcticus

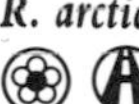 

No prickles; 3-lobed lvs; infl long-stkd, 1–3 fls, many fr parts. *Ht:* 20 cm; *D:* N; *Fl:* 7–9

Bramble

R. fruticosus

Curved prickles; fr of 20+ parts, no bloom (unlike *R. caesius*). *Ht:* 1.5 m *D:* T; *Fl:* 5–9

Water avens  

Geum rivale

Hairy. Top lflt large. Fls nodding, spls purple, styles persist in fr. *Ht:* 45 cm; *D:* T; *Fl:* 5–9

Herb bennet   

G. urbanum

Stem lvs simple above, lobed lower down. Fls uprt, spls green. *Ht:* 45 cm; *D:* T (not far N); *Fl:* 6–8

Alpine avens 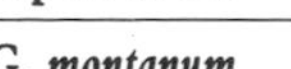

G. montanum

Rhizomatous. Top lflt round. Fls 3 cm, often 6 ptls, feathery fr. *Ht:* 7 cm; *D:* C, S; *Fl:* 7–8

Mountain avens   

Dryas octopetala

Many v hry lvs; 7–10 ptls, sticky black hrs on spls, feathery fr. *Ht:* 6 cm; *D:* S mts, N; *Fl:* 6–7

Lady's mantle

Alchemilla vulgaris

Large lvs, lobes half radius, green below; no ptls. *Ht:* 30 cm; *D:* W, C; *Fl:* 6–9

Alpine lady's mantle

Alchemilla alpina

Creeping; lf blades cut almost to centre; fls 3 mm. *Ht:* 15 cm; *D:* N, W; *Fl:* 6–8

Agrimony

Agrimonia eupatoria

Hairy, hooked spines on fls persist in fr. *Ht:* 60 cm; *D:* T (not far N); *Fl:* 6–8

Meadowsweet

Filipendula ulmaria

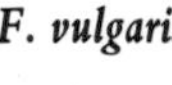

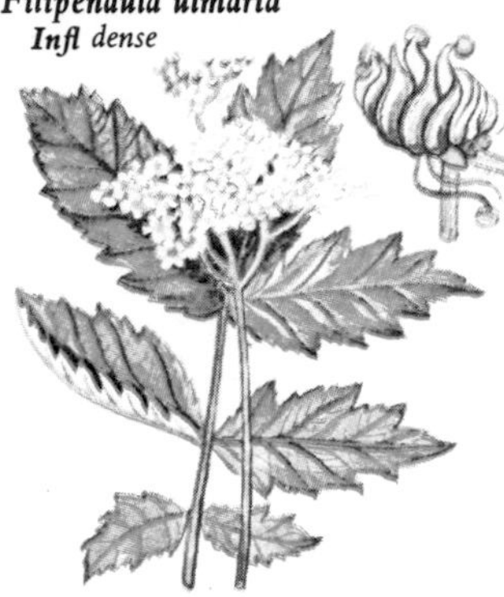

Leaves pinnate, 2–5 big lflts alt with small prs; 5 ptls, fr spirally twisted. *Ht:* 1 m; *D:* T; *Fl:* 6–9

Great burnet

Sanguisorba officinalis

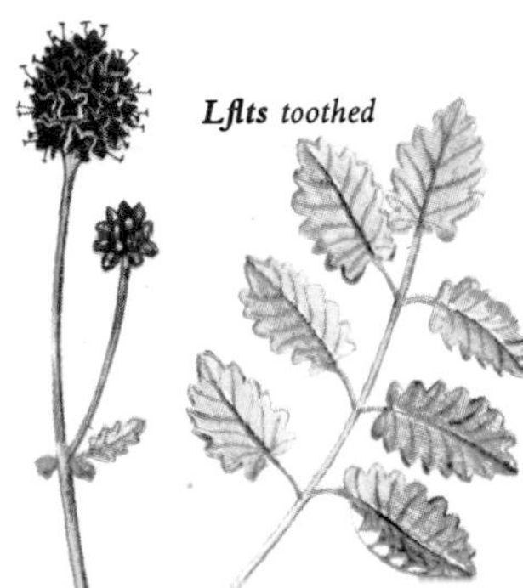

Pinnate lvs, 3–7 prs lflts; 4 red spls, no ptls, 4 stms; ♂, ♀ parts in same fl. *Ht:* 80 cm; *D:* T; *Fl:* 6–9

Salad burnet

S. minor

Scrambles to 60 cm; 4 green spls, no ptls, many stms; ♂ fls atop round infl, ♀ below. *D:* W, C; *Fl:* 5–8

Dropwort

F. vulgaris

Basal lvs jagged, 8–20 prs large lflts between small prs; 6 ptls. *Ht:* 60 cm; *D:* T (not N); *Fl:* 5–8

Parsley piert

Aphanes arvensis

Creeps to 20 cm. Lvs have 3 lobed lflts. Fls v small with only spls and stipules. *D:* W, C; *Fl:* 4–10

Goat's beard spiraea

Aruncus dioicus

Rhizomatous. Fl shs to 2 m; lvs 2× cut, serrate. Infl pyramidal, fls unstkd. *D:* C mts; *Fl:* 6–8

Pea family Leguminosae

Compound leaves have stipules and maybe tendrils. Flowers have an erect (standard) petal, two wing petals and two petals joined into a keel; 5 sepals form a tube. The fruit is a pod.

Red clover 

Trifolium pratense

Erect or straggling per. Lvs have 3 lflts, often with pale V mark. Stipules contracted to a fine point. Fls in dense globular heads. Forage crop. *Ht:* 30 cm; *D:* T; *Fl:* 5–9

Zig-zag clover  

T. medium

Straggling per. Like *T. pratense* but lflts narrower and stipules oblong. Fl head arises from a pair of lvs. *Ht:* 30 cm; *D:* T; *Fl:* 6–9

Mountain clover 

T. montanum

Hairy per like *T. hybridum*. Lflts to 4 cm long, elliptical. Fl heads often paired on v long, hry stks. *Ht:* to 60 cm; *D:* C, S; *Fl:* 5–7

White clover

T. repens

Creeping hrlss per, roots at nodes. Lflts broader near tip, white V mark, stipules oval. Spls short-toothed. *Ht:* 30 cm; *D:* T; *Fl:* 6–9

Haresfoot clover

T. arvense

Softly hry ann. Brs straggling, hry. Infl cylindrical, downy, long-stkd. Ptls half spl length. *Ht:* 10 cm; *D:* T (not far N); *Fl:* 6–9

Alsike clover

T. hybridum

Erect per. Lflts elliptic. Stipules oval, long, fine points. Teeth on spl tube 2 × tube length. Infl long-stkd. *Ht:* 40 cm; *D:* T; *Fl:* 6–9

Lesser yellow trefoil

T. dubium

Infl of up to 26 fls

Standard ptl folds round fr unlike *T. campestre* (hop trefoil). *Ht:* 15 cm; *D:* T (not far N); *Fl:* 5–10

Strawberry clover

T. fragiferum

Lflts serrated. Spls inflate round fr swelling head. *Ht:* 20 cm; *D:* T (not far N); *Fl:* 7–9

Sulphur clover

T. ochroleucon

Hairy per; lflts to 3 cm, 2 unstkd lvs round fl head; 1 v long spl tooth. *Ht:* 30 cm; *D:* W, C, S; *Fl:* 6–7

Fenugreek

T. ornithopodioides

Delicate hrlss ann. Stipules lance-shaped. Infl has 1–3 short stkd fls. Fr curved. *Ht:* 10 cm; *D:* T; *Fl:* 5–9

Suffocated clover

T. suffocatum

Prostrate, hrlss ann. Lflts toothed, triangular, to 5 mm, stipules pointed. Infls at sh tips, dense unstkd. *Ht:* 5 cm; *D:* S, W; *Fl:* 4–8

Birdsfoot trefoil

Lotus corniculatus

Infl of 2–6 fls

Pods twist spirally when split

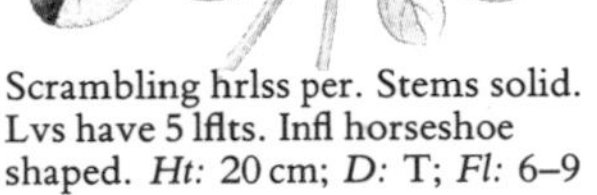

Scrambling hrlss per. Stems solid. Lvs have 5 lflts. Infl horseshoe shaped. *Ht:* 20 cm; *D:* T; *Fl:* 6–9

Marsh birdsfoot trefoil

L. uliginosus

Erect or climbing per, sometimes hry. Stem hollow. Lflts to 2 cm. Infl with 5–12 fls on long, slim stks. *Ht:* 40 cm; *D:* W, C, S; *Fl:* 6–8

Dragon's teeth

Tetragonolobus maritimus

Like *Lotus* but lvs short-stkd, 3-lobed, big stipules; fls sol. *Ht:* 20 cm; *D:* C, S; *Fl:* 5–7

Bush vetch

V. sepium

Trailing, hrlss to 1 m with tendrils; 2–6 fls in infl, spl teeth not equal. *D:* T; *Fl:* 5–8

Upright vetch

V. orobus

Has 6–9 lflt prs, no tendrils, toothed stipules; infl 6–20 fls. *Ht:* 30 cm; *D:* W; *Fl:* 6–9

Birdsfoot

Ornithopus perpusillus

Prostrate, hry; 4–13 lflt prs, lowest near stem. Infl of 3–6 fls; fruit constricted. *Ht:* 35 cm; *D:* W, C; *Fl:* 5–8

Wood vetch

V. sylvatica

Scrambling, hrlss, has tendrils; 6–9 lflt prs, stipules toothed; top spl teeth short. *Ht:* 1 m; *D:* N, C, E; *Fl:* 6–8

Common vetch

Vicia sativa

Scrambling with tendrils; dark spot on stipules. Fls in 1s or 2s, spl teeth equal. *Ht:* 1 m; *D:* T; *Fl:* 5–9

Tufted vetch

V. cracca

Clambers to 2 m; 8–12 lflt prs; infl 10–14 fls, top spl teeth short. *D:* T; *Fl:* 6–8

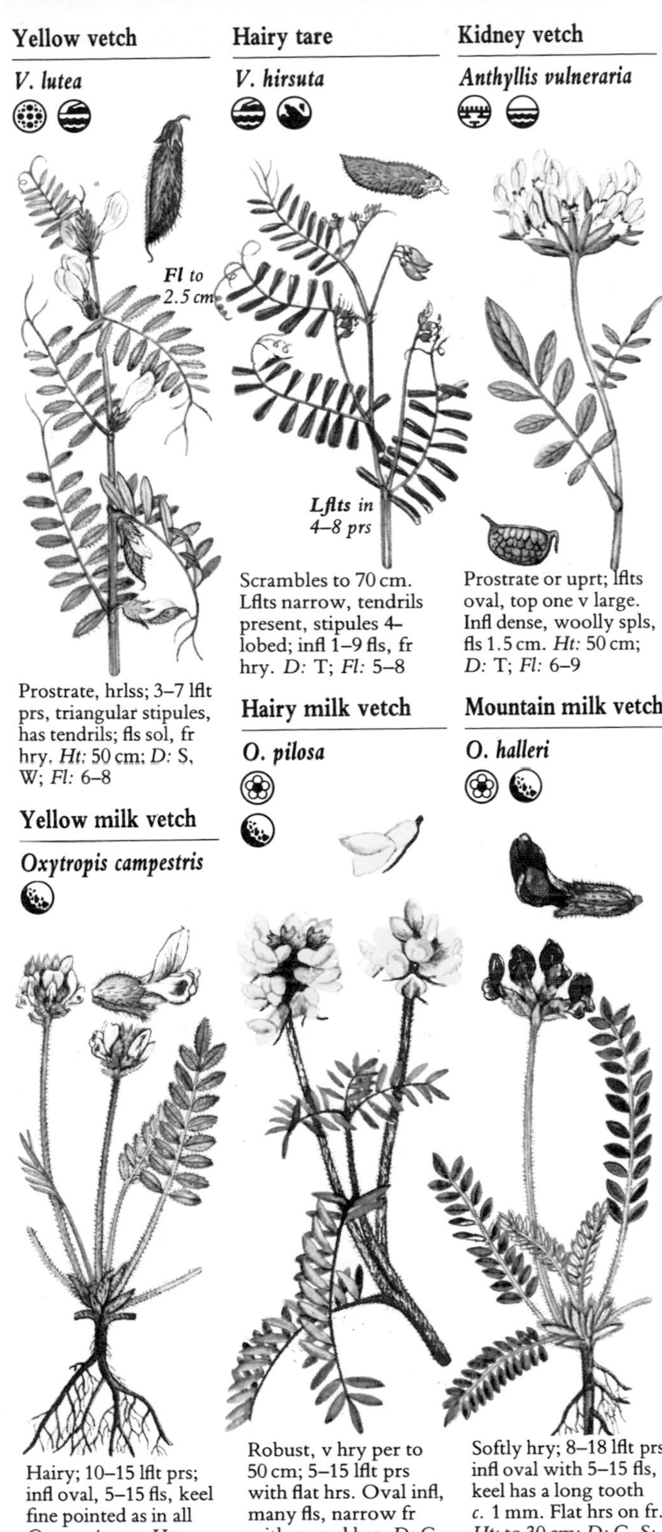

Yellow vetch

V. lutea

Prostrate, hrlss; 3–7 lflt prs, triangular stipules, has tendrils; fls sol, fr hry. *Ht:* 50 cm; *D:* S, W; *Fl:* 6–8

Hairy tare

V. hirsuta

Scrambles to 70 cm. Lflts narrow, tendrils present, stipules 4-lobed; infl 1–9 fls, fr hry. *D:* T; *Fl:* 5–8

Kidney vetch

Anthyllis vulneraria

Prostrate or uprt; lflts oval, top one v large. Infl dense, woolly spls, fls 1.5 cm. *Ht:* 50 cm; *D:* T; *Fl:* 6–9

Yellow milk vetch

Oxytropis campestris

Hairy; 10–15 lflt prs; infl oval, 5–15 fls, keel fine pointed as in all *Oxytropis* spp. *Ht:* 15 cm; *D:* N, S; *Fl:* 6–8

Hairy milk vetch

O. pilosa

Robust, v hry per to 50 cm; 5–15 lflt prs with flat hrs. Oval infl, many fls, narrow fr with spread hrs. *D:* C, E; *Fl:* 6–8

Mountain milk vetch

O. halleri

Softly hry; 8–18 lflt prs; infl oval with 5–15 fls, keel has a long tooth *c.* 1 mm. Flat hrs on fr. *Ht:* to 30 cm; *D:* C, S; *Fl:* 6–7

Purple milk vetch

Astragalus danicus

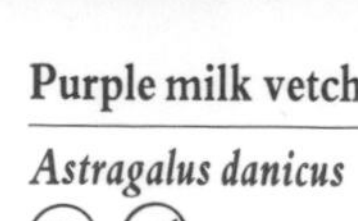

Delicate per, silky hrs. Fl sh to 2 × lf length; fr 2-celled. *Ht:* 25 cm; *D:* T; *Fl:* 5–7

Alpine milk vetch

A. alpinus

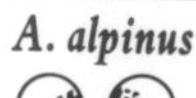

Prostrate; lflts hrlss above. Loose infl, 5–15 fls, spls hry. *Ht:* 30 cm; *D:* N, S; *Fl:* 7–8

Yellow alpine milk vetch

A. frigidus

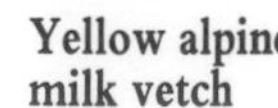

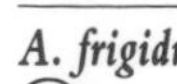

Lfls oval in 3–8 prs

Erect, hrlss; loose infl, 5–20 fls, teeth on spl tube triangular. *Ht:* 35 cm; *D:* N, S; *Fl:* 7–8

Wild lentil

A. cicer

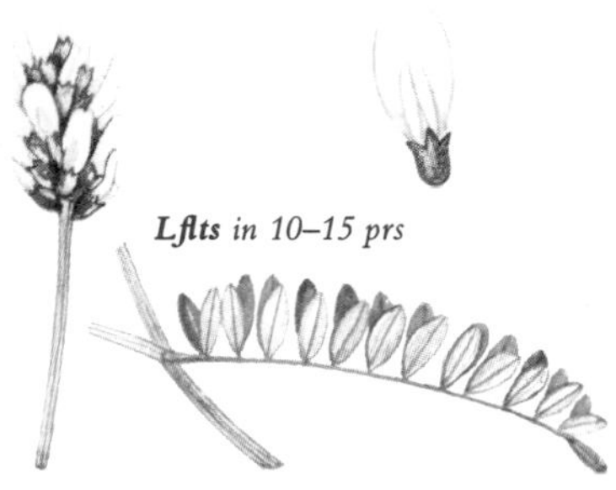

Scrambling. Fl shs just shorter than lvs. Spl teeth half tube length. *Ht:* 65 cm; *D:* C; *Fl:* 6–7

Wild liquorice

A. glycophyllos

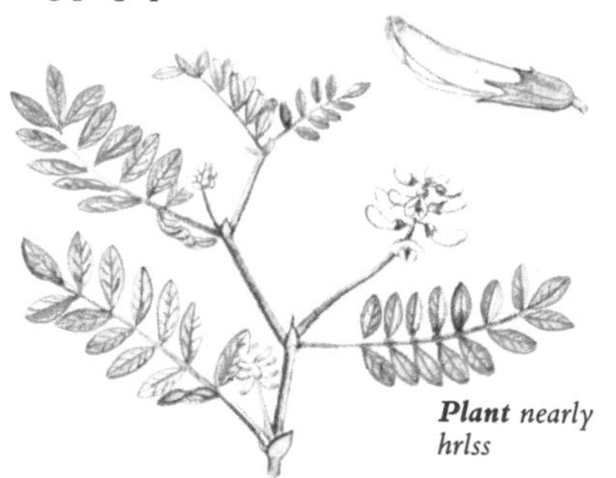

Straggles to 1.5 m. Only 4–7 lflt prs. Fl shs under half lf length, fr curved. *D:* T; *Fl:* 5–8

Norwegian milk vetch

A. norvegicus

Erect, hrlss; 6–7 lflt prs. Fl shs 2 × length of lvs; fr flat, oval. *Ht:* 30 cm; *D:* T; *Fl:* 7–8

Crown vetch

Coronilla varia

***Fr** 4-angled*

Spreading, hrlss; 7–12 lflt prs. Long-stkd infl, 10–20 fls. *Ht:* 1 m; *D:* T; *Fl:* 5–8

Scorpion vetch

C. coronata

***Ptls** 1 cm*

***Infl** long-stkd*

***Fr** to 3 cm*

Stout, glaucous; 3–7 lflt prs; infl 12–20 fls; fr 4-angled. *Ht:* 60 cm; *D:* C; *Fl:* 5–7

Lesser scorpion vetch

C. minima

Woody per. Leaflets unstkd, 2–6 prs. Infl of up to 15 fls, ptls to 8 mm, Pod 4-angled to 3.5 cm. *Ht:* 30 cm; *D:* SW; *Fl:* 4–6

Small scorpion vetch

C. vaginalis

***Ptls** to 1 cm*

Woody per to 50 cm. Oval, short-stkd lflts in 2–6 prs. Infl of 4–6 fls; pod to 3 cm long has 6 angles and 4 wings. *D:* C; *Fl:* 5–6

Scorpion senna

C. emerus

Has 2–4 prs glaucous fine-pointed lflts, infl 2–6 fls, fr hangs. *Ht:* 80 cm; *D:* C; *Fl:* 4–6

Horseshoe vetch

Hippocrepis comosa

***Fls** 1 cm long*

Hairless, to 40 cm, woody base; lflts 4–5, obovate. Fl sh long, infl of 5–8 flowers, fruit has horseshoe-shaped parts. *D:* W, C; *Fl:* 5–7

Meadow vetchling

Lathyrus pratensis

Yellow vetchling

L. aphaca

Grass vetchling

L. nissolia

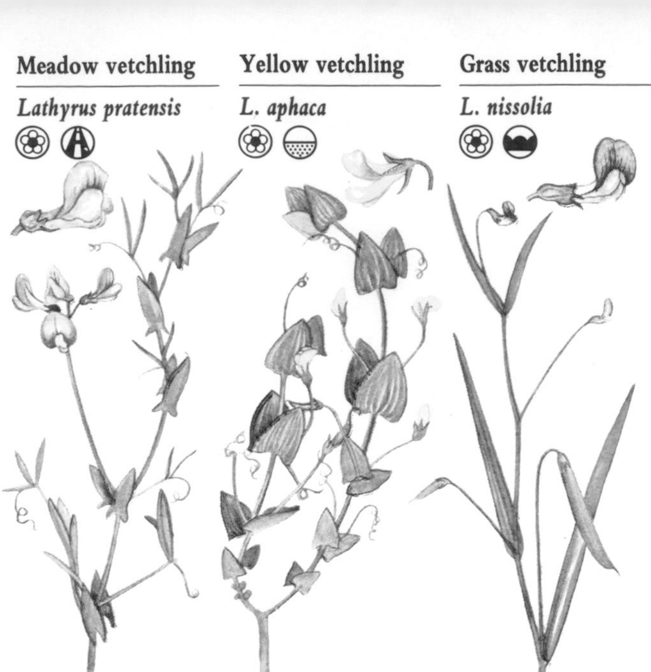

Plant hrlss

Clambers, angled shs, fine hrs; 1 pr pointed lflts, a tendril and arrow-shaped stipules. Fl stk long, fr flat. *Ht:* 1 m; *D:* T; *Fl:* 5–8

Hairless, to 1 m. No lflts but triangular stipules to 3 cm. Fls sol, long-stkd, long spl teeth, fr curved. *D:* W, C, S; *Fl:* 6–8

Erect to 90 cm; no lflts or tendrils but has grass-like shs. *D:* W, C, S; *Fl:* 5–7

Spring pea

L. vernus

Narrow-leaved everlasting pea

L. sylvestris

Bitter vetchling

L. montanus

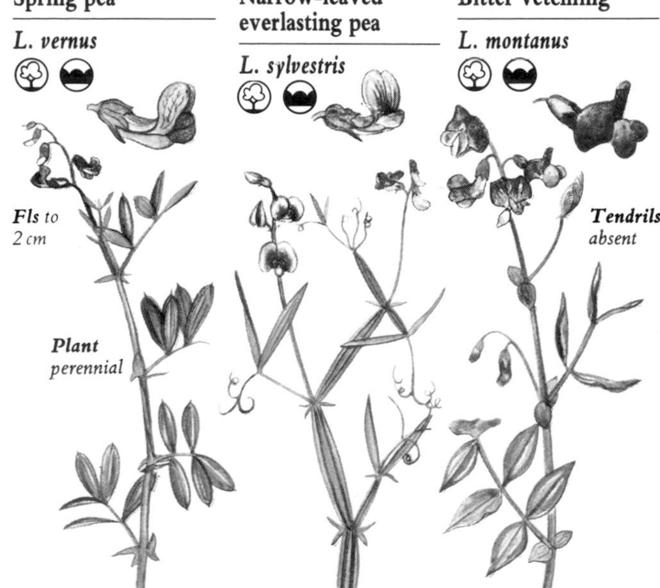

Fls *to 2 cm*

Plant *perennial*

Tendrils *absent*

Erect, usually hrlss. Stem angled, 2–4 lflt prs, no tendrils; infl 3–10 spaced fls, fr hrlss. *Ht:* 50 cm; *D:* T (not GB); *Fl:* 4–6

Bushy, hrlss, winged stem; 1 lflt pr, single tendril; stipules thin, spread. Infl 3–8 fls, fr winged. *Ht:* 1.5 m; *D:* T (not N); *Fl:* 6–8

Rhizomatous. Winged stem. Lflts narrow, 2–4 prs. Infl 2–8 fls, flat hrs on flower shs and spls. *Ht:* 30 cm; *D:* S, W, C; *Fl:* 6–7

Marsh pea

L. palustris

Scrambles to 1.2 m; 2–3 lflt prs and branched tendril per lf. Infl of 2–6 fls; fr flat. *D:* T; *Fl:* 5–7

Tuberous pea

L. tuberosus

Has rt tubers, stem angled; lvs have 1 lflt pr, 1 tendril; fr cylindrical. *Ht:* 1 m; *D:* T (not N); *Fl:* 6–7

Sea pea

L. japonicus

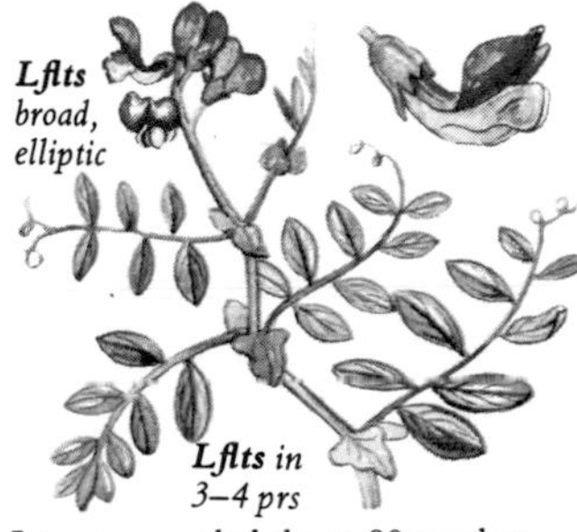

Low per, angled shs to 90 cm; has tendrils, stipules triangular, infl 5–15 fls, fr rigid. *D:* W, N; *Fl:* 6–8

Goat's rue

Galega officinalis

Stout, uprt; 4–8 lflt prs, arrow-shaped stipules. Fl shs equal lvs; fr straight. *D:* E, C, S; *Fl:* 6–7

Common melilot

Melilotus officinalis

Sprawling or uprt; many 6 mm fls, fr ribbed, hrlss, brown. *Ht:* 2 m; *D:* T; *Fl:* 7–9

White melilot

M. alba

Keel and wing ptls shorter than standard; fr hrlss, brown. *Ht:* 1 m; *D:* T; *Fl:* 7–8

Tall melilot

M. altissima

Like *M. officinalis* but to 1.5 m. All ptls equal; fr hry, black. *D:* T (not E); *Fl:* 6–8

Bladder senna 

Colutea arborescens

Shrubby, v branched; lvs pinnate, stipules pointed. Infl of 3–8 fls, fr inflated. *Ht:* 4 m; *D:* S; *Fl:* 5–7

Spotted medick  

Medicago arabica

Prostrate, hrlss; lflts toothed, in 3s, black blotch; 1–4 fls in infl; fr coiled. *Ht:* 45 cm; *D:* S, W; *Fl:* 4–8

Black medick  

M. lupulina

Prostrate. Lflt tips notched with projecting nerve. Fr curled. *Ht:* 35 cm; *D:* T (not far N); *Fl:* 4–8

Sickle medick  

M. falcata

Scrambling. Infl loose, each fl on sh longer than spls, fr curved. *Ht:* 50 cm; *D:* T (not N); *Fl:* 6–8

Rest harrow

Ononis repens

Creeping, no spines but sticky hrs; fl wings equal keel. *Ht:* 45 cm; *D:* W, C; *Fl:* 6–9

Small rest harrow

O. reclinata

Sticky, uprt, no spines. Lflts v hry, fl shs bend back in fr. *Ht:* 7 cm; *D:* S, W; *Fl:* 6–7

Hairy rest harrow

O. pusilla

Erect, hry, woody base. Fls unstkd, spls and ptls 1 cm. *Ht:* 20 cm; *D:* S; *Fl:* 6–8

Spiny rest harrow

Ononis spinosa

Pod hry

Woody uprt stems spiny with 2 lines of hrs; keel ptls longer than wings. *Ht:* 45 cm; *D:* W, C; *Fl:* 6–9

Large yellow rest harrow

Ononis natrix

Dwarf shrub, stickily hry. Lvs variable oval to narrow; infl loose, ptls veined. *Ht:* 45 cm; *D:* S, W; *Fl:* 5–8

Sainfoin

Onobrychis viciifolia

***Pod** hry*

***Lflts** in 6–12 prs*

Upright per; pinnate lvs, lflts narrow with pointed tips. Loose infl, to 50 fls. *Ht:* 60 cm; *D:* T; *Fl:* 6–8

Hedysarum

Hedysarum hedysaroides

***Lflts** oval, blunt in 3–10 prs*

Hairless; lvs pinnate; infl of 15–35 fls each 2 cm, colour varies. Drooping fr has a flange. *Ht:* 30 cm; *D:* S, C; *Fl:* 7–8

Star-fruited fenugreek

Trigonella monspeliaca

Prostrate, hry; lvs 3-lobed, lflts obovate; fls 4 mm, unstkd, gps of 4–14. Fr just curved, hanging. *Ht:* 25 cm; *D:* C, S; *Fl:* 3–6

Classical fenugreek

T. foenum-graecum

***Fr** 1 cm*

Erect, sparsely hry. Lflts narrow, fine-toothed; fls short-stkd in prs in lf axils, fr curved. *Ht:* 35 cm; *D:* C, S; *Fl:* 4–5

Petty whin

Genista anglica

Shrub with spines to 2 cm, some curved; lvs hrlss, no stipules; spl tube 2-lipped. *Ht:* 45 cm; *D:* W; *Fl:* 5–6

German greenweed

G. germanica

Spiny, hry shrub to 60 cm. Infl loose, spls and fl shs very hairy, standard ptl pointed at tip. *D:* SW; *Fl:* 5–9

Dyer's greenweed

G. tinctoria

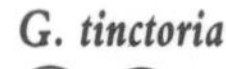

Woody, uprt, no spines; shs grooved. Lvs hry at edges; infl long. *Ht:* 60 cm; *D:* T (not far N); *Fl:* 7–9

Broom

Cytisus scoparius

Erect hry shrub to 2 m, stems ridged; lvs 3-lobed, fall easily. Fl 2 cm. *D:* W, S, C; *Fl:* 5–6

Black broom

Lembotropis nigricans

Erect shrub, no spines. Long infl of drooping buds and fls. *Ht:* 1 m; *D:* C, S; *Fl:* 6–7

Winged broom

Chamaespartium sagittale

Mat-forming, fl shs broad-winged, lvs hry below, infl dense. *Ht:* 40 cm; *D:* C; *Fl:* 5–9

Clustered broom

Chamaecytisus supinus

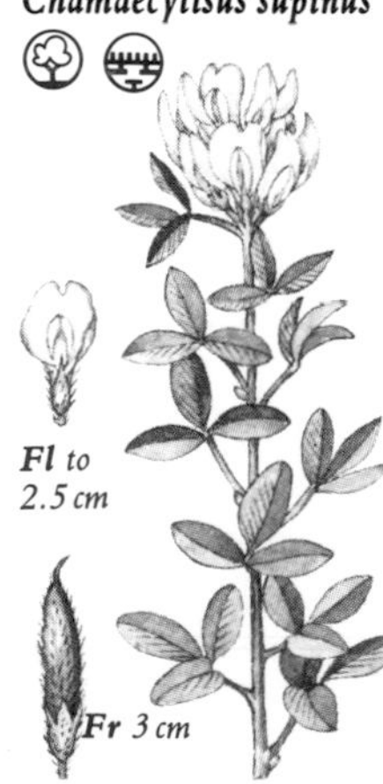

Hairy but no spines; lvs 3-lobed. Infl of 2–8 fls, spls hry. *Ht:* 70 cm; *D:* C, S; *Fl:* 5–7

Gorse	Western dwarf gorse	Dwarf gorse
Ulex europaeus	*U. gallii*	*U. minor*

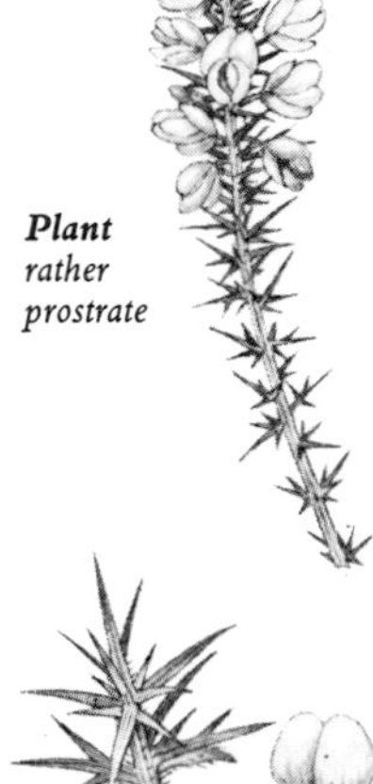

Gorse — Shrub, many ridged spines to 2 cm, young plants have 3-lobed lvs. Spls hry. *Ht:* 1.5 m; *D:* W; *Fl:* 2–6

Western dwarf gorse — Hairy; unfurrowed spines *c.* 2 cm. Spls ⅔ ptl length, wings longer than keel. *Ht:* 60 cm; *D:* W; *Fl:* 7–9

Dwarf gorse — Spines *c.* 1 cm, not furrowed. Spls as long as ptls, wings as long as keel. *Ht:* to 1 m; *D:* W; *Fl:* 7–9

Wood sorrel family Oxalidaceae

Herbs with a fleshy rootstock and often alternate, palmate leaves. The solitary or sparsely grouped flowers have 5 petals and sepals and 10 stamens. The fruit is a capsule.

Wood sorrel  

Oxalis acetosella

Creeping rhizomatous per. Lvs 3-lobed, lflts to 2 cm. Fls sol, to 3 cm on long thin stks. Fr to 4 mm. *Ht:* 10 cm; *D:* T; *Fl:* 4–6

Yellow oxalis  

O. corniculata

***Stems** hry, rooting*

***Stk** of each fl c. 1 cm*

Weak, prostrate. Lvs 3-lobed with small stipules, lflts deeply cut at tips. Long-stkd infl of 1–6 fls. *Ht:* 10 cm; *D:* S; *Fl:* 6–9

Geranium family Geraniaceae

Herbs or shrubs having alternate, lobed or compound leaves with stipules. Flowers have 5 separate petals and 5 sepals in a tube which persists round the long-beaked fruit.

Bloody cranesbill  

Geranium sanguineum

Meadow cranesbill  

G. pratense

Bushy herb with creeping rhizome. Lvs in narrow segments with flat white hrs. Fls sol, to 3.6 cm, fr to 3 cm. *Ht:* 25 cm; *D:* T; *Fl:* 7–8

Perennial. Erect hry stems. Lvs have deeply cut lobes. Paired fls on long stks which bend back in fr. Fr *c.* 2.5 cm. *Ht:* 50 cm; *D:* T; *Fl:* 6–9

Hedgerow cranesbill 

G. pyrenaicum

Perennial with many sticky hrs. Fls in pairs. Fr stks bent back but tips erect. *Ht:* 40 cm; *D:* S, W; *Fl:* 6–8

Shining cranesbill 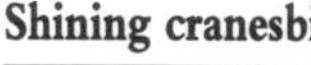 

G. lucidum

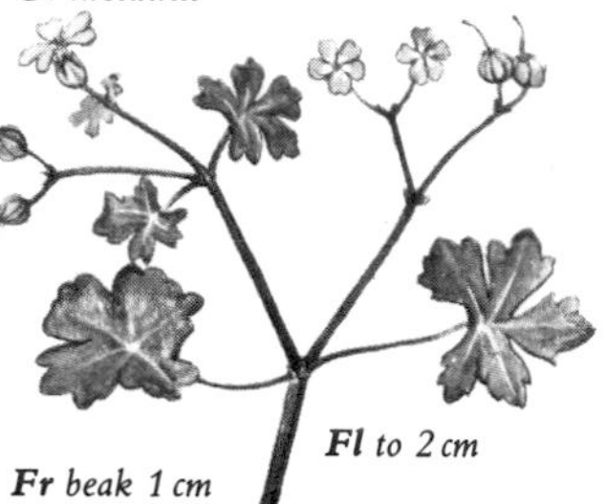

Annual branched from ground. Lvs glossy, reddish, cut to half lf width. Fls on spread, up-curved stks. *Ht:* 25 cm; *D:* T (not NE); *Fl:* 5–8

Herb Robert  

G. robertianum

Wood cranesbill   

G. sylvaticum

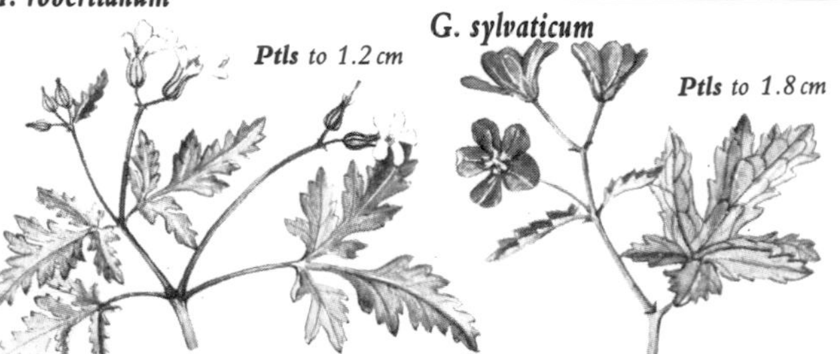

Biennial or ann. Shoots much-branched, delicate, reddish. Lvs lobed, lobes divided. Fl stks uprt. *Ht:* 30 cm; *D:* T (not far N); *Fl:* 5–9

Perennial. Stems have sticky hrs above. Lvs hry, 7-lobed. Fls in pairs. Fl stks erect in fruit. *Ht:* 50 cm; *D:* T; *Fl:* 6–7

Long-stalked cranesbill

G. columbinum

Dove's foot cranesbill

G. molle

Cut-leaved cranesbill

G. dissectum

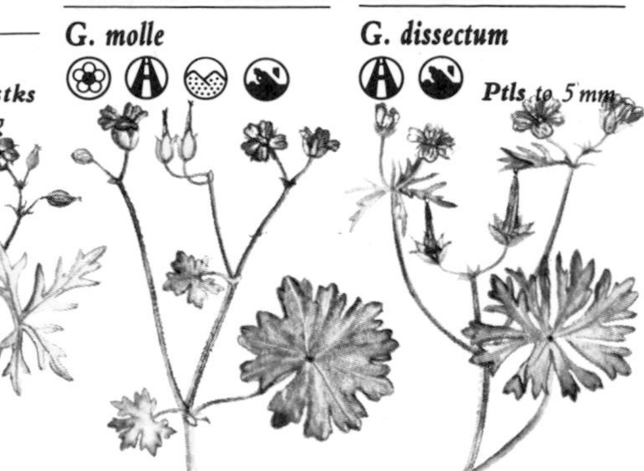

Branching ann. Flat hrs on stems and spl veins. Fr hrlss. *Ht:* 30 cm; *D:* T (not far N); *Fl:* 6–7

Annual covered with soft white hrs. Lvs round. *Ht:* 30 cm; *D:* T (not far N); *Fl:* 4–9

Straggling. Hrs on shs down-pointed, on spls sticky. *Ht:* 40 cm; *D:* T (not far N); *Fl:* 5–8

Marsh cranesbill

G. palustre

Hairy per. Lvs toothed. Few fls in infl. Fr stks bend back. *Ht:* 40 cm; *D:* T (not N); *Fl:* 7–8

Common storksbill

Erodium cicutarium

Hairy. Lvs compound, lflts cut. Ptls longer than spls. *Ht:* 30 cm; *D:* T; *Fl:* 6–9

Soft storksbill

E. malacoides

Flowers in gps of 3–7. Sticky hrs on fl stks and spls. *Ht:* 30 cm; *D:* SW; *Fl:* 2–6

Sea storksbill

E. maritimum

Musk storksbill

E. moschatum

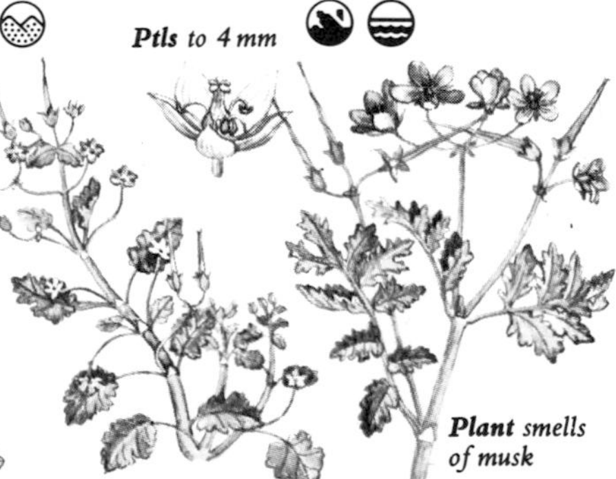

Flat ann. Hrs bristly. Lvs lobed to half width. Fls sol or paired. *D:* NW; *Fl:* 5–9

Annual, many white hrs. Ptls just longer than spls. *Ht:* 30 cm; *D:* S, W: *Fl:* 5–7

Flax family Linaceae

Herbs with simple, usually alternate leaves without stipules. The flowers usually have 5 petals, sepals and stamens and an ovary with 3–5 cells. The fruit is a capsule that splits vertically.

Perennial flax

Linum perenne

Hairless perennial with rigid, upright stems. Numerous alternate leaves 1–2 cm long. Spls rounded, less than half fr length, ptls to 2 cm. Fr stks erect. A variable sp. *Ht:* 45 cm; *D:* C, E; *Fl:* 6–7

Pale flax

L. bienne

Hairless ann or per; stems uprt, branched. Ptls to 1.2 cm, spls oval, pointed tips, more than half fr length. Ancestor of cultivated flax. *Ht:* 45 cm; *D:* W, S; *Fl:* 5–9

Purging flax

L. catharticum

Delicate ann, slender stems. Lvs opposite, oval, rounded to 1.2 cm. Many fls in loose infl, fl shs fine, ptls 6 mm, spls pointed. Fr 3 mm, same length as spls. Seeds purgative. *Ht:* 15 cm; *D:* T; *Fl:* 6–9

Yellow flax

L. flavum

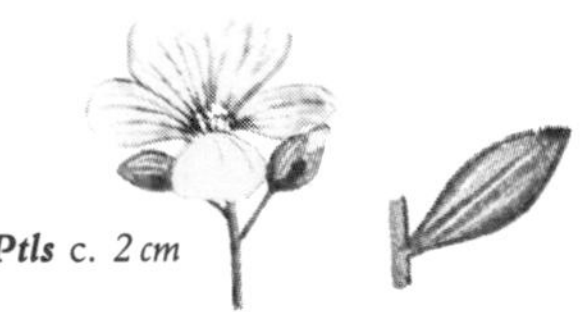

Lvs *to 3 cm*

Robust per. Erect shs from dense base. Lvs broadest near tip. Infl branched 20–40 clustered flowers pointed spls with hry edges. Spls just longer than fr. *Ht:* 45 cm; *D:* C, S; *Fl:* 5–8

Allseed

Radiola linoides

Tiny ann to 8 cm. Stems slender, branched, bushy. Lvs opp, 3 mm long. Fls *c.* 2 mm across in flat-topped clusters have 4 ptls and spls. Fr spherical, *c.* 1 mm diam. *D:* T (not NE); *Fl:* 7–8

Spurge family Euphorbiaceae

Annual or perennial herbs with alternate leaves. Male and female flowers are usually separate but may be grouped together in a cup-like structure. The ovary has two or three cells.

Sea spurge 

Euphorbia paralias

Stiff, hrlss, glaucous per; erect usually unbranched stems. Thick fleshy lvs have obscure midrib below. Fls in terminal clusters, ♂ and ♀ joined in a cup. Fr hrlss. *Ht:* to 40 cm; *D:* W, S; *Fl:* 8–11

Wood spurge 

E. amygdaloides

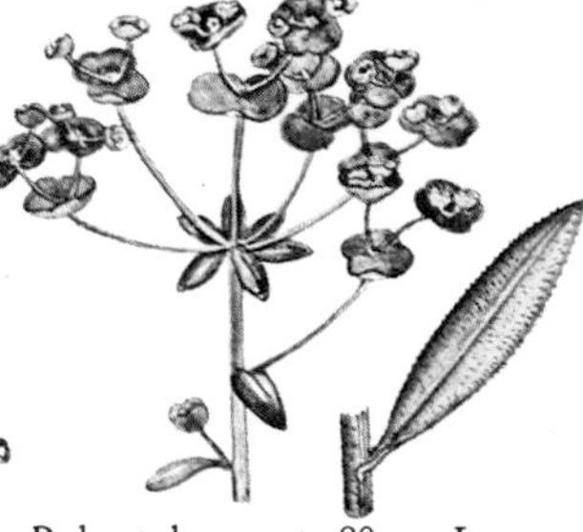

Robust, hry per to 80 cm. Lvs on veg shs taper to stk at base, lvs on fl shs do not. Infl a 5–10 rayed umbel with kidney-shaped bracts below. *D:* NW, C, S; *Fl:* 3–5

Portland spurge 

E. portlandica

Like a small version of *E. paralias* but stems unbranched. Lvs fleshy, prominent midrib below, tapered to base. Often reddens with age. *Ht:* 25 cm; *D:* W; *Fl:* 5–9

Purple spurge 

E. peplis

Prostrate ann, usually with 4 main branches from base. Lvs to 1 cm, enlarged on one side at base and with divided stipules. Infl to 2 mm long, fr a hairless, 3-sided capsule. *Ht:* 4 cm; *D:* T; *Fl:* 7–9

Dwarf spurge 

E. exigua

Hairless, glaucous, to 30 cm. Lvs to 3 cm, untoothed, narrow, tips pointed. Infl an umbel with 3 rays, bracts below lvs broader than true lvs. *D:* T (not E); *Fl:* 6–10

Petty spurge

Euphorbia peplus

Hairless ann, stem simple or branched. Lvs to 3 cm, oval, untoothed. Infl a 3-rayed umbel with stklss bracts. *Ht:* 30 cm; *D:* T; *Fl:* 4–11

Sun spurge

E. helioscopia

Hairless, uprt, few brs. Infl 5-rayed, bracts round at base. *Ht:* 35 cm; *D:* T; *Fl:* 5–10

Annual mercury

Mercurialis annua

Near hrlss; erect shs v branched; lvs stkd. ♂ and ♀ plants separate, ♂ fls in spike, ♀ sol, unstkd. *Ht:* 40 cm; *D:* T; *Fl:* 7–10

Dog's mercury

M. perennis

Patch-forming, hry. Shs uprt, no brs. ♂ and ♀ plants separate, ♂ fls clustered, stkd, ♀ sol, long-stkd. *Ht:* 30 cm; *D:* T; *Fl:* 2–4

Caper spurge

Euphorbia lathyris

Glaucous, hrlss; lvs opp, broad, round at base. Infl 2–6 brs, fr to 2 cm. *Ht:* 1 m; *D:* S, W, C; *Fl:* 6–7

Cypress spurge

E. cyparissias

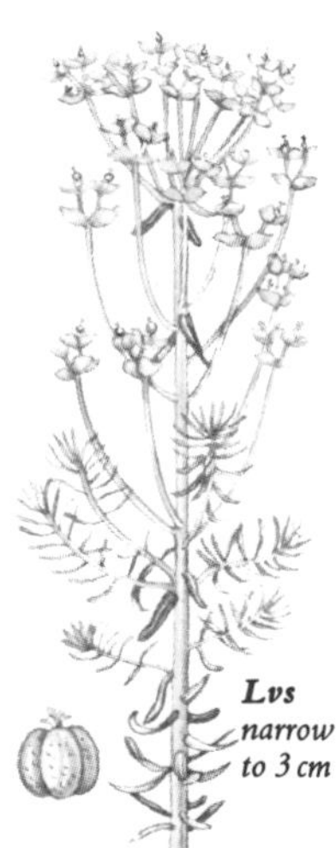

Has rhizome; dense shs hrlss, often branched. Many alt lvs. Infl of 5–9 brs. *Ht:* 20 cm; *D:* T (not far N); *Fl:* 5–8

Rue family Rutaceae

Herbs or shrubs with glandular leaves. The flowers have 4–5 free sepals and petals, 8 or 10 stamens and free styles.

Rue  

Ruta graveolens

Strong-smelling hrlss per to 45 cm. Lower lvs stkd, v divided. Infl loose, spls narrow, pointed, ptls toothed. *D:* S, SC; *Fl:* 5–7

Milkwort family Polygalaceae

Herbs with simple leaves with no stipules. Asymmetrical flowers have 5 sepals (two petal-like) and 3–5 petals.

Common milkwort 

Polygala vulgaris

Scrambling stems, lvs narrow, alt to 1 cm at base, 3 cm above. Colour variable. *Ht:* 20 cm; *D:* T; *Fl:* 5–9

Chalk milkwort 

P. calcarea

Prostrate per. Lvs in rosette to 2 cm, glossy, obovate, top lvs smaller. *Ht:* 15 cm; *D:* W; *Fl:* 5–7

Shrubby milkwort    

P. chamaebuxus

Dwarf shrub to 15 cm. Lvs oval or linear; fls sol or in prs, long-keeled. *D:* WC, S; *Fl:* 4–9

Thyme-leaved milkwort 

P. serpyllifolia

Like *P. vulgaris* but lower lvs in opp prs, upper alt. More compact infl. *Ht:* 20 cm; *D:* W, C; *Fl:* 5–8

Balsam family Balsaminaceae

Herbs with no stipules at their leaf bases. The flowers have 3 or 5 sepals which are often petal-like and 5 petals, the upper one large and the lower ones united in two pairs. The ovary develops into a 5-celled, many-seeded fruit.

Himalayan balsam

Impatiens glandulifera

Erect, robust annual 1–2 m high. Stem stout, translucent and reddish. Leaves opposite or in groups of 3 around stem, stalked and sharply toothed. Flowers to 4 cm across with short, bent spurs and 3 sepals borne in groups of 5–10 at shoot tips. *D:* T; *Fl:* 7–10

Touch-me-not balsam

I. noli-tangere

Upright hrlss ann. Lvs to 12 cm stkd with teeth to 3 mm. Fls to 4 cm grouped in lf axils have 3 spls, the lowest with a curved spur. Name comes from seeds which shoot out if fruit is touched. *Ht:* 40 cm; *D:* T (not far N); *Fl:* 7–9

Orange balsam

I. capensis

Like *I. noli-tangere* but lvs to 8 cm with fewer smaller teeth. Fl spur curved. *Ht:* to 80 cm; *D:* W; *Fl:* 6–8

Small balsam

I. parviflora

Annual to 1 m. Lvs alternate with many teeth. Fls *c.* 1 cm, spur straight. *D:* T (not Scand); *Fl:* 7–11

Mallow family Malvaceae

Herbs and shrubs with leaves often palmately lobed. Grouped or single flowers have 5 free petals and 5 sepals either free or joined and often with an extra outer sepal whorl (epicalyx).

Common mallow

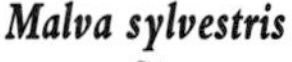

Malva sylvestris

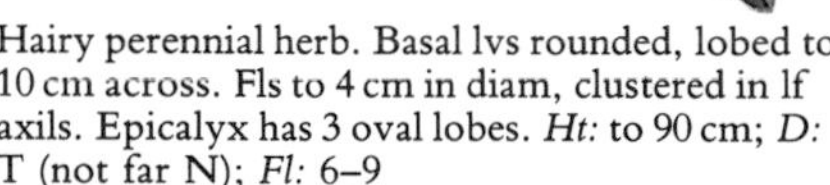

Hairy perennial herb. Basal lvs rounded, lobed to 10 cm across. Fls to 4 cm in diam, clustered in lf axils. Epicalyx has 3 oval lobes. *Ht:* to 90 cm; *D:* T (not far N); *Fl:* 6–9

Dwarf mallow

M. neglecta

Often prostrate. Lvs to 7 cm diam. Epicalyx 3-lobed. *Ht:* 40 cm; *D:* T (not far N); *Fl:* 6–9

Musk mallow

M. moschata

Leaves deeply cut. Fls sol to 6 cm. Epicalyx 3-lobed. *Ht:* 60 cm; *D:* T (not N); *Fl:* 7–8

Marsh mallow

Althaea officinalis

Softly hry. Short-stkd fls to 4 cm. Epicalyx 6-lobed. *Ht:* 1 m; *D:* T (not N); *Fl:* 8–9

Rough mallow

A. hirsuta

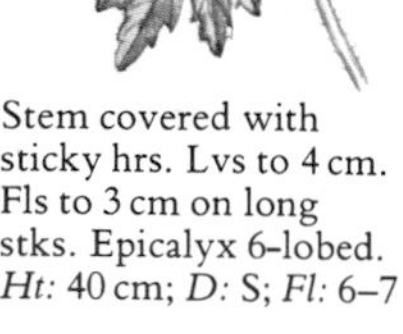

Stem covered with sticky hrs. Lvs to 4 cm. Fls to 3 cm on long stks. Epicalyx 6-lobed. *Ht:* 40 cm; *D:* S; *Fl:* 6–7

Thymelaea family Thymelaeaceae

Shrubs with alternate, unlobed leaves with no stipules. Flowers have 4 or 5 lobed sepals placed at the end of the enlarged, tube-shaped, petal-like flower stalks.

Spurge laurel

Daphne laureola

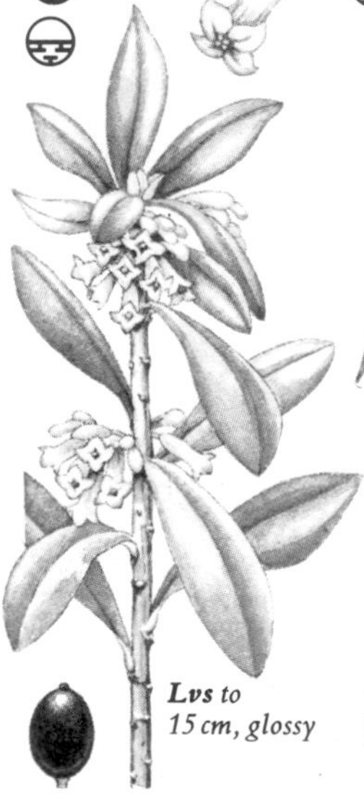

Lvs to
15 cm, glossy

Evergreen, shs erect, lvs clustered at tips; fls 1 cm, 8 stamens, 4 spls, infl 5–10 fls; fr 1.2 cm, black. *Ht:* 70 cm; *D:* S, W; *Fl:* 2–4

Mezereon

D. mezereum

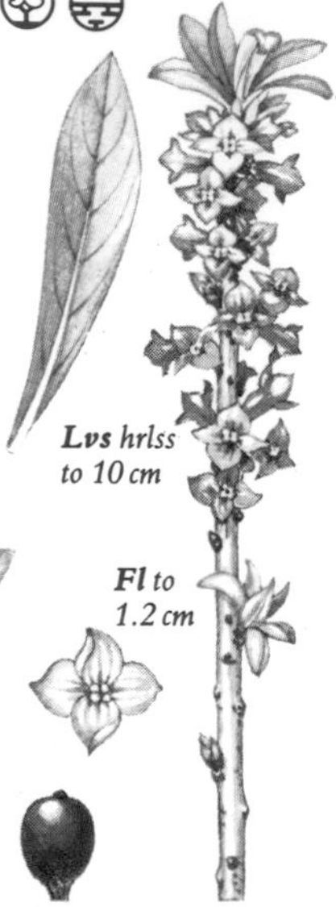

Lvs hrlss
to 10 cm
Fl to
1.2 cm

Erect, decid. Gps of 2–4 fls appear before lvs over old lf scars; 4 spls equal tube in length; fr 1 cm, red. *Ht:* 65 cm; *D:* C, S; *Fl:* 2–4

Annual thymelaea

Thymelaea passerina

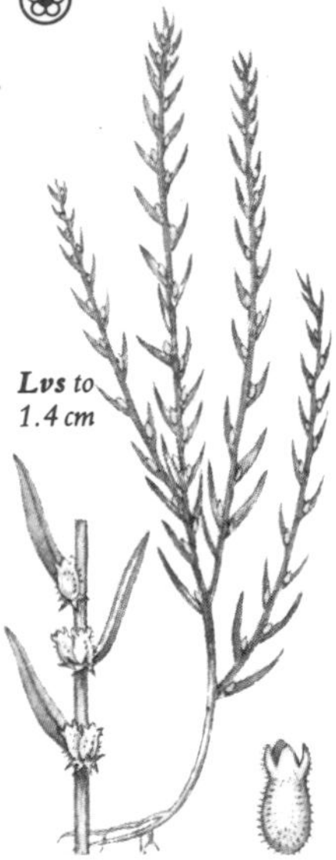

Lvs to
1.4 cm

Erect, hrlss. Gps of 1–3 fls to 4 mm in lf axils with 2 tiny bracts and tuft of hrs, spls blunt. *Ht:* 35 cm; *D:* S, W, C; *Fl:* 7–10

St John's wort family Guttiferae

Herbs or shrubs with simple opposite leaves often with resinous glands. The flowers have 5 petals and sepals and many stamens.

Perforate St John's wort

Hypericum perforatum

Fl 2 cm
Lvs elliptic,
stklss, to 2 cm
Shs have 2
raised lines

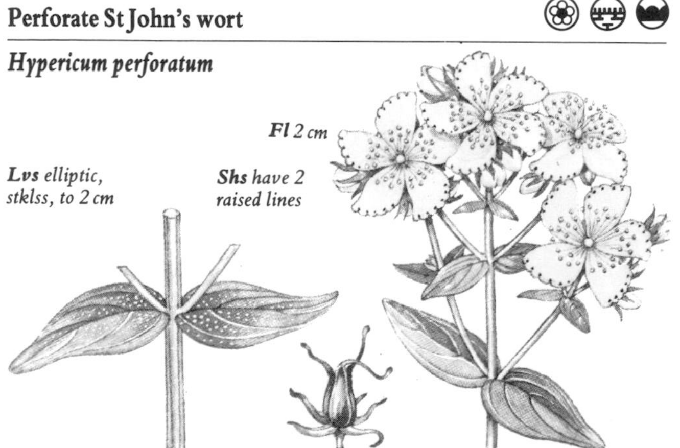

Erect, hrlss. Lvs show translucent glands if held to light. Spls half ptl length, no black glands at edge. *Ht:* 70 cm; *D:* T (not far N); *Fl:* 6–9

Slender St John's wort

H. pulchrum

Lvs to *1 cm*

Shs uprt

Translucent glands on lvs; spls round, under half ptl length, black glands at edge. *Ht:* 45 cm; *D:* NW; *Fl:* 6–8

Hairy St John's wort

H. hirsutum

Fl 1.5 cm

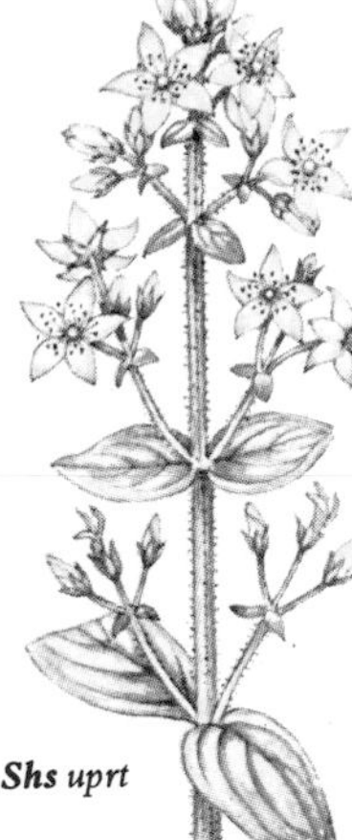

Shs uprt

Hairy, few brs; infl of many fls, spls half ptl length have black glands. *Ht:* 70 cm; *D:* T (not NE); *Fl:* 7–8

Trailing St John's wort

H. humifusum

Spls *almost equal ptls*

Prostrate per, delicate stems to 20 cm, 2 raised lines; translucent glands on lvs. Few 1 cm fls in infl, spl size varies. *D:* W, C; *Fl:* 6–9

Marsh St John's wort

H. elodes

Fl 1.5 cm

Very hry, few fls in infl, spls fine-toothed, stamens in 3 gps. *Ht:* 20 cm; *D:* W; *Fl:* 6–9

Tutsan

H. androsaemum

Fl 2 cm

Stem has 2 lines; spls unequal, stamens long, fr a berry. *Ht:* 70 cm; *D:* W; *Fl:* 6–8

Square-stemmed St John's wort

H. tetrapterum

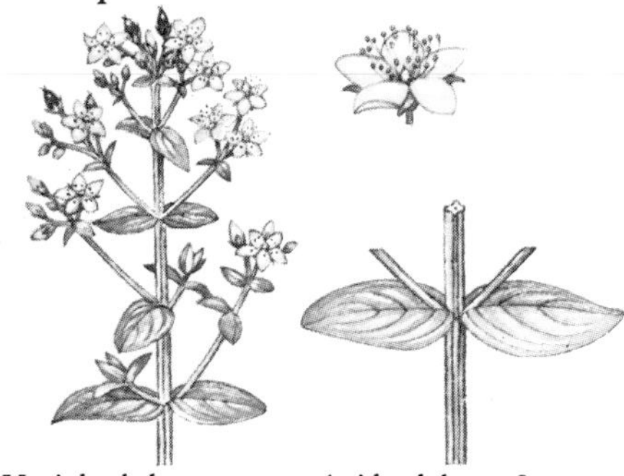

Upright, hrlss per, stems 4-ridged, lvs to 2 cm. Many 1 cm fls in infl, spls narrow, pointed, ⅔ ptl length. *Ht:* 55 cm; *D:* T (not far N); *Fl:* 6–9

Violet family Violaceae

Herbs whose leaves have stipules. Often spurred, solitary flowers have parts in fives and two bracts on their stalks.

Sweet violet

Viola odorata

Down-pointed hrs on lf stk; fls frag, spls blunt. *Ht:* 10 cm; *D:* T (not far N); *Fl:* 2–4

Common dog violet

V. riviniana

Near-hrlss, rosette of lvs; appendages on spls, spur notched. *Ht:* 15 cm; *D:* T; *Fl:* 4–6

Early dog violet

V. reichenbachiana

No hrs on fl shs, spl appendages small, spur unnotched. *Ht:* 15 cm; *D:* W, C; *Fl:* 3–5

Hairy violet

V. hirta

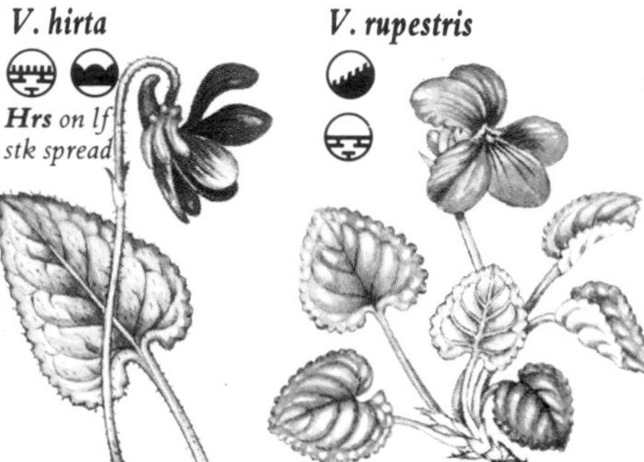

Not frag. Lvs hry, more pointed than *V. odorata*, spls round. *Ht:* 20 cm; *D:* T; *Fl:* 4

Teesdale violet

V. rupestris

Many short hrs, central lf rosette, lvs round, hry stks, fr hry. *Ht:* 3 cm; *D:* T; *Fl:* 5

Bog violet

V. persicifolia

Fl *to 1.5 cm, rounded*

Erect, lf blade longer than stk. Fls purple-veined, spur green. *Ht:* 15 cm; *D:* T; *Fl:* 5–6

Marsh violet

V. palustris

No uprt stems, lf blade to 4 cm. Fl 1 cm, ptls pale, dark veins, spls blunt. *D:* T; *Fl:* 4–7

Heath violet

V. canina

Creeping per, no lf rosette. Lvs not as notched at base as other spp. *Ht:* 20 cm; *D:* T; *Fl:* 4–6

Wild pansy 

V. tricolor

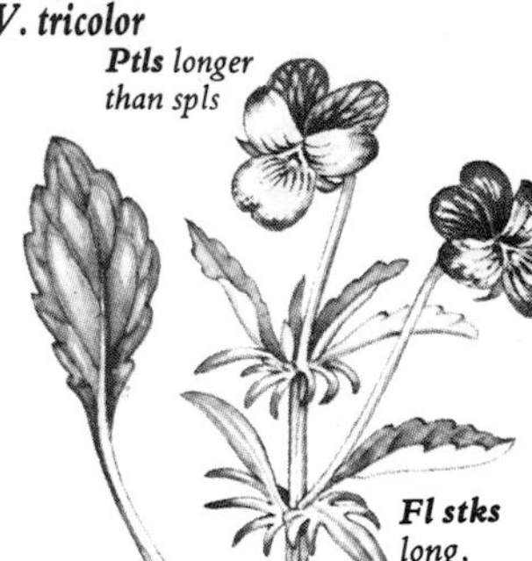

Stipules lobed, centre lobe not indented; spur longer than spl appendages. *Ht:* 30 cm; *D:* T; *Fl:* 4–9

Field pansy  

V. arvensis

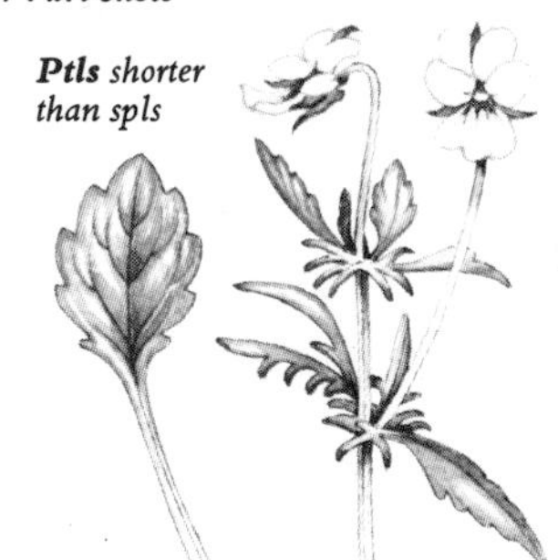

Centre stipule lobe indented. Spur equals spl appendages, fl less than 2 cm. *Ht:* 30 cm; *D:* T; *Fl:* 4–10

Rockrose family Cistaceae

Shrubs or herbs with opposite, hairy, unlobed leaves. Flowers have 3 or 5 sepals, 5 petals and many stamens.

Common rockrose 

Helianthemum nummularium

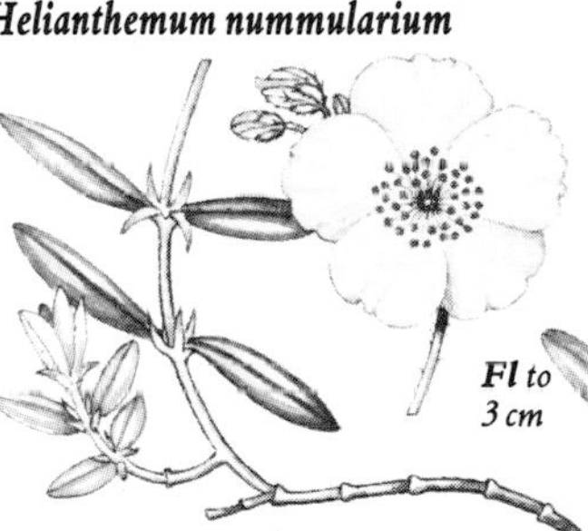

Straggles to 30 cm. Lvs stipuled, woolly below. Infl loose, style not bent. *D:* T (not far N); *Fl:* 6–9

White rockrose 

H. apenninum

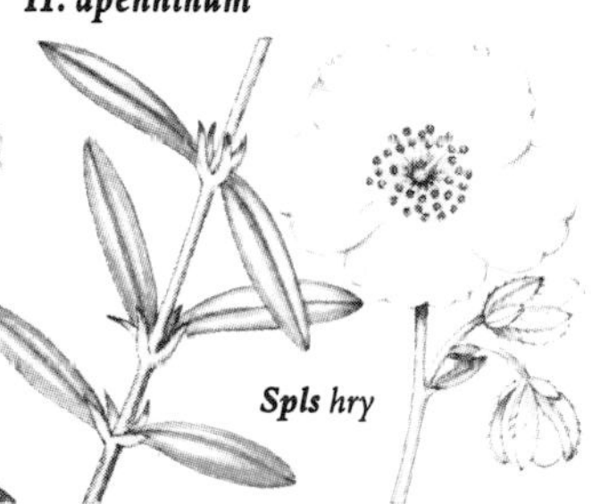

Like *H. nummularium* except in fl col. Lvs woolly all over, curled edges. *Ht:* 25 cm; *D:* SW; *Fl:* 5–7

Hoary rockrose

H. canum

Leaves small, oval, no stipules, small fl, bent style. *Ht:* 10 cm; *D:* C, S; *Fl:* 5–7

Spotted rockrose

Tuberaria guttata

Erect, hry lvs unstkd, stipuled, terminal infl, no styles. *Ht:* 20 cm; *D:* S, W; *Fl:* 5–8

Common fumana

Fumana procumbens

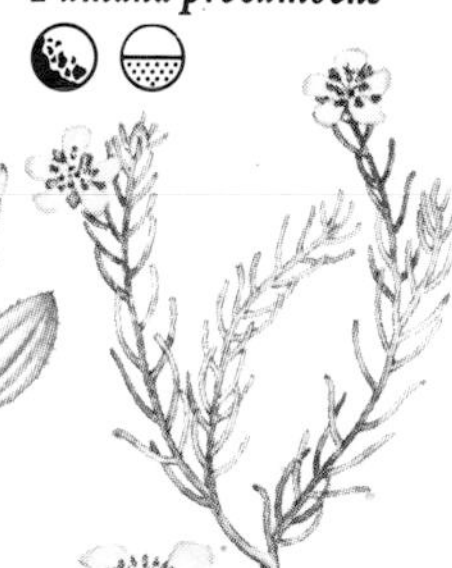

Prostrate, brs 30 cm; lvs alt, no stipules; fls sol, stks as long as lvs. *D:* S, W; *Fl:* 5

Water chestnut family Trapaceae

Annual aquatics with large woody fruits. Leaves in a rosette have inflated stalks. Flower parts are in fours.

Water chestnut

Trapa natans ***Floating lf blades*** *to 4 cm*

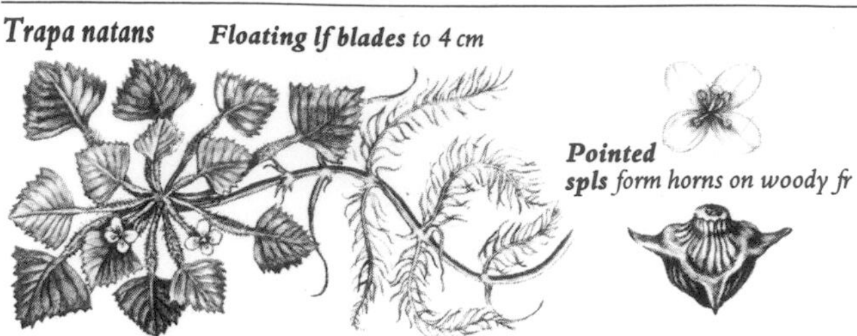

Pointed spls *form horns on woody fr*

Robust submerged stems unbranched to 2 m. Lf stks to 17 cm, hry, swollen. Fls in lf axils, ptls 8 mm. Locally cultivated. *D:* S, C; *Fl:* 6–7

Willowherb family Onagraceae

Annuals or perennials. Single or terminally grouped flowers usually have 4 unjoined petals and sepals and 8 stamens.

Rosebay willowherb

Epilobium angustifolium

Fl *to 3 cm*

Lvs *narrow*

Erect, lfy per. Lvs spiral, serrate; 2 top ptls larger than lower 2, stamens and style protrude; fr 7 cm. *Ht:* 1 m; *D:* T; *Fl:* 7–9

Broad-leaved willowherb

E. montanum

Fl *to 9 mm*

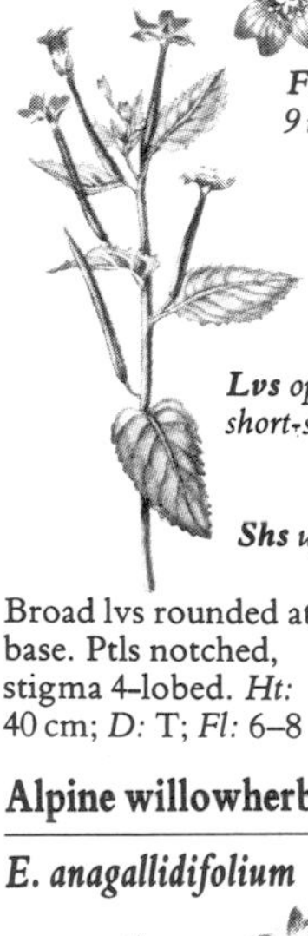

Lvs *opp, short-stkd*

Shs *uprt*

Broad lvs rounded at base. Ptls notched, stigma 4-lobed. *Ht:* 40 cm; *D:* T; *Fl:* 6–8

Marsh willowherb

E. palustre

Stem *has no raised lines*

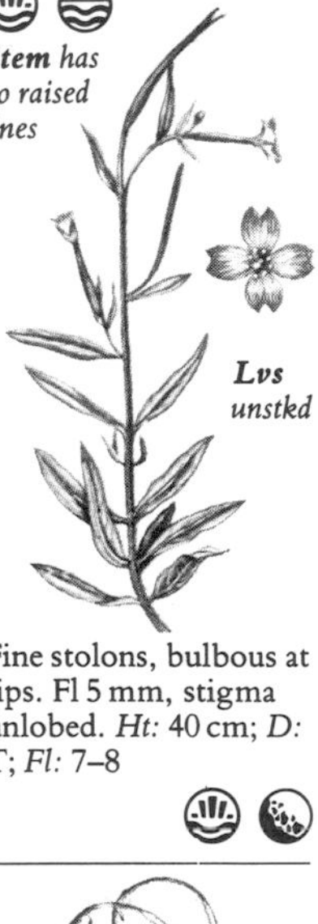

Lvs *unstkd*

Fine stolons, bulbous at tips. Fl 5 mm, stigma unlobed. *Ht:* 40 cm; *D:* T; *Fl:* 7–8

Alpine willowherb

E. anagallidifolium

Fl *to 5 mm*

Lvs *to 2 cm*

Stems prostrate, 2 faint ridges, erect fl shs to 10 cm. Lvs in prs. *D:* T (not far N); *Fl:* 7–8

Great willowherb

E. hirsutum

Fl 2 cm

Very hry; stigma 4-lobed, longer than stms. *Ht:* 1.2 m; *D:* T (not far N); *Fl:* 7–8

Large-flowered evening primrose

Oenothera erythrosepala

Robust, stem hry to 1 m, lvs spiral, buds big, ridged, spls red striped, 4 ptls to 5 cm. *D:* W, C; *Fl:* 6–9

Hoary willowherb

E. parviflorum

Fl under 1 cm

Plant softly hry

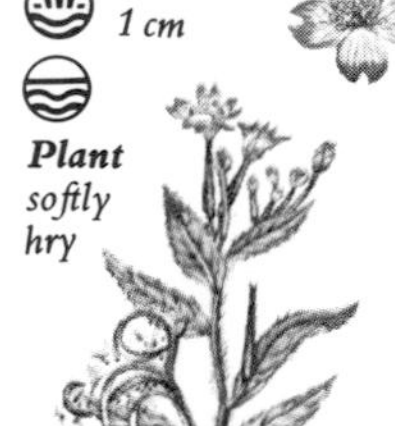

Leaves do not run into stem; 4-lobed stigma equals stms. *Ht:* 80 cm; *D:* T (not N); *Fl:* 7–8

Enchanter's nightshade

Circaea lutetiana

Has stolons and few hrs; 2 deep-notched ptls and spls. *Ht:* 50 cm; *D:* T; *Fl:* 6–8

American willowherb

E. adenocaulon

Fl to 6 mm

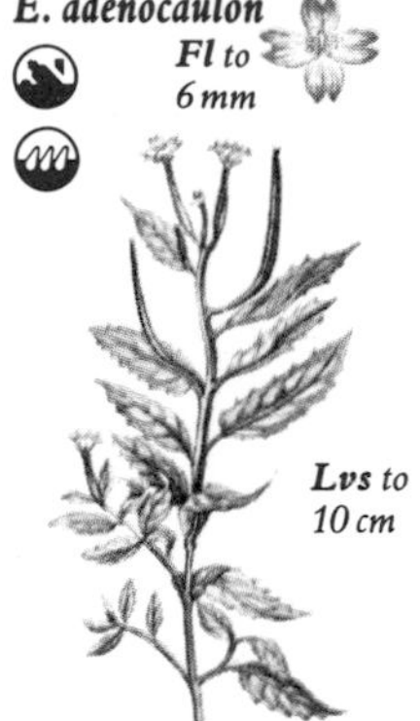

Lvs to 10 cm

Stem hry, 4 raised lines; lvs short-stalked; stigma unlobed. *Ht:* 80 cm; *D:* NW; *Fl:* 6–8

Alpine enchanter's nightshade

C. alpina

Fr hooked

Lvs opp, stkd

Has tuberous stock, fl shs space out in fr, ptls notched. *Ht:* 20 cm; *D:* N; *Fl:* 7–8

Hampshire purslane

Ludwigia palustris

Lvs to 2 cm in opp prs

Fl 3 mm

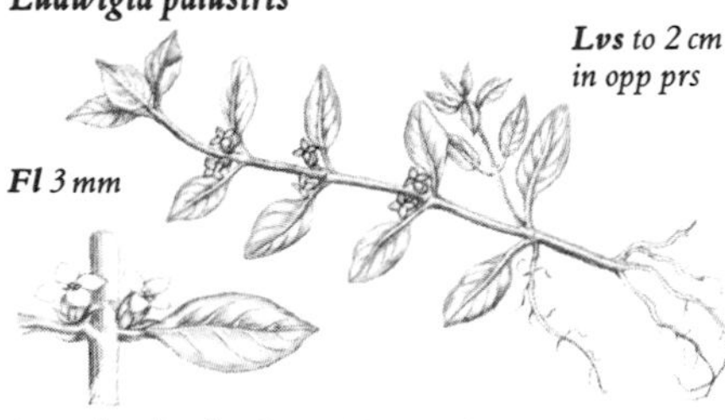

Aquatic, shs slender to 30 cm. Fls sol in axils, 4 spread spls, no ptls. *D:* W, C, S; *Fl:* 6

Sea heath family Frankeniaceae

Dwarf shrubs with opposite leaves. Flowers have 4–6 sepals and petals and 6 stamens. The fruit is a capsule.

Sea heath  

Frankenia laevis

Delicate mat-forming, prostrate woody per resembling spp of *Erica* (p 93). Lvs densely crowded. *Ht:* to 15 cm; *D:* W; *Fl:* 7–8

Cucumber family Cucurbitaceae

Mostly succulent, tendrilled, hairy annual climbers. Flowers have parts in fives and petals often joined at the base.

White bryony  

Bryonia cretica

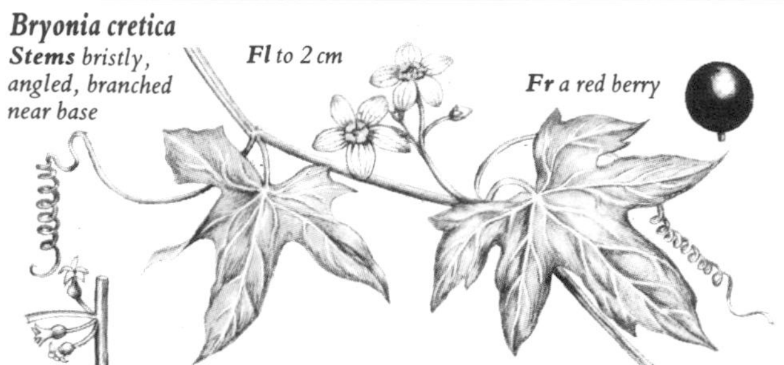

Scrambles to 3 m. Tendrils arise from stem near lvs. ♂, ♀ fls on separate plants, veined ptls longer than spls, 3 stigmas 2 × cut. *D:* S, W; *Fl:* 5–9

Loosestrife family Lythraceae

Herbs or shrubs with whorled leaves without stipules. The petals are joined to the sepals which are united in a tube.

Purple loosestrife 

Lythrum salicaria

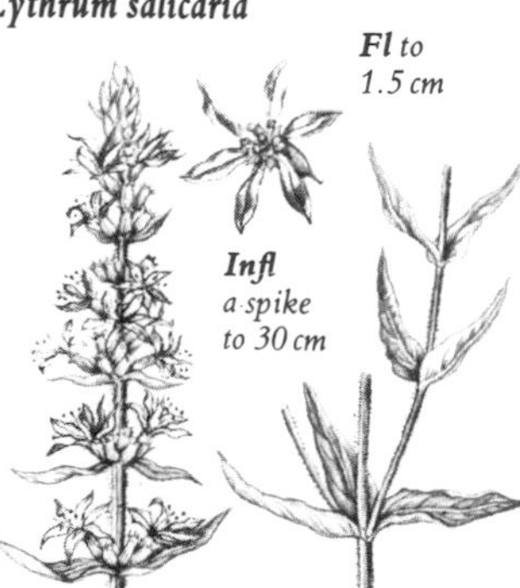

Stem 4-angled; lvs unstkd, opp or in whorls of 3. Fls have 4–6 ptls. *Ht:* 1 m; *D:* T (not far N); *Fl:* 6–8

Grass poly  

L. hyssopifolia

Much branched, hrlss. Fls 5 mm, sol in lf axils, 6 stamens. *Ht:* 15 cm; *D:* S, W, C; *Fl:* 6–7

Water milfoil family Haloragaceae

Marestail family Hippuridaceae

Aquatics often with whorled leaves. Solitary marestail flowers hve no sepals or petals and one stamen. Water milfoil flowers have tiny petals and sepals and 8 stamens.

Spiked water milfoil 

Myriophyllum spicatum

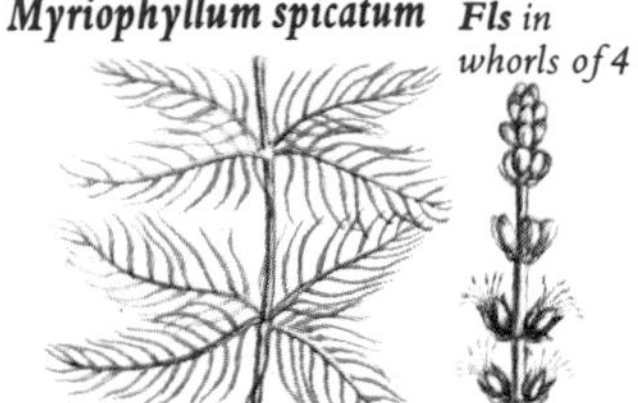

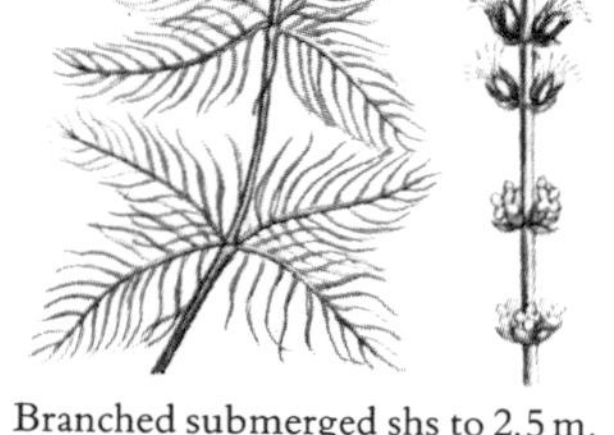

Branched submerged shs to 2.5 m. Lvs 4 per whorl, 13–35 narrow lobes, fl bracts entire. *D:* T; *Fl:* 6–7

Whorled water milfoil 

M. verticillatum

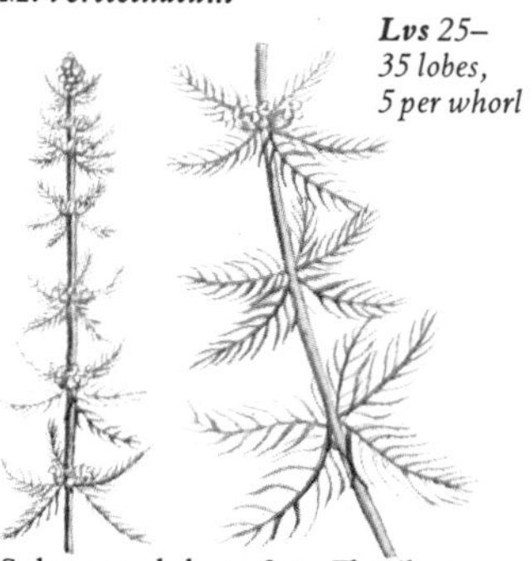

Submerged shs to 3 m. Fl spike to 25 cm above water, fls in whorls of 5, bracts pinnate. *D:* T; *Fl:* 7–8

Alternate-leaved water milfoil 

M. alterniflorum

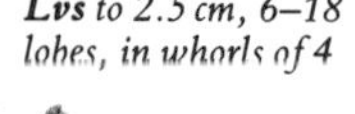

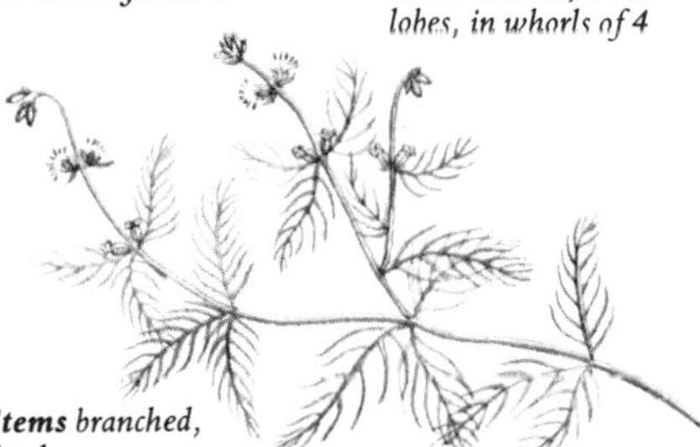

Submerged shs to 1.2 m. Fl spike droops in bud, fls in whorls, ♀ at base, ♂ above, bracts pinnate below, simple above. *D:* W, C, N; *Fl:* 5–8

Marestail

Hippuris vulgaris

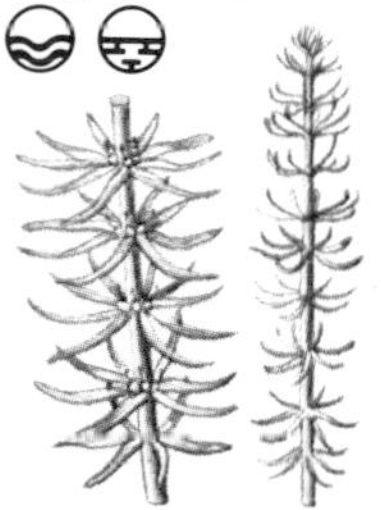

Emergent, with rhizome. Lvs unlobed in whorls of 6–12. *Ht:* 60 cm; *D:* T; *Fl:* 6–7

Dogwood family Cornaceae

Mostly trees and shrubs rather than herbs. Flowers have parts in fours (the sepals are small) above the ovary.

Dwarf cornel

Cornus suecica

Perennial, shs erect. Lvs in opp prs, parallel veins. Infl an umbel of 8–25 fls to 2 mm with 4 bracts to 8 mm. *Ht:* 15 cm; *D:* N; *Fl:* 7–8

Ivy family Araliaceae

Evergreen woody climbers. Flowers in umbels have sepals joined in a 5-toothed tube and 5 petals and stamens.

Ivy

Hedera helix

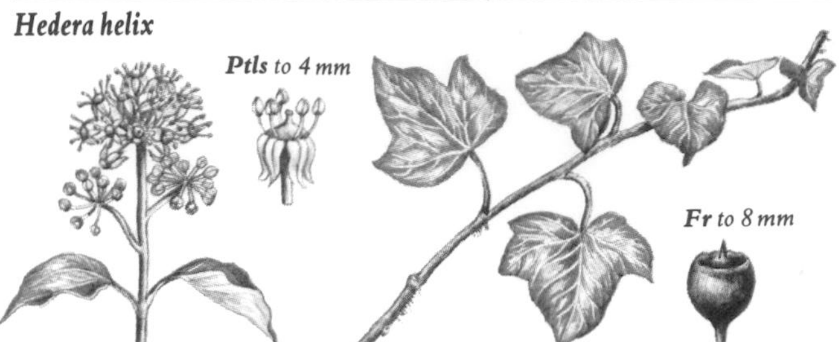

Climbs to 30 m, using rts on trees. Lvs hrlss, 3–5 lobes; infl gps of umbels on climbing shs only, fr berry-like. *D:* W, C, S; *Fl:* 9–11

Carrot family Umbelliferae

Herbs, often with hollow, furrowed stems. Leaves have sheathing stalks. Flowers in groups of umbels with bracts and/or bracteoles have parts in fives and sepals united in a tube.

Hogweed

Heracleum sphondylium

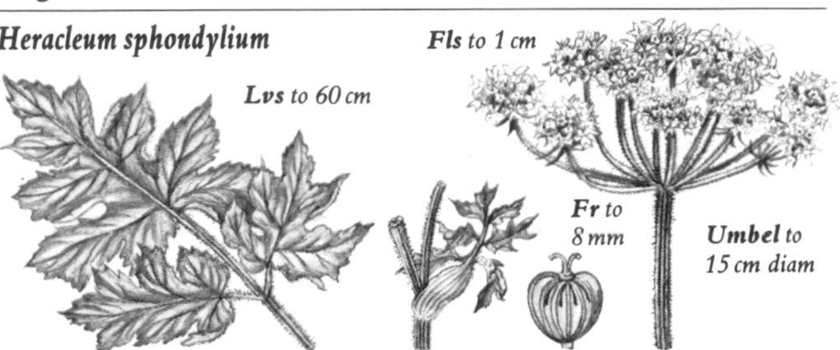

Bristly, stems hollow; lvs 1-pinnate. Bracteoles but no bracts in infl, outer fls have unequal ptls. *Ht:* 1.5 m; *D:* T (not far N); *Fl:* 6–9

Upright hedge parsley

Torilis japonica

Umbel 5–15 rays, 4–6 bracts, hooked spines on fr. *Ht:* 1 m; *D:* T (not far N); *Fl:* 7–8

Knotted bur parsley

T. nodosa

Short-stkd umbel, no bracts, long bracteoles. Fr spines straight. *Ht:* 20 cm; *D:* S, W; *Fl:* 5–7

Spreading bur parsley

T. arvensis

Umbel 3–5 rays, 1 or no bracts, spines on fr curved. *Ht:* 25 cm; *D:* W, S, C; *Fl:* 7–9

Cow parsley

Anthriscus sylvestris

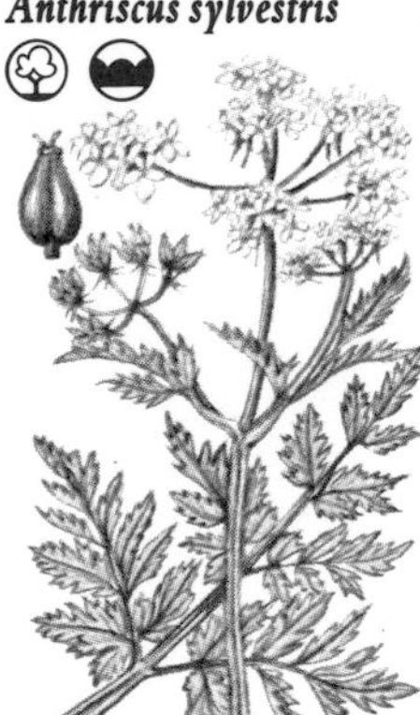

Umbel 4–10 rays, no hrs or bracts; fr to 5 mm, smooth. *Ht:* 80 cm; *D:* T; *Fl:* 4–6

Bur chervil

A. caucalis

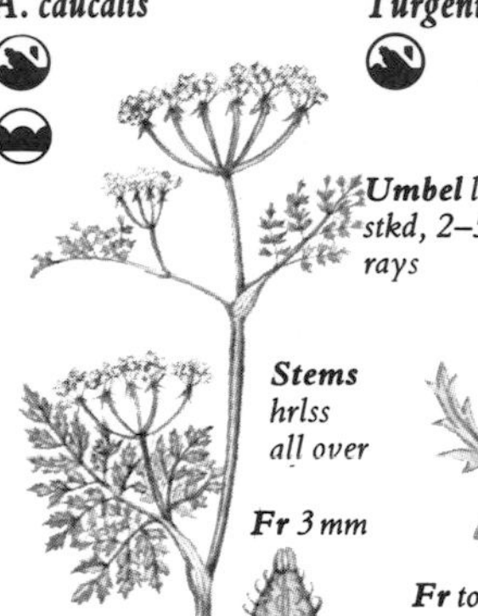

Umbel has bracteoles, no bracts; spines on fr hooked. *Ht:* 35 cm; *D:* W, C, S; *Fl:* 5–6

Greater bur parsley

Turgenia latifolia

Leaves 1-pinnate, hry below; fr has rows of spines. *Ht:* 45 cm; *D:* S, C; *Fl:* 5–8

Small bur parsley

Caucalis platycarpos

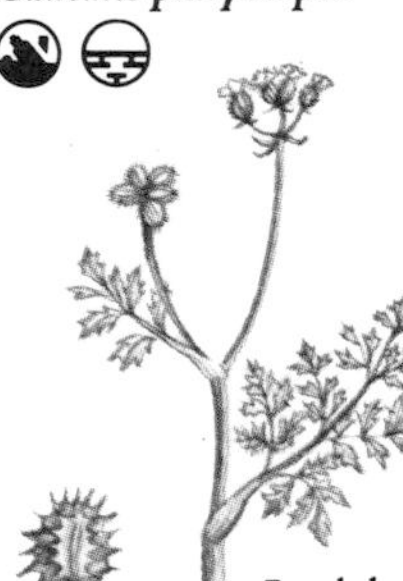

Sepal tube has obvious teeth; fr has spineless ridges. *Ht:* 20 cm; *D:* T (not far N); *Fl:* 6–7

Stone parsley

Sison amomum

Fetid smell, hrlss; umbel 3–6 rayed, fr round. *Ht:* 80 cm; *D:* S, W; *Fl:* 7–9

Cambridge milk parsley

Selinum carvifolia

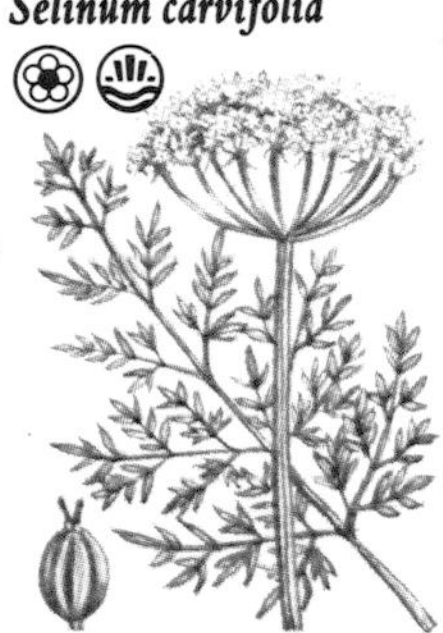

Stems solid, hrlss, winged ridges, no spl teeth; fr 4 mm. *Ht:* 80 cm; *D:* T; *Fl:* 7–10

Rough chervil

Chaerophyllum temulentum

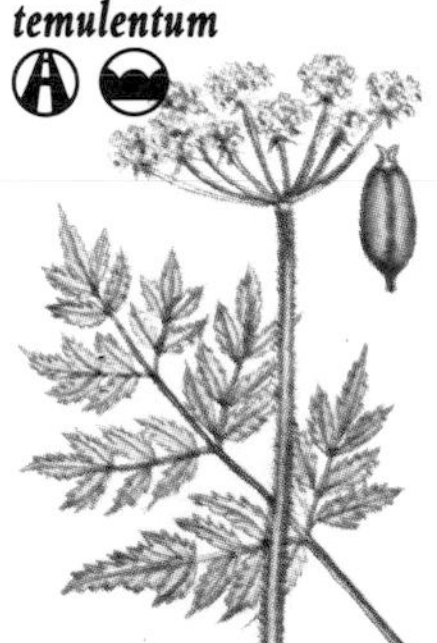

Stems bristly, spotted; bracts reflexed in fr; fr tapered. *Ht:* 80 cm; *D:* T (not N); *Fl:* 6–7

Hemlock

Conium maculatum

Stems spotted; infl 10–20 rays, fr 3 mm, wavy ridges. *Ht:* 2 m; *D:* T (not N); *Fl:* 6–7

Coriander

Coriandrum sativum

Leaves 1–2 pinnate; ptls vary in size, frs stick in groups. *Ht:* 55 cm; *D:* S; *Fl:* 6

Pignut

Conopodium majus

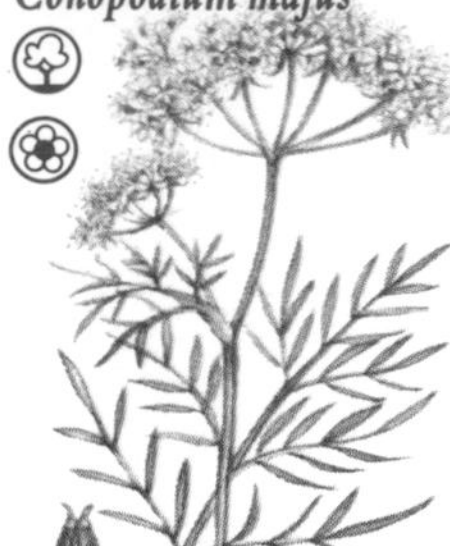

Hairless, hollow stem. Umbels to 7 cm, 6–12 rays. Fr 4 mm has prominent uprt styles; tubers edible. *Ht:* 40 cm; *D:* W; *Fl:* 5–6

Great pignut

Bunium bulbocastanum

Stem solid. Fr to 3 mm has curved, short styles. *Ht:* 50 cm; D: *S, C;* Fl: *6–7*

Fool's parsley

Aethusa cynapium

Umbel 10–20 rays, 3–4 bracteoles on outer part, no bracts; fr to 4 mm. *Ht:* 1 m; *D:* T; *Fl:* 7–8

Wild carrot

Daucus carota

Infl to 7 cm diam

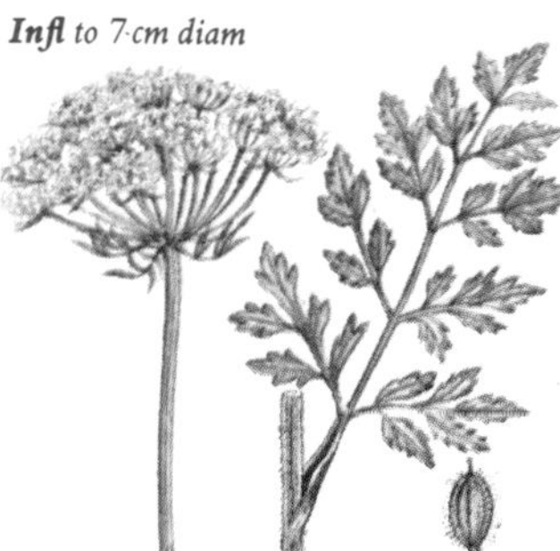

Bristly, stem solid, many rays in infl, bracts lobed; fr ridged, spiny. *Ht:* 80 cm; *D:* T; *Fl:* 6–8

Moon carrot

Seseli libanotis

Stems have fibrous base. Umbels long-stkd to 6 cm diam, many bracts and bracteoles. *Ht:* 45 cm; *D:* T (not far N); *Fl:* 7–8

Caraway

Carum carvi

Leaves 2-pinnate. No bracts or bracteoles; fr strong smelling. *Ht:* 40 cm; *D:* T; *Fl:* 6–7

Whorled caraway

C. verticillatum

Leaves 1-pinnate, look whorled. Some bracts and bracteoles. *Ht:* 45 cm; *D:* W; *Fl:* 7–8

Honewort

Trinia glauca

Plant glaucous

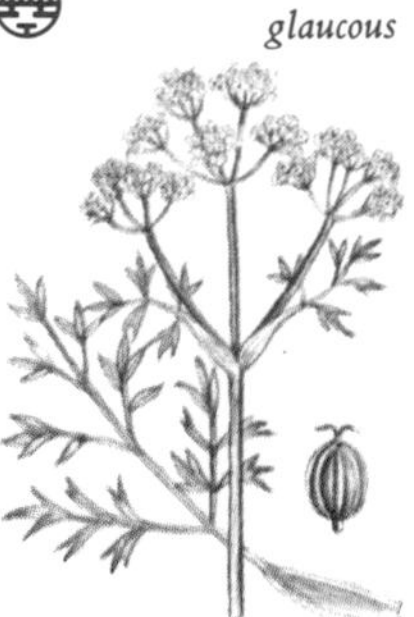

Male umbels 1 cm, ♀ 3 cm on separate plants. *Ht:* 15 cm; *D:* W, C, S; *Fl:* 5–6

Greater water parsnip

Sium latifolium

Leaves 1-pinnate, 4–6 lflt prs, serrate; infl 20+ rays; fr oval. *Ht:* 1.5 m; *D:* T; *Fl:* 7–8

Lesser water parsnip

Berula erecta

Leaves 1-pinnate, 7–10 lflt prs; infl 10–20 rays. *Ht:* to 1 m; *D:* T (not far N); *Fl:* 7–9

Spignel

Meum anthamaticum

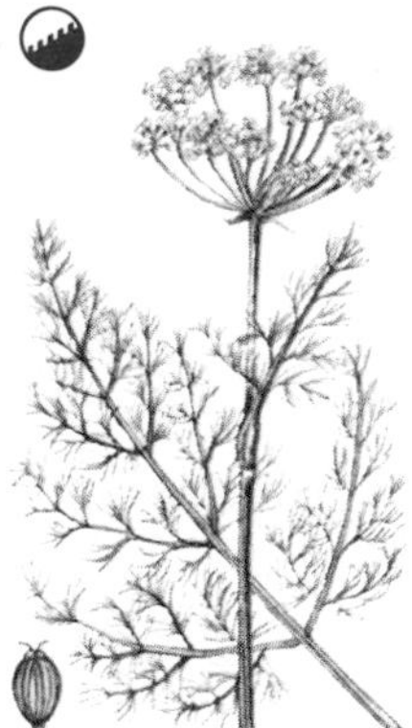

Aromatic, lf segments fine; umbel 6–15 rays; fr to 1 cm. *Ht:* 45 cm; *D:* W, C; *Fl:* 6–7

Angelica

Angelica sylvestris

Stems have bloom (unlike *A. archangelica*); lvs 2–3 pinnate, stks inflated. *Ht:* 1.5 m; *D:* T; *Fl:* 7–9

Cowbane

Cicuta virosa

Plant *v poisonous*

Leaflets narrow, serrate. Many bracteoles longer than fl stks. *Ht:* to 1.3 m; *D:* T; *Fl:* 7–8

Sermountain

Laserpitium latifolium

Umbel has many bracts, few bracteoles. Fr to 1 cm has wavy wings. *Ht:* 1.2 m; *D:* T (not UK); *Fl:* 6–8

Sweet cicely

Myrrhis odorata

Strongly aromatic. Some fls ♂ only. Fr to 2.5 cm. *Ht:* to 1 m; *D:* W, mts in S; *Fl:* 5–6

Corn parsley

Petroselinum segetum

Lower brs spreading; lvs 1-pinnate, umbels irregular. *Ht:* to 1 m; *D:* W; *Fl:* 8–9

Milk parsley

Peucedanum palustre

Umbel has 4 bracts bent back, long thin bracteoles. *Ht:* to 1.5 m; *D:* T; *Fl:* 7–9

Hog's fennel

P. officinale

Linear, tangled lflts; infl 20+ rays, often no bracteoles. *Ht:* 1 m; *D:* S, C; *Fl:* 7–9

Field eryngo

Eryngium campestre

Basal lvs pinnate, stkd. Bracts spiny, bracteoles 2–3 × fl length. *Ht:* 45 cm; *D:* C, S; *Fl:* 7–8

Sea holly

E. maritimum

***Fl** 8 mm*

Glaucous. Bracts spiny, toothed, bracteoles just longer than fls. *Ht:* 45 cm; *D:* T; *Fl:* 7–8

Rock samphire

Crithmum maritimum

Fleshy per to 30 cm. Lf segs cylindrical; many bracts and bracteoles in umbel. Fr to 6 mm, egg-shaped. *D:* T (not N); *Fl:* 6–8

Burnet saxifrage

Pimpinella saxifraga

Basal lvs 1-pinnate, stem lvs 2-pinnate; no bracts or bracteoles. *Ht:* 1 m; *D:* T; *Fl:* 7–8

Greater burnet saxifrage

P. major

Stems rigid, brittle; lvs 1-pinnate; no bracts or bracteoles. *Ht:* 1 m; *D:* T; *Fl:* 6–7

Ground elder

Aegopodium podagraria

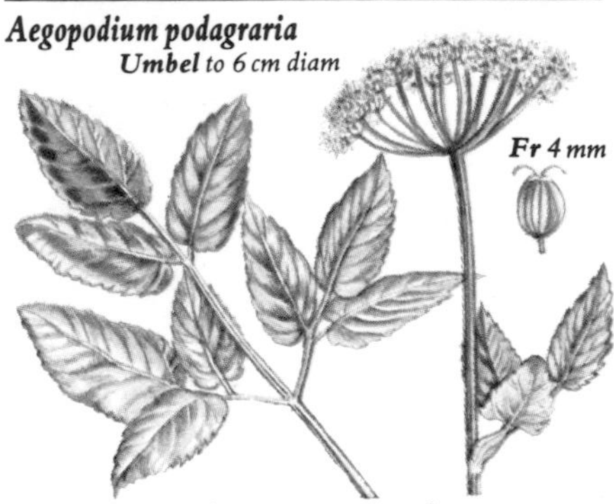

Creeps to 1 m. Lf segments *c.* 5 cm long, serrate. No bracts or bracteoles. *D:* T; *Fl:* 5–7

Shepherd's needle

Scandix pecten-veneris

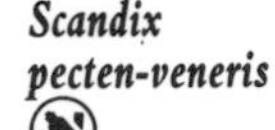

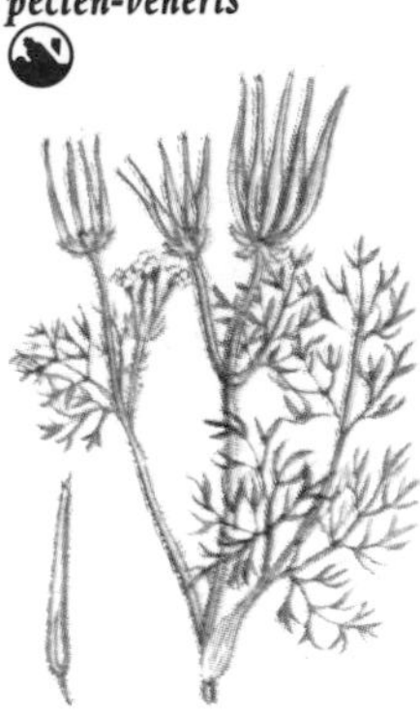

Umbels 2–3 rays; bracteoles lobed, 1 cm; fr ridged. *Ht:* 35 cm; *D:* W, C, S; *Fl:* 4–7

Hemlock water dropwort

Oenanthe crocata

Has rt tubers; lvs 3–4 pinnate to 50 cm; v poisonous. *Ht:* 1.2 m; *D:* W; *Fl:* 6–7

Fine-leaved water dropwort

O. aquatica

Umbel short-stkd

Lvs 3-pinnate

Roots fibrous; lower lvs submerged; umbels opp lvs. *Ht:* 1.2 m; *D:* T (not far N); *Fl:* 6–9

Parsley water dropwort

O. lachenalii

Pinnate part of lf longer than solid stk. Fr 2 mm, stk swollen. *Ht:* 1 m; *D:* W; *Fl:* 6–9

Wild celery

Apium graveolens

Top stem lvs 3-lobed, no bracts or bracteoles; celery smell. *Ht:* 40 cm; *D:* T; *Fl:* 6–8

Water dropwort

O. fistulosa

Pinnate part of lf shorter than hollow stk. *Ht:* 45 cm; *D:* W, C, S; *Fl:* 7–9

Fool's watercress

A. nodiflorum

Often prostrate to 1 m; umbels unstkd, no bracts, 5 bracteoles. *D:* T; *Fl:* 7–8

Sickle hare's ear

Bupleurum falcatum

Hollow-stemmed per; bracteoles shorter than fls. *Ht:* to 1.3 m; *D:* S, C, E; *Fl:* 7–10

Smallest hare's ear

B. tenuissimum

Umbels to 5 mm in lf axils; fls shorter than bracteoles. *Ht:* 35 cm; *D:* S, W, C; *Fl:* 7–9

Thorow-wax

B. rotundifolium

Glaucous, lvs round, encircling stem, oval bracteoles. *Ht:* 20 cm; *D:* C, S; *Fl:* 6–7

Scots lovage

Ligusticum scoticum

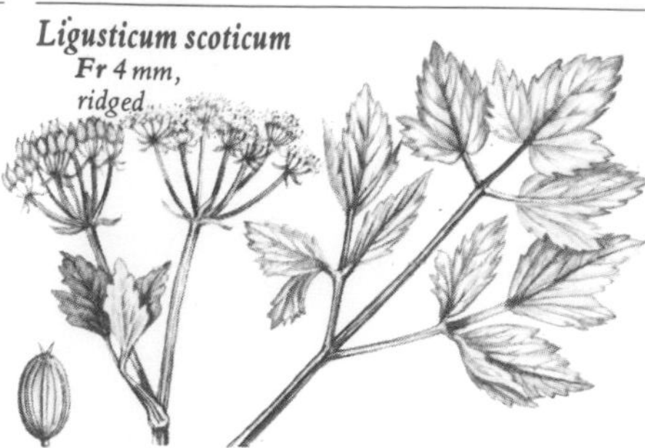

Hairless per to 90 cm. Upper lvs 3-lobed, serrate, basal lvs 2-pinnate. *D:* N; *Fl:* 7

Fennel

Foeniculum vulgare

Glaucous, strong smell. Lvs cut into v fine segs. *Ht:* 1 m; *D:* T (not N); *Fl:* 7–10

Alexanders

Smyrnium olusatrum

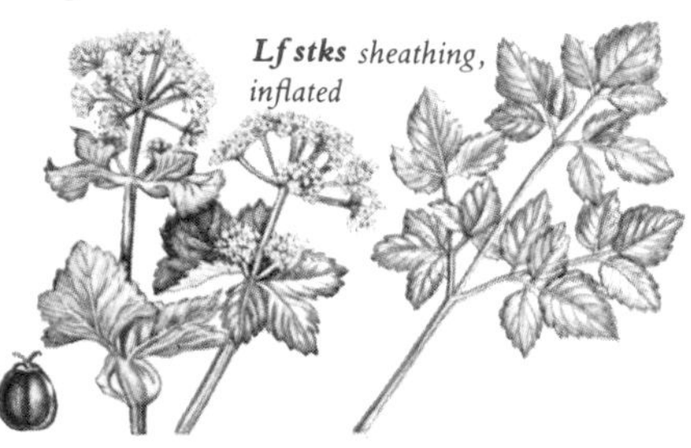

Leaves pinnate, shiny with 3-lobed segs; fr 8 mm, black. *Ht:* to 1.5 m; *D:* S; *Fl:* 4–6

Marsh pennywort

Hydrocotyle vulgaris

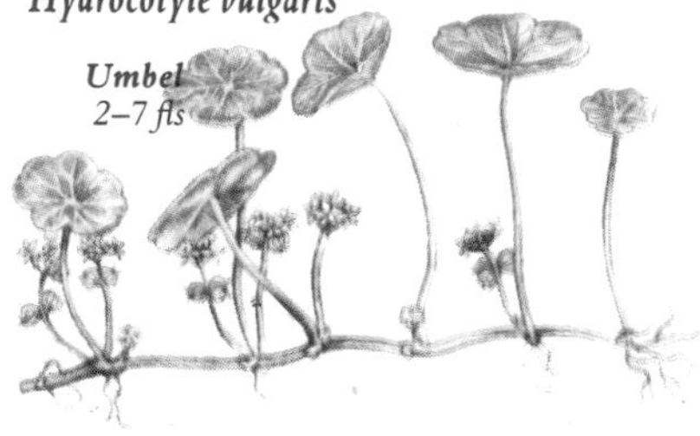

Creeping per. Lvs circular to 5 cm diam on long erect stks to 25 cm. *D:* W, C, S; *Fl:* 7–10

Pepper saxifrage

Silaum silaus

Hairless per; lvs 2–3 pinnate, fine-toothed segs. *Ht:* to 1 m; *D:* W, C, E; *Fl:* 6–8

Astrantia

Astrantia major

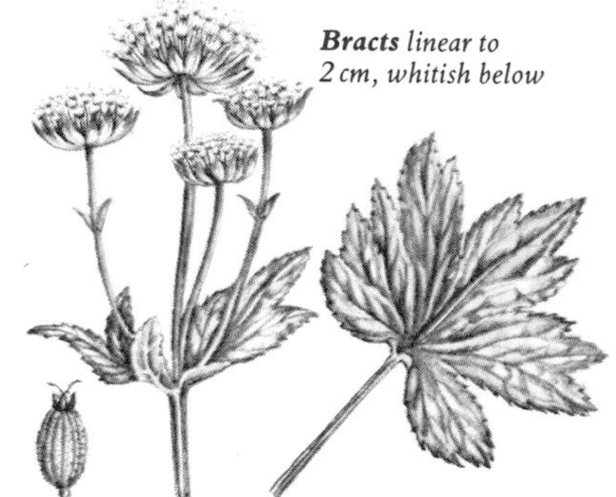

Has creeping stock. Basal lvs to 15 cm, palmate; some fls ♂ only. *Ht:* 60 cm; *D:* C; *Fl:* 5–7

Sanicle

Sanicula europaea

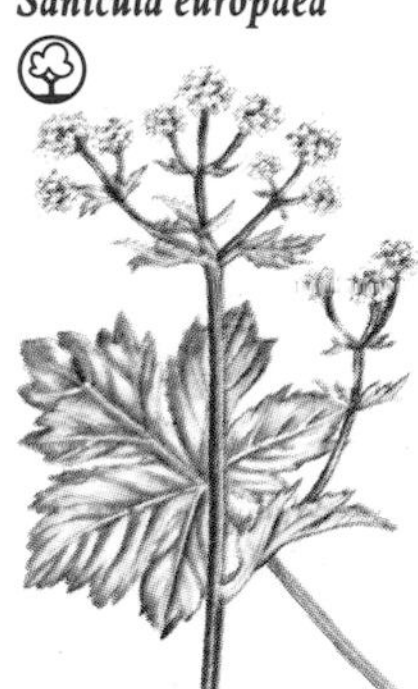

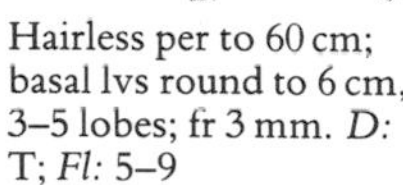

Hairless per to 60 cm; basal lvs round to 6 cm, 3–5 lobes; fr 3 mm. *D:* T; *Fl:* 5–9

Wild parsnip

Pastinaca sativa

Leaves 1-pinnate, shs hollow; fr to 8 mm, pointed. *Ht:* 1.2 m; *D:* T (not far N); *Fl:* 7–8

Bladderseed

Physospermum cornubiense

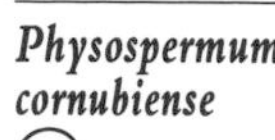

Leaves and umbels long-stkd; fr 5 mm, styles bent back. *Ht:* 55 cm; *D:* S; *Fl:* 7–8

Diapensia family Diapensiaceae

Arctic perennials and dwarf shrubs. Sepals and petals are in a 5-lobed tube, the stigma is three-lobed.

Diapensia

Diapensia lapponica

Woody, cushion-forming per to 5 cm. Lvs unlobed, narrowing to short stk. Fls sol, fl stks to 3 cm. Spl tube 5 mm. *D:* N; *Fl:* 5–6

Wintergreen family Pyrolaceae

Perennial evergreen herbs with rhizomes. The symmetrical flowers have parts in fives and the petals are not united in a tube. The 5-celled ovary has a single stigma.

Common wintergreen

Pyrola minor

Round-leaved wintergreen

P. rotundifolia

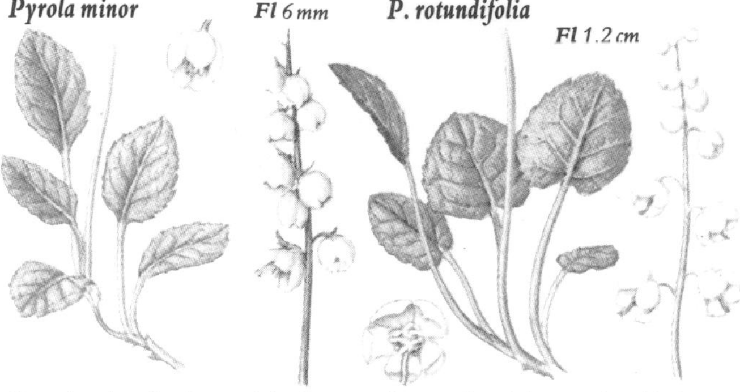

Creeping; lvs alt, short-stkd. Fls spherical, style straight, stigma 5-lobed. *Ht:* 20 cm; *D:* T; *Fl:* 6–8

Leaves alt, stk longer than blade. Long, curved style makes ring under stigma. *Ht:* 25 cm; *D:* T; *Fl:* 7–9

Yellow wintergreen

P. chlorantha

Umbellate wintergreen

Chimaphila umbellata

Like *P. rotundifolia* but lvs pale above, obovate; fls yellow-green. *Ht:* 20 cm; *D:* T (not W); *Fl:* 7–9

Leaves serrate, appear whorled; fls in an umbel, v short styles, ptls spread. *Ht:* 20 cm; *D:* N, C, E; *Fl:* 6–7

One-flowered wintergreen

Moneses uniflora

Toothed wintergreen

Orthilia secunda

Yellow birdsnest

Monotropa hypopitys

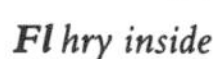

Leaves opp, rounded, short-stkd. Fl shs to 15 cm, fls sol wide open. *D:* T; *Fl:* 6–8

Leaves serrate; fl shs 10 cm, fls all to one side, stigmas projecting. *D:* T; *Fl:* 7–8

Has no green parts. Waxy stems to 30 cm, fls drooping, fr erect. *D:* T; *Fl:* 6–8

Heather family Ericaceae

Dwarf shrubs with simple evergreen leaves. The flowers, usually in clusters, have petals fused into a tube to which the stamens are not attached and a single style.

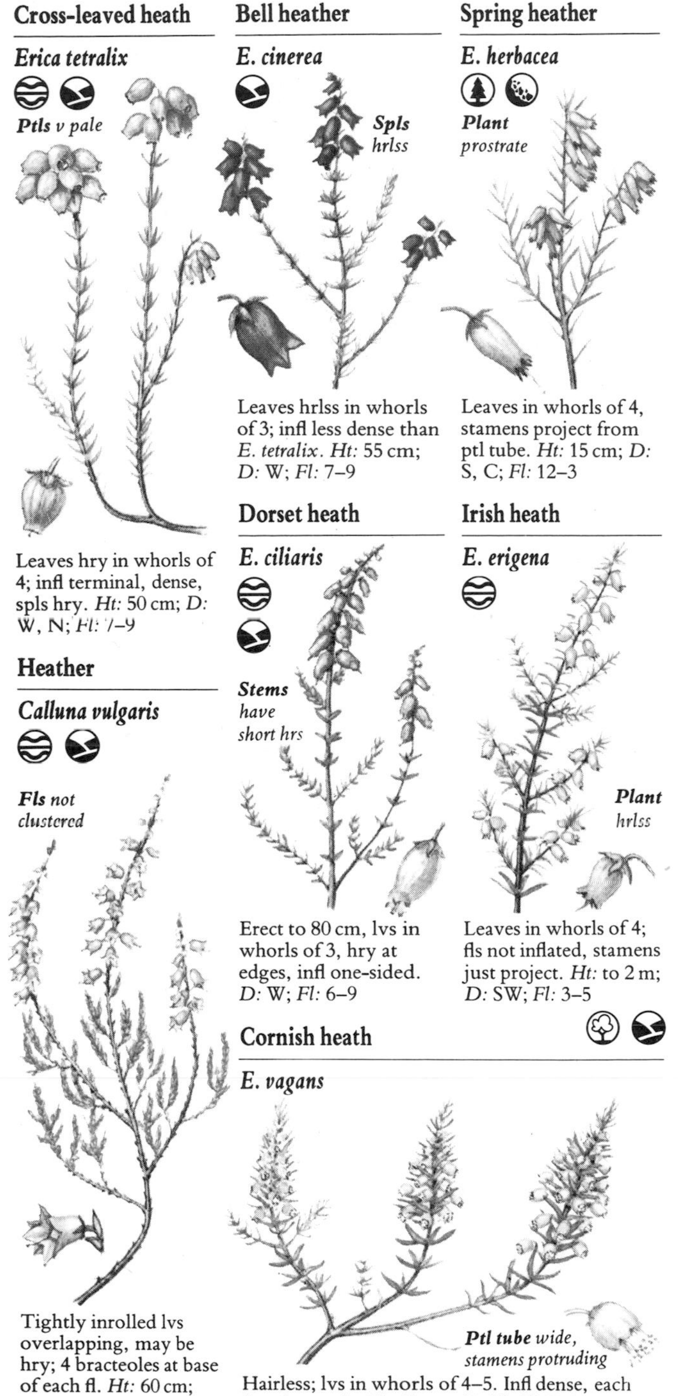

Cross-leaved heath

Erica tetralix

Leaves hry in whorls of 4; infl terminal, dense, spls hry. *Ht:* 50 cm; *D:* W, N; *Fl:* 7–9

Bell heather

E. cinerea

Leaves hrlss in whorls of 3; infl less dense than *E. tetralix*. *Ht:* 55 cm; *D:* W; *Fl:* 7–9

Spring heather

E. herbacea

Leaves in whorls of 4, stamens project from ptl tube. *Ht:* 15 cm; *D:* S, C; *Fl:* 12–3

Heather

Calluna vulgaris

Tightly inrolled lvs overlapping, may be hry; 4 bracteoles at base of each fl. *Ht:* 60 cm; *D:* T; *Fl:* 7–9

Dorset heath

E. ciliaris

Erect to 80 cm, lvs in whorls of 3, hry at edges, infl one-sided. *D:* W; *Fl:* 6–9

Irish heath

E. erigena

Leaves in whorls of 4; fls not inflated, stamens just project. *Ht:* to 2 m; *D:* SW; *Fl:* 3–5

Cornish heath

E. vagans

Hairless; lvs in whorls of 4–5. Infl dense, each fl on long stk. *Ht:* 60 cm; *D:* W; *Fl:* 7–8

St Dabeoc's heath

Daboecia cantabrica

Stems hry, lvs white below. Infl 3–10 fls, 4 hry spls. *Ht:* 35 cm; *D:* W; *Fl:* 7–9

Bilberry

Vaccinium myrtillus

Deciduous, stems green, v ridged; berry black with bloom. *Ht:* 45 cm; *D:* T; *Fl:* 4–6

Cowberry

V. vitis-idaea

Evergreen, lvs round, glossy above; fl 6 mm, bell shaped. *Ht:* 20 cm; *D:* N, C; *Fl:* 6–8

Cranberry

V. oxycoccos

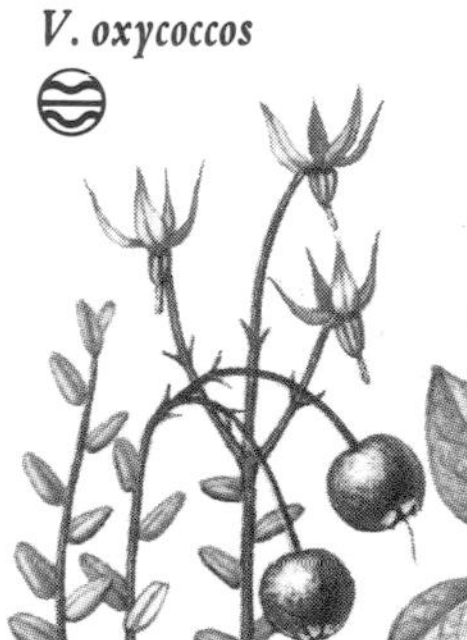

Creeps to 80 cm, shs slender, lvs oval. Ptl tube cut almost to base *D:* N, C; *Fl:* 6–8

Bog whortleberry

V. uliginosum

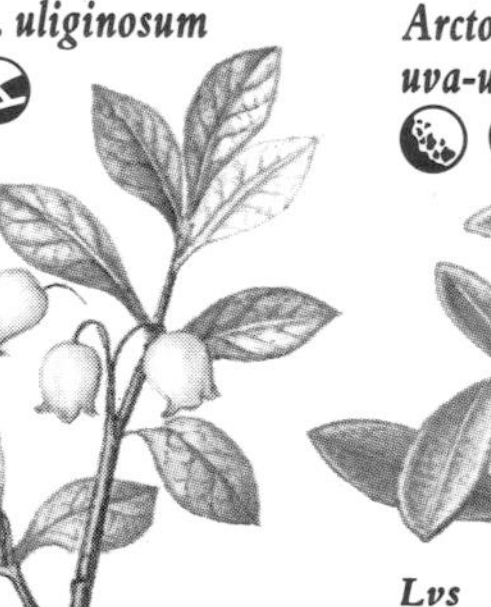

Stems round, lvs untoothed, decid; fr has bloom. *Ht:* 40 cm; *D:* N, C; *Fl:* 5–6

Alpine bearberry

Arctostaphylos uva-ursi

Prostrate evergreen to 2 m. Infl 5–12 fls, fr to 8 mm, red, tastes dry. *D:* T; *Fl:* 5–7

Black bearberry

A. alpinus

Prostrate, decid to 2 m; serrate lvs strongly veined; fr juicy, black to 1 cm. *D:* S mts, N; *Fl:* 5–8

Wild azalea

Loiseleuria procumbens

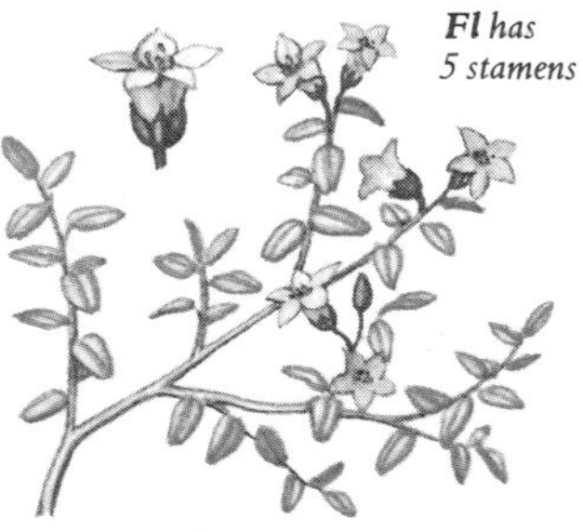

Prostrate, evergreen to 30 cm, lvs numerous, opp to 8 mm; ptls have spreading lobes. *D:* T; *Fl:* 5–7

Mountain heather

Phyllodoce caerulea

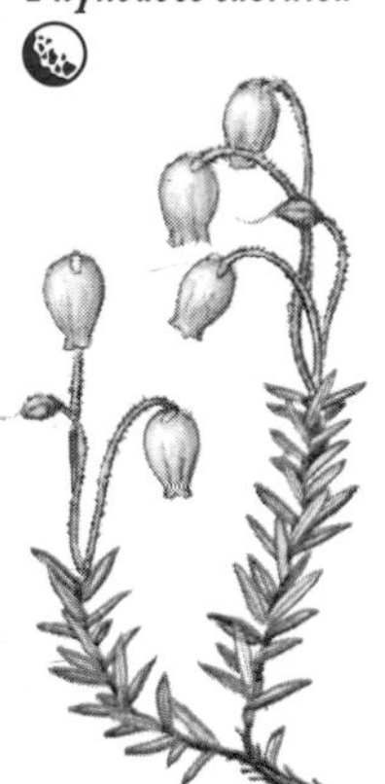

Erect evergreen; lvs dense, fls to 8 mm, long-stkd, 5 stamens in terminal infl. *Ht:* 10 cm; *D:* N; *Fl:* 6–7

Leatherleaf

Chamaedaphne calyculata

Erect evergreen, lvs slightly serrate, scaly below to 4 cm; infl 5–20 drooping fls. *Ht:* 35 cm; *D:* NE; *Fl:* 6–7

Bog rosemary

Andromeda polifolia

Creeping evergreen to 30 cm. Lvs elongate to 3.5 cm, darker above; fls long-stkd, infl 2–8 fls. *D:* T; *Fl:* 5–6

Ledum

Ledum palustre

Many rust coloured hrs on stems and lf undersides; fls long-stkd, infl dense. *Ht:* 80 cm; *D:* N, C; *Fl:* 6–7

Rhododendron

Rhododendron ponticum

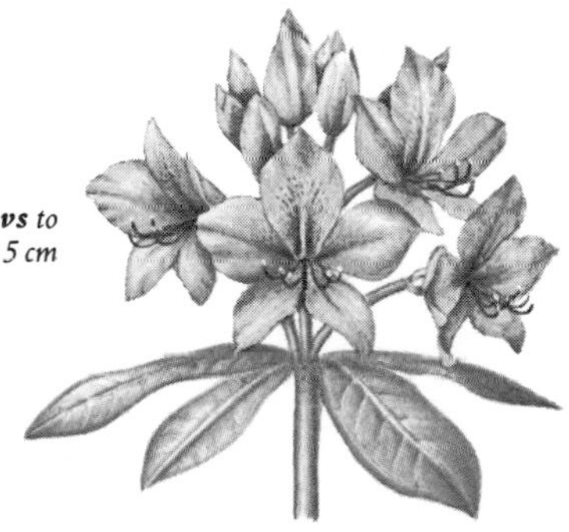

Evergreen to 3 m; lvs hrlss, paler below. Infl dense, fls open, bell shaped, 10 stamens. *D:* W; *Fl:* 5–6

Crowberry family Empetraceae

Heath-like dwarf evergreens with 6 sepal and petal lobes that are not brightly coloured and three stamens.

Crowberry

Empetrum nigrum

Prostrate evergreen to 30 cm, stems red. Lvs linear, white line below; fls in lf axils in gps of 1–3; fr round, black. *D:* S mts, N; *Fl:* 5–6

Primrose family Primulaceae

Simple-leaved herbs. Symmetrical tubular flowers have parts in fives and stamens joined to the petal tube interior.

Primrose

Primula vulgaris

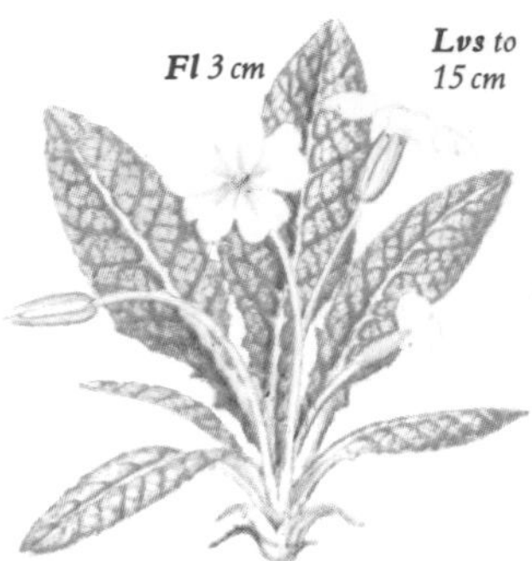

Leaves hrlss above thin gradually to base; indiv fl shs to 10 cm have long hrs. *D:* W, S; *Fl:* 12–5

Cowslip

P. veris

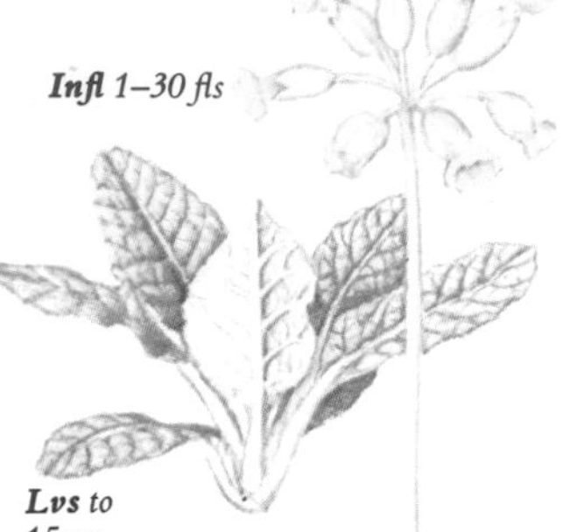

Hairy lvs narrow sharply; orange-spotted fls on common 20 cm sh (scape). *D:* T (not far N); *Fl:* 4–5

Birdseye primrose

P. farinosa

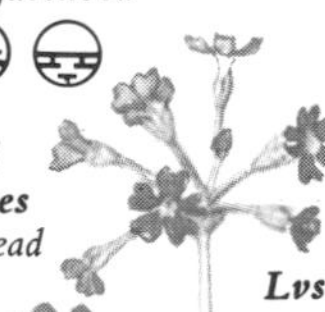
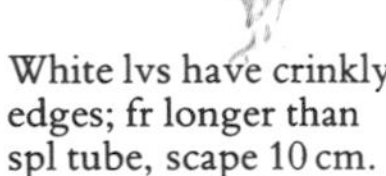

White lvs have crinkly edges; fr longer than spl tube, scape 10 cm. *D:* mts T; *Fl:* 5–6

Scottish primrose

P. scotica

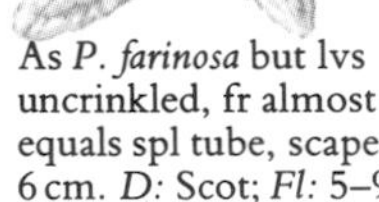
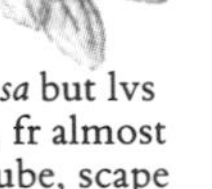
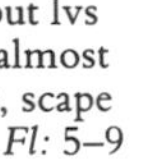

As *P. farinosa* but lvs uncrinkled, fr almost equals spl tube, scape 6 cm. *D:* Scot; *Fl:* 5–9

Scandinavian primrose

P. scandinavica

Like *P. scotica* but scape to 10 cm, fl to 1 cm, longer bracts. *D:* Scand mts; *Fl:* 6–9

Oxlip

P. elatior

Leaves as *P. veris* but hrs curled; scape to 30 cm, hry; spl tube has dark ridges. *D:* S, W, C; *Fl:* 4–5

Auricula

P.auricula

Broad lvs hrlss, succ, thick at edges; scape to 16 cm, infl to 30 fls. *D:* Alps, Carp; *Fl:* 5–7

Cyclamen

Cyclamen purpurascens

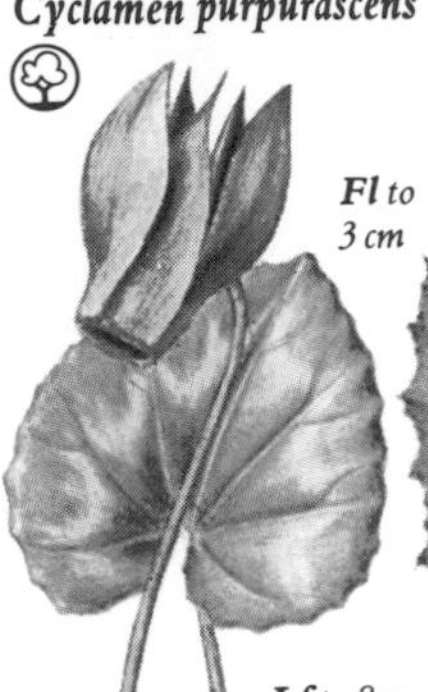

Tuberous base to 3 cm, lf edges rounded, ptl lobes clawless below, fl sh to 15 cm. *D:* C, S; *Fl:* 6–10

Sowbread

C. hederifolium

Corm to 15 cm; lvs to 14 cm, angled edges. Ptl lobes to 2 cm, clawed at base; fl sh to 30 cm, coiled fr stk. *D:* S; *Fl:* 8–11

Alpine snowbell

Soldanella alpina

Round, long-stkd lvs to 4 cm wide. Fl to 1.3 cm, many narrow lobes, fl sh to 15 cm. *D:* S, C; *Fl:* 4–7

Chickweed wintergreen

Trientalis europaea

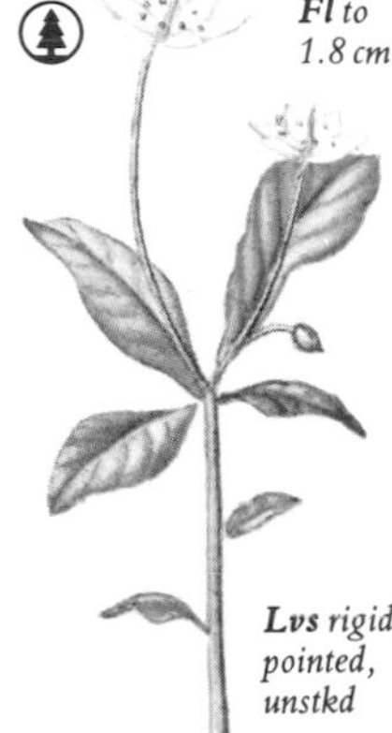

Erect, hrlss stems to 25 cm not branched; 1 or 2 fls on stks to 7 cm from lf whorl. *D:* S mts, N; *Fl:* 6–7

Large androsace

Androsace maxima

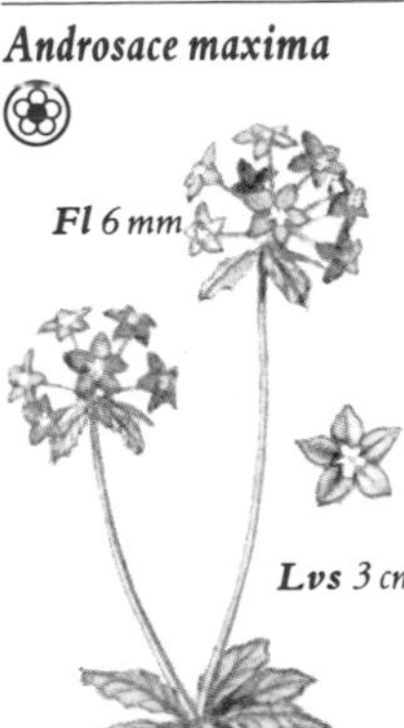

Annual; 1 to sev 8 cm scapes, bracts large, lfy; spls longer than ptls. *D:* S, C; *Fl:* 4–5

White androsace

A. lactea

Fl stks long

Tufted per; lvs linear sessile; sev scapes to 15 cm. Stolons present. *D:* S, C; *Fl:* 6–8

Scarlet pimpernel

Anagallis arvensis

Prostrate, stems square; lvs opp, spots below; fl stks slim, globular fr. *Ht:* 20 cm; *D:* T; *Fl:* 6–8

Bog pimpernel

A. tenella

Stems round; lvs opp, shorter than slim fl shs. Ptl tube longer than spls. *Ht:* 10 cm; *D:* W; *Fl:* 6–8

Yellow loosestrife

Lysimachia vulgaris

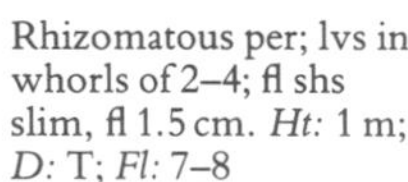

Rhizomatous per; lvs in whorls of 2–4; fl shs slim, fl 1.5 cm. *Ht:* 1 m; *D:* T; *Fl:* 7–8

Tufted loosestrife

L. thyrsiflora

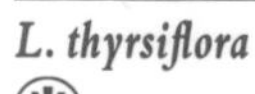

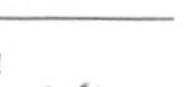

Rhizomatous per, lvs in opp prs, dotted black. Infl dense in lf axils. *Ht:* 45 cm; *D:* T (not S); *Fl:* 6–7

Sea milkwort

Glaux maritima

Creeping succ, opp lvs in 4 ranks; unstkd fls in lf axils, no ptls, 5 ptl-like spls. *Ht:* 20 cm; *D:* T; *Fl:* 6–8

Water violet

Hottonia palustris

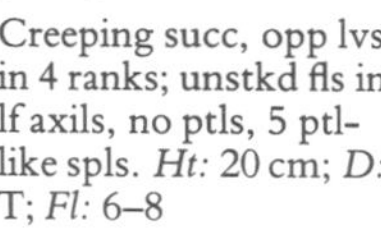

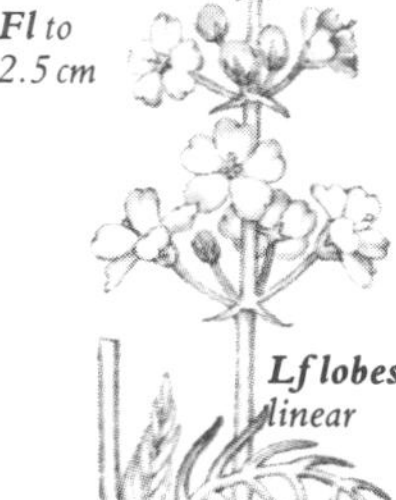

Floating, hrlss; lvs pinnate in whorls; fl scape 30 cm erect. *D:* T (not far N); *Fl:* 5–6

Yellow pimpernel

L. nemorum

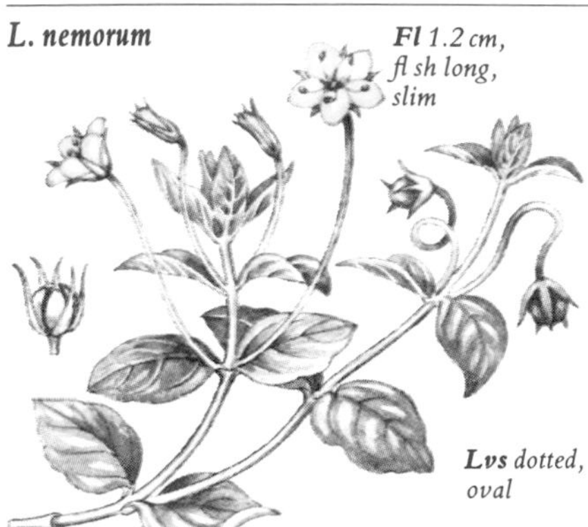

Slender prostrate per; lvs opp, short-stkd. Fls sol, fr globular. *Ht:* 30 cm; *D:* W, C; *Fl:* 5–9

Creeping Jenny

L. nummularia

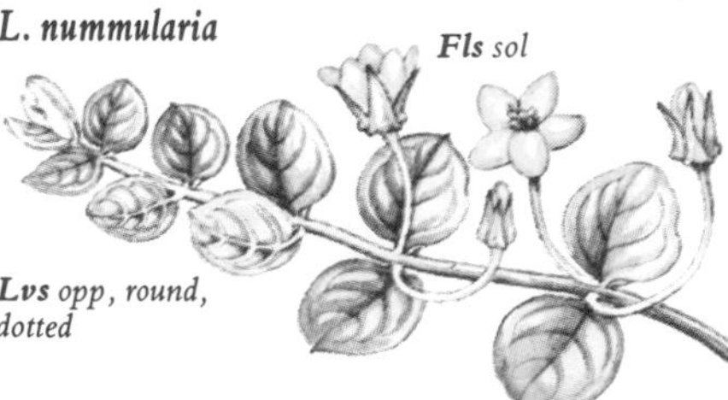

Prostrate stems to 60 cm little branched. Fl shs robust, shorter than lvs. *D:* T; *Fl:* 6–8

Brookweed

Samolus valerandi

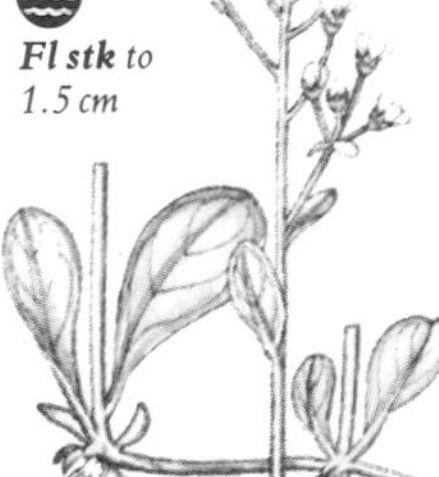

Stems lfy, no brs, lvs alt; fl stks slim in lf axils. *Ht:* 35 cm; *D:* W, C; *Fl:* 6–8

Sea lavender family Plumbaginaceae

Simple-leaved perennials. Clustered flowers have parts in fives—sepals in a tube and petals just joined below.

Thrift   

Armeria maritima

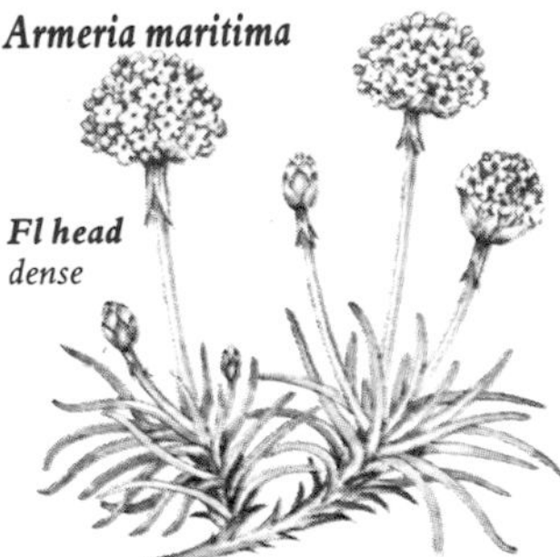

Dense basal lf rosette, lvs narrow, l-veined. Scape to 30 cm, short-stkd 8 mm fls, lobes of spl tube sharply pointed. *D:* T; *Fl:* 4–10

Jersey thrift   

A. alliacea

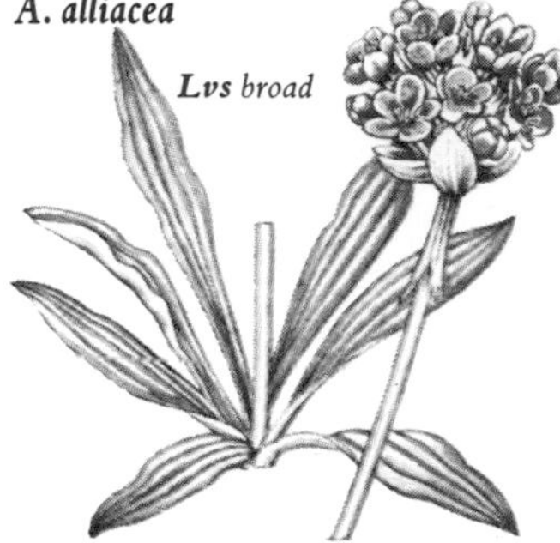

As *A. maritima* but scape to 60 cm; lvs 3–5 veined; points on spl tube long, hr-like. *D:* SW; *Fl:* 6–9

Sea lavender 

Limonium vulgare

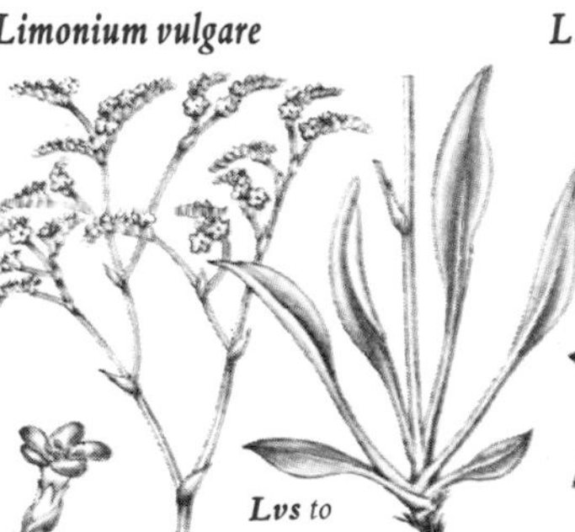

Leaves succ, veins pinnate; scape to 30 cm, many fls on short stks, infl branched. *D:* S; *Fl:* 7–10

Rock sea lavender  

L. binervosum

Like *L. vulgare* but lvs smaller, rounder, no pinnate veins, 3 veins below. *Ht:* 20 cm; *D:* W; *Fl:* 7–9

Gentian family Gentianaceae

Hairless herbs with simple stalkless opposite leaves and tubular 4–5 lobed flowers. The stamens join the petals.

Marsh gentian 

Gentiana pneumonanthe

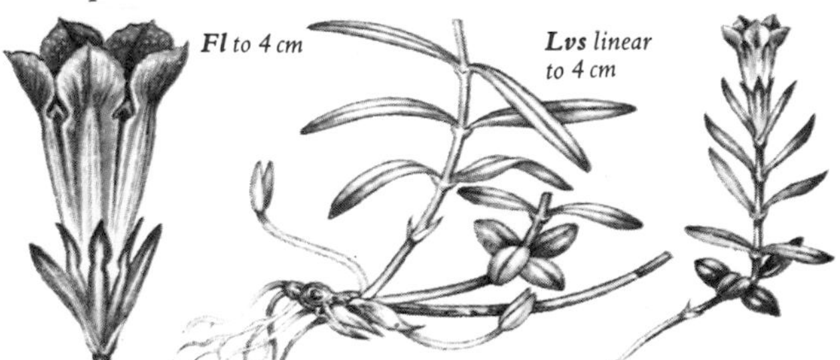

Erect per to 40 cm. Terminal infl 1–7 fls, spl lobes joined by membrane as in all *Gentiana* spp, ptl lobes 3-veined. *D:* T (not far N); *Fl:* 8–9

Spring gentian

Gentiana verna

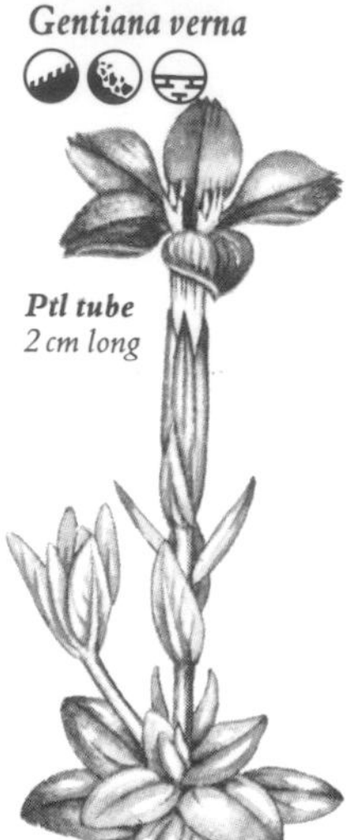

Perennial; lvs to 1.5 cm in rosettes make a compact cushion. Fls sol, terminal, spl tube ridged. *Ht:* 4 cm; *D:* C; *Fl:* 4–6

Alpine gentian

G. nivalis

Delicate uprt ann; fls sol, ptl tube to 1.5 cm. *Ht:* to 15 cm; *D:* N, S; *Fl:* 7–9

Cross gentian

G. cruciata

Flowers in terminal gps, ptl tube 2 cm, 4-lobed. *Ht:* 35 cm; *D:* S, C, E; *Fl:* 6–9

Purple gentian

G. purpurea

Erect per to 30 cm. Fls clustered at apex and in lf axils, ptls spotted. *D:* C; *Fl:* 7–8

Great yellow gentian

G. lutea

Robust, uprt per to 1.2 m. Fls crowded in lf axils and at apex, ptl tube has 5–9 lobes longer than tube. *D:* C, S mts; *Fl:* 6–8

Slender gentian

Gentianella tenella

Flowers much shorter than fl shs, spl tube deeply cut. *Ht:* 7 cm; *D:* T (not UK); *Fl:* 7–8

Autumn gentian

Gentianella amarella

Sepal tube cut to under ¾ of length, 4 or 5 equal spl lobes. *Ht:* 20 cm; *D:* N, C; *Fl:* 7–10

Field gentian

Gentianella campestris

Flower parts in 4s, 2 outer lobes of spl tube much longer than other 2. *Ht:* 20 cm; *D:* N, C; *Fl:* 7–10

Fringed gentian

G. ciliata

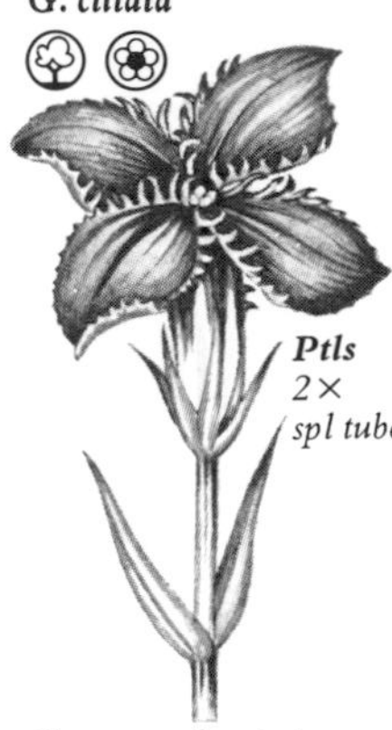

Flowers sol or in loose clusters, 4 ptl lobes, fringed at edges. *Ht:* 17 cm; *D:* T (not N, W); *Fl:* 8–10

Northern gentian

G. aurea

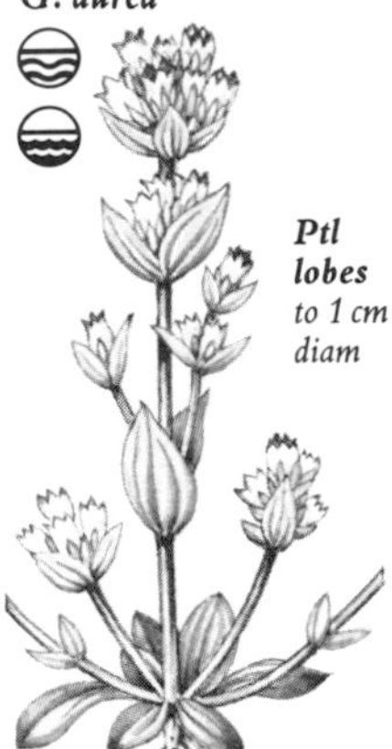

Flowers in dense terminal gps, 4 or 5 ptl lobes. *Ht:* 10 cm; *D:* Arct; *Fl:* 7–8

Common centaury

Centaurium erythraea

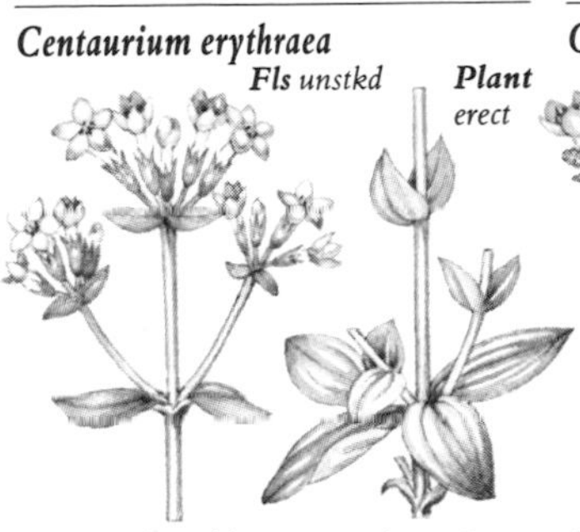

Rounded oval lvs to 5 cm long, 2 cm diam in basal rosette. *Ht:* 30 cm; *D:* T (not far N); *Fl:* 6–10

Seaside centaury

C. littorale

Leaves in basal rosette 2 cm long, under 5 mm diam, fls unstkd. *Ht:* 15 cm; *D:* NW, EC; *Fl:* 7–8

Yellow wort

Blackstonia perfoliata

Glaucous ann; fls to 1.5 cm, 6–8 ptl and spl lobes. *Ht:* 30 cm; *D:* W, C, S; *Fl:* 6–10

Marsh felwort

Swertia perennis

Petal and spl tubes 4–5 lobed, cut nearly to base. *Ht:* 45 cm; *D:* mts T (not UK); *Fl:* 7–9

Yellow centaury

Cicendia filiformis

Delicate ann, long-stkd fls to 5 mm, 4 ptl lobes. Lvs to 6 mm. *Ht:* 8 cm; *D:* W, S; *Fl:* 6–10

Bogbean family Menyanthaceae

Alternate-leaved aquatics. The 5 petals and sepals are in deep-lobed tubes; the stamens join the petal tube.

Bogbean 

Menyanthes trifoliata

Flower stks and 3-lobed lvs above water. Ptl tube 1.5 cm, fringed edges. *Ht:* 20 cm; *D:* T; *Fl:* 5–7

Fringed water lily 

Nymphoides peltata

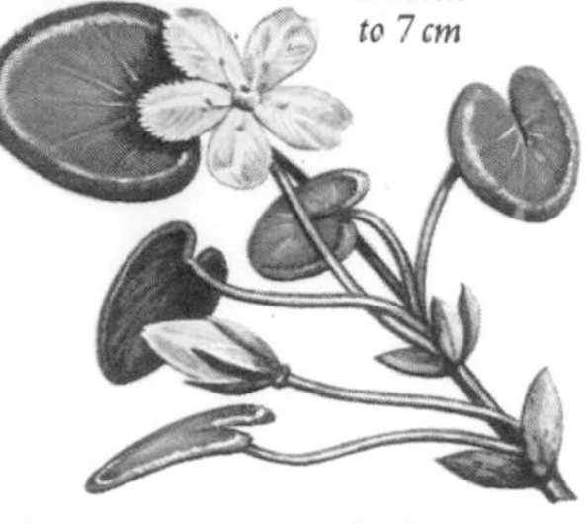

Leaves 8 cm, v notched at base. Fls 3 cm, long-stkd, fringed ptl lobes. *D:* T (not far N); *Fl:* 7–8

Periwinkle family Apocynaceae

Woody plants with symmetrical 5-part flowers. The petal lobes twist in bud and the stamens join the petal tube.

Lesser periwinkle 

Vinca minor

Greater periwinkle  

V. major

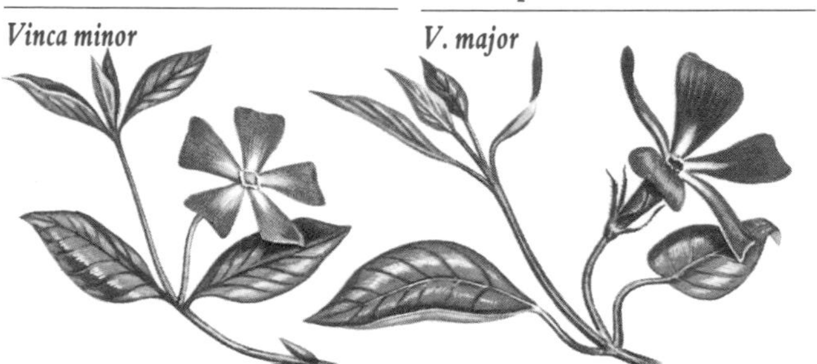

Creeps to 60 cm. Lvs v short-stkd, hrlss; fls sol to 3 cm, spl tube hrlss. *D:* S, W, C; *Fl:* 3–5

Scrambles to 1 m. Lf stks to 1 cm, fl shs uprt, fls to 5 cm, spl lobes hry at edge. *D:* W, C; *Fl:* 4–6

Milkweed family Asclepiadaceae

Perennials often with milky sap. Tubular flowers have parts in fives; stamens fused in a ring join the stigma.

Vincetoxicum  

Vincetoxicum hirundinaria

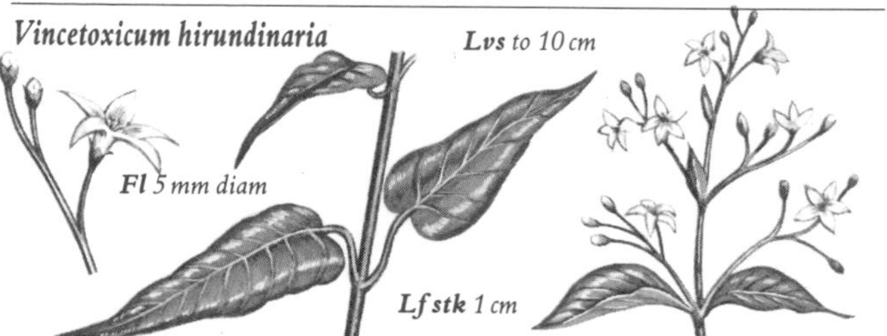

Perennial herb to 1.2 m. Lvs broadly oval. Infl both axillary and terminal has 6–10 fls on long stks. *D:* T (not UK); *Fl:* 6–9

Bedstraw family Rubiaceae

Herbs or woody plants with unlobed, small whorled leaves. Small densely grouped flowers have parts in fours or fives, tiny or no sepals, petals in a tube and inferior ovaries.

Wild madder

Rubia peregrina

Fr
succ

Robust evergreen, stem 4-angled, down-pointed prickles; lvs leathery, prickly. *Ht:* 1 m; *D:* S, W; *Fl:* 6–8

Squinancywort

Asperula cynanchica

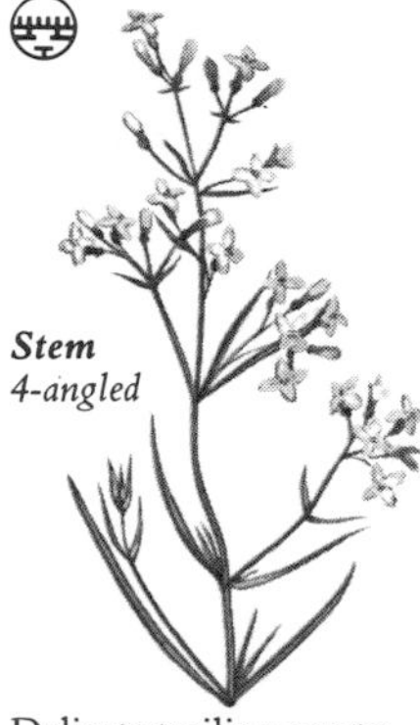

Delicate trailing per to 40 cm; lvs linear, 4 per whorl, fls 6 mm. *D:* T; *Fl:* 6–8

Blue woodruff

A. arvensis

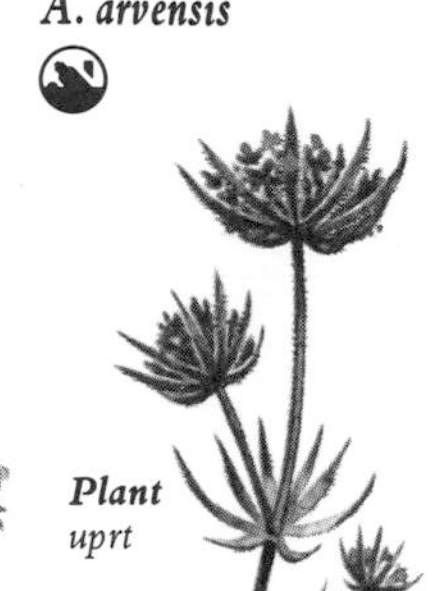

Leaves 6–9 per whorl; fls 4 mm, hry bracts longer than fls. *Ht:* 20 cm; *D:* T; *Fl:* 4–6

Hedge bedstraw

Galium mollugo

Lvs *broad,*
6–8
whorl

Stout per to 1.2 m. Prickles at lf edge point forwards. Infl large, dense. *D:* T; *Fl:* 6–9

Woodruff

Galium odoratum

Creeping per, rhizomatous; erect shs to 45 cm. Prickles at lf edges point forwards. Long ptl tube equals ptl lobes. *D:* T; *Fl:* 5–6

Lady's bedstraw

G. verum

Mat-forming, erect shs to 1 m; lvs fine, 2 cm, 8–12 per whorl, fls 3 mm. *D:* T; *Fl:* 7–8

Heath bedstraw

G. saxatile

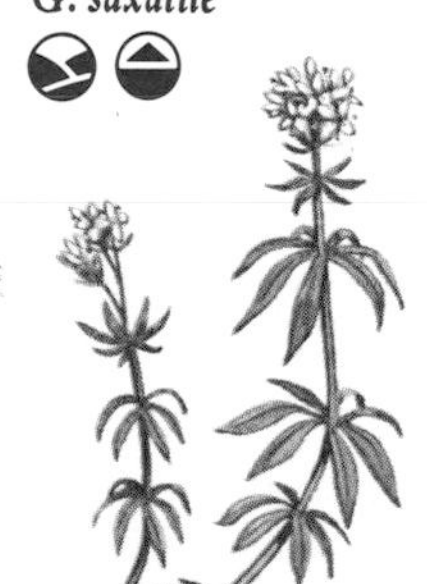

Prostrate with fl shs to 20 cm. Prickles at lf edges point forwards. *D:* W, WC; *Fl:* 6–8

Crosswort

Cruciata laevipes

Scrambles to 70 cm. Lvs 4 per whorl, hry, broad, 3-veined. *D:* W, S, C; *Fl:* 5–6

Slender bedstraw

Galium pumilum

Low shs to 30 cm, few prickles pointing backwards; fls long-stkd. *D:* W, C; *Fl:* 6–7

Northern bedstraw

G. boreale

Erect, stiff shs to 45 cm. Lvs 3-veined, 4 per whorl; loose infl. *D:* T; *Fl:* 7–8

Common cleavers

G. aparine

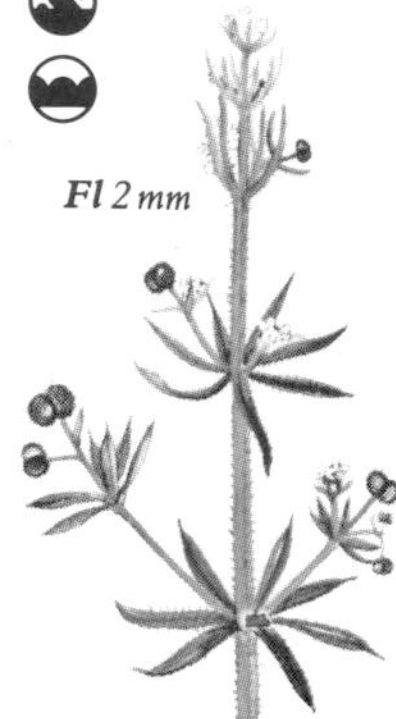

Very prickly; fls on axillary stks have whorls of bracts. *Ht:* 1 m; *D:* T; *Fl:* 6–8

False cleavers

G. spurium

As *G. aparine* but fls 1 mm, only 2 bracts on fl stk, lvs narrow. *Ht:* 1 m; *D:* T; *Fl:* 7

Marsh bedstraw

G. palustre

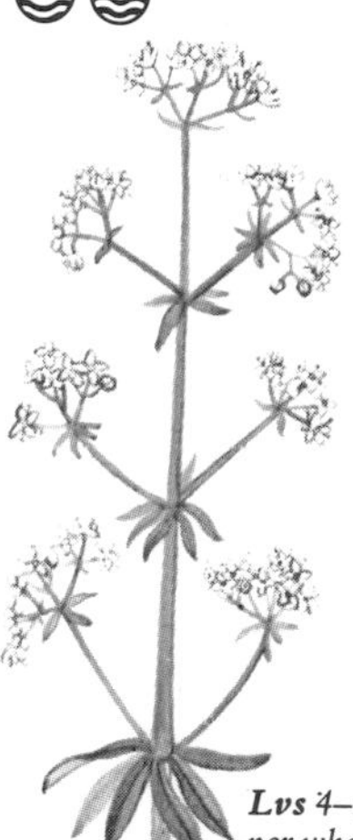

Delicate, scrambling to 1.2 m. Lvs blunt-tipped; infl spread, loose, v branched. *D:* T; *Fl:* 6–7

Field madder

Sherardia arvensis

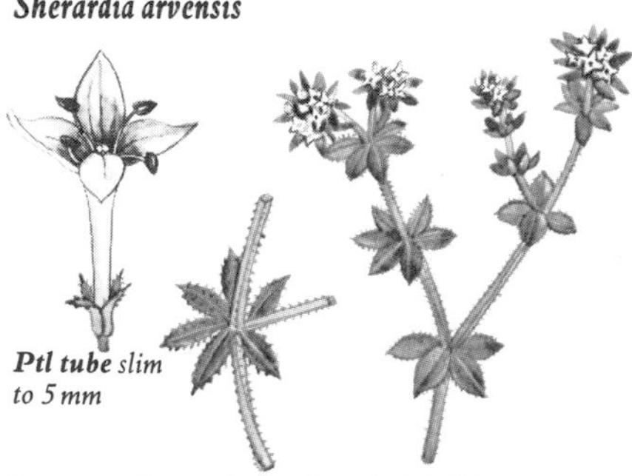

Prostrate shs to 40 cm. Terminal infl has many bracts, spls evident, esp in fr. *D:* T; *Fl:* 5–10

Jacob's ladder family Polemoniaceae

Symmetrical-flowered herbs. The 5-lobed sepal and petal tubes and 5 stamens lie above the 3-stigma ovary.

Jacob's ladder

Polemonium caeruleum

Erect lfy shs from rhizome. Lvs pinnate, 6–12 lflt prs. Fls to 3 cm diam, v short ptl tube, stamens fill fl mouth. *Ht:* 60 cm; *D:* N, C; *Fl:* 6–7

Convolvulus family Convolvulaceae

Climbers with a milky sap. Flowers have 5 petals in a funnel and 5 free sepals. The stamens join the petal tube.

Field bindweed

Convolvulus arvensis

Climbs anticlockwise to 75 cm. Fls 2 cm, fl stk has 2 bracts well below spls. Lvs 4 cm. *D:* T; *Fl:* 6–9

Common dodder

Cuscuta epithymum

Parasite on heather, gorse; lvs are scales, shs red; styles longer than ovary. *Ht:* 1 m; *D:* T (not far N); *Fl:* 7–9

Greater dodder

C. europaea

Parasite on hops and nettles. Stems robust, styles shorter than ovary. *Ht:* 1 m; *D:* T (not far N); *Fl:* 8–9

Hedge bindweed

Calystegia sepium

Climber. Fls 6 cm, swollen bracts longer than and enclosing spls. *Ht:* 2 m; *D:* T (not far N); *Fl:* 7–9

Sea bindweed

Calystegia soldanella

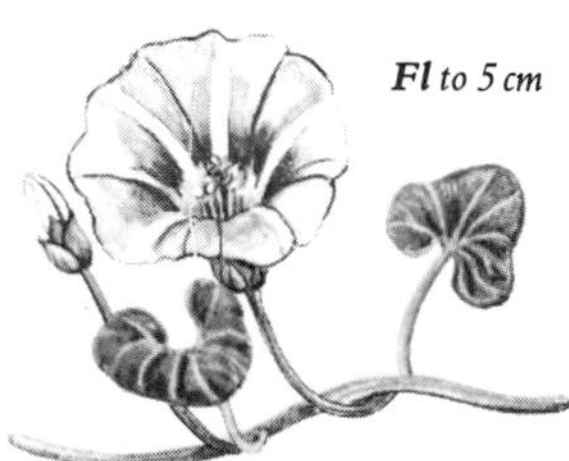

Prostrate shs to 60 cm. Lvs 3 cm, long-stkd, kidney-shaped; bracts smaller than spls. *D:* W; *Fl:* 6–8

Borage family Boraginaceae

Coarse-haired herbs. The coiled inflorescence has the oldest flowers below. Tubular pink or blue flowers have 5 joined petals and sepals, one style and a 4-lobed ovary.

Common comfrey

Symphytum officinale

***Fl** to 1.7 cm*

Erect, much branched per to 1.2 m. Lf bases form wings down stem, lower lvs largest, to 25 cm; fr 4 black nutlets. *D:* T; *Fl:* 5–6

Tuberous comfrey

S. tuberosum

Swollen tuberous rts, stems to 50 cm, little branched; lower lvs to 14 cm, smaller than middle ones, no wings. *D:* W, C, S; *Fl:* 6–7

Hound's tongue

Cynoglossum officinale

***Fl** 1 cm diam*

Softly hry greyish bi to 90 cm. Fr covered with barbed spines all equal length. *D:* T (not far N); *Fl:* 6–8

Green hound's tongue

C. germanicum

Like *C. officinale* but greener, hrs rougher; lvs near-hrlss above, outer fr spines longer than inner. *Ht:* 60 cm; *D:* W, C; *Fl:* 5–7

Green alkanet

Petaglottis sempervirens

***Lvs** to 30 cm, lower ones stkd*

Coarse-hrd per to 1 m. Long-stkd infls in lf axils. Fl 1 cm has white scales in mouth of ptl tube. *D:* SW; *Fl:* 5–6

Borage

Borago officinalis

***Lvs** to 20 cm, lower ones stkd*

Robust ann to 60 cm Fls 2 cm diam on long stks to 4 cm, stamens protruding, purple. *D:* C, S; *Fl:* 6–8

Nonea

Nonea pulla

Erect ann or per to 50 cm. Fls to 1.5 cm, ptl tube 2 × spls. *D:* E, EC; *Fl:* 4–5

Alkanet

Anchusa officinalis

Erect v branched per to 80 cm. Infl dense, stms not protruding. *D:* C, S; *Fl:* 6–8

Bugloss

A. arvensis

Bristly uprt ann to 60 cm. Lvs wavy at edges; ptl tube just curved. *D:* T; *Fl:* 5–9

Common gromwell

Lithospermum officinale

Much branched per to 80 cm. Lvs have obvious side nerves. Nuts white, glossy. *D:* T; *Fl:* 6–7

Purple gromwell

Buglossoides purpurocaeruleum

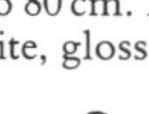
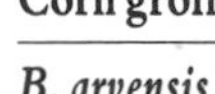
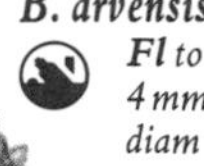

Creeping per, uprt fl shs to 60 cm. Ptls 1.5 cm, 2 × spl length. *D:* S, C; *Fl:* 5–6

Corn gromwell

B. arvensis

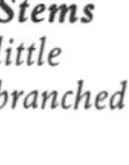

Erect ann to 50 cm. Lvs have no obvious side veins; nut brown, warty. *D:* T; *Fl:* 5–7

Lungwort

Pulmonaria officinalis

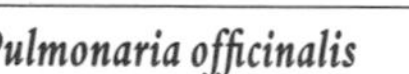

Short-hrd per to 30 cm. Fl 1 cm, tufts of hrs alternate with stamens. *D:* C, S, W; *Fl:* 3–5

Tufted forgetmenot

Myosotis laxa

Has flattened hrs on lvs, spls and rounded stems. Fl 4 mm. *Ht:* 30 cm; *D:* T; *Fl:* 5–8

Wood forgetmenot

M. sylvatica

Erect per to 45 cm, spread hrs on lvs and stems, curled hrs on spls. Fr stks 2 × spls. *D:* T (not N); *Fl:* 5–9

Early forgetmenot

M. ramosissima

***Fl** 2 mm*

Delicate, has spread hrs. *M. discolor* sim, but fls yellow. *Ht:* 25 cm; *D:* T (not N); *Fl:* 4–6

Field forgetmenot

M. arvensis

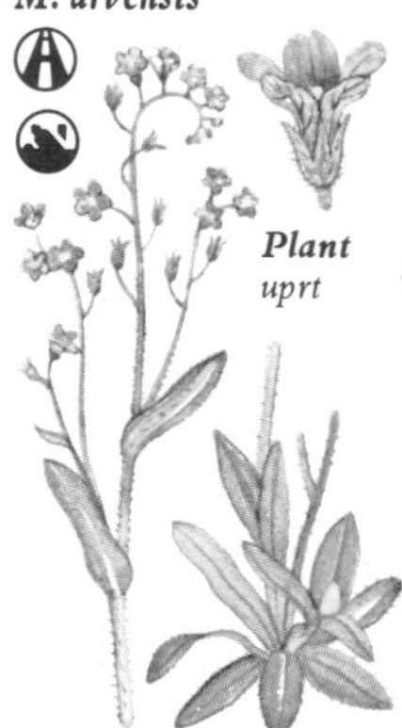

Spread hrs on lvs and spls. Fr stks 2 × spl length; fls 5 mm. *Ht:* 20 cm; *D:* T; *Fl:* 4–9

Creeping forgetmenot

M. secunda

Hairs on stem spread, on spls flat. Fr stks 3–5 × spl length. *Ht:* 45 cm; *D:* W; *Fl:* 5–8

Marsh forgetmenot

M. scorpioides

Flat hrs on lvs and spls. Stems ridged; fr stks 2 × spls. *Ht:* 30 cm; *D:* C, N; *Fl:* 5–9

Bur forgetmenot

Lappula squarrosa

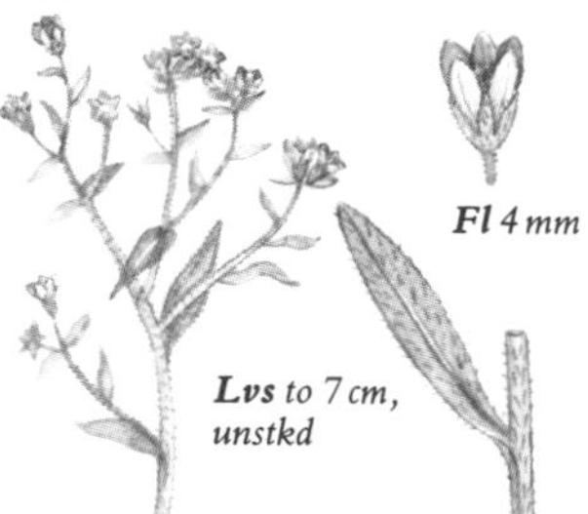

Delicate bristly ann, erect shs to 70 cm. Fr has 2 rows of hooked spines. *D:* T (not NW); *Fl:* 6–7

Madwort

Asperugo procumbens

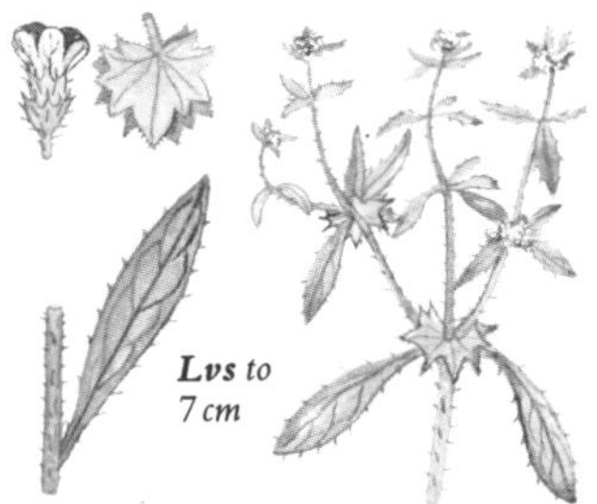

Coarsely hry trailing ann. Spls. enlarge into 2-lipped fr covering. *Ht:* 45 cm; *D:* N, C, E; *Fl:* 5–7

Oyster plant

Mertensia maritima

Straggling hrlss succ per to 60 cm, fl stks to 1 cm, stamens just protruding. *D:* NW; *Fl:* 6–8

Navelwort

Omphalodes scorpioides

Straggles to 40 cm. Fls to 4 mm sol in lf axils, obvious lobes at ptl tube mouth. *D:* C, E; *Fl:* 4–5

Viper's bugloss

Echium vulgare

Roughly hry. Ptl tube lobes unequal, 4 protruding stamens. *Ht:* 65 cm; *D:* T; *Fl:* 6–9

Vervain family Verbenaceae

Plants whose flowers have 5 sepals in a tube, 5 petals, often in a two-lipped tube and usually 4 stamens.

Vervain

Verbena officinalis

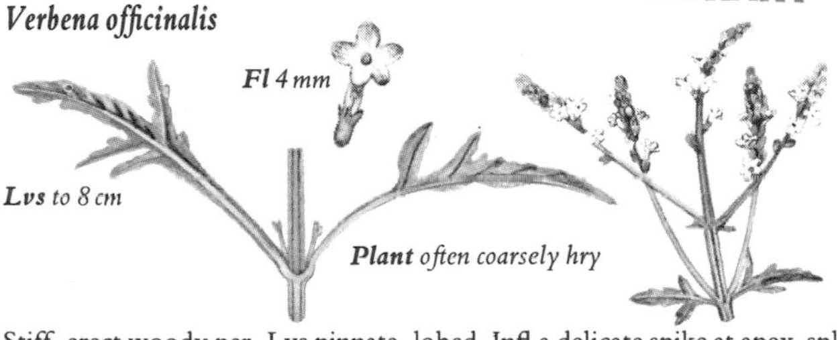

Stiff, erect woody per. Lvs pinnate, lobed. Infl a delicate spike at apex, spl tube ribbed. Fr 4 nutlets. *Ht:* 45 cm; *D:* T (not N); *Fl:* 7–9

Water starwort family Callitrichaceae

Slender aquatics with simple leaves. Separate male and female flowers on the same plant have no sepals or petals.

Water starwort

Callitriche stagnalis

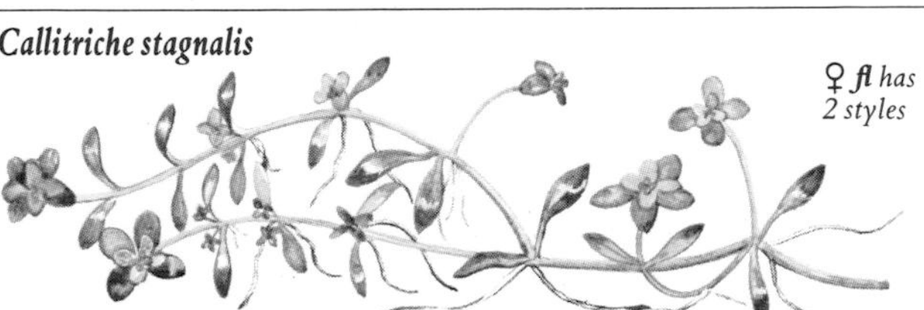

Submerged lvs narrow, floating lvs spathulate in rosette. Stems to 60 cm, fr 2 mm, strongly keeled; ♂ fl has 1 stamen. *D:* T; *Fl:* 5–9

Mint family Labiatae

Square-stemmed herbs with opposite leaves. Flowers in axillary whorls have two-lipped petal and sepal tubes (the sepal tube 5 lobed, the petal tube three-lobed below) and 4 stamens.

White dead nettle

Lamium album

Henbit dead nettle

L. amplexicaule

Red dead nettle

L. purpureum

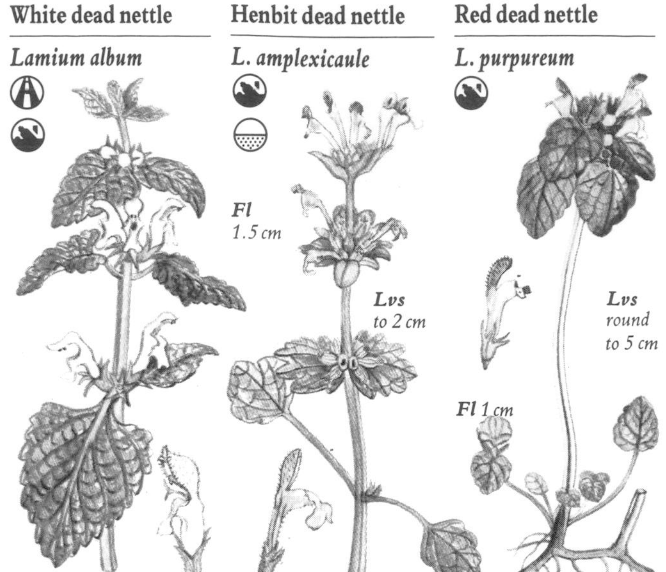

Rhizomatous per; uprt hry stems to 60 cm. Fls 2 cm have ring of hrs near ptl tube base. *D:* T; *Fl:* 5–12

Annual, lvs round, long-stkd, bracts not stkd; spread white hrs on spl tube. *Ht:* 15 cm; *D:* T; *Fl:* 4–8

Bushy ann to 45 cm. Lvs and bracts stkd; ring of hrs nr ptl base. *D:* T; *Fl:* 3–10

Spotted dead nettle

L. maculatum

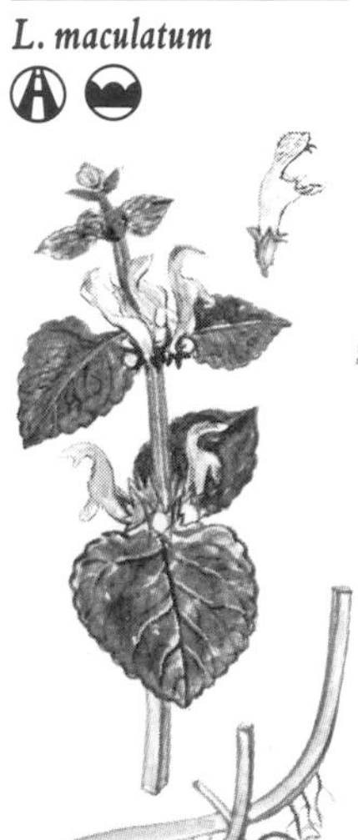

Creeping, uprt shs to 40 cm. Lvs have pale patch. Fls 2 cm, ring of hrs in ptl tube. *D:* S, C; *Fl:* 5–10

Common hemp nettle

Galeopsis tetrahit

Straggling coarsely hry ann to 1 m. Fls to 2 cm, white, pink or purple, ptls often spotted. *D:* T; *Fl:* 7–9

Red hemp nettle

G. angustifolia

Hairy ann to 80 cm, lvs to 8 cm narrow. Fls to 2.5 cm, ptl tube far longer than spls. *D:* W, S, C; *Fl:* 7–10

Large-flowered hemp nettle

Galeopsis speciosa

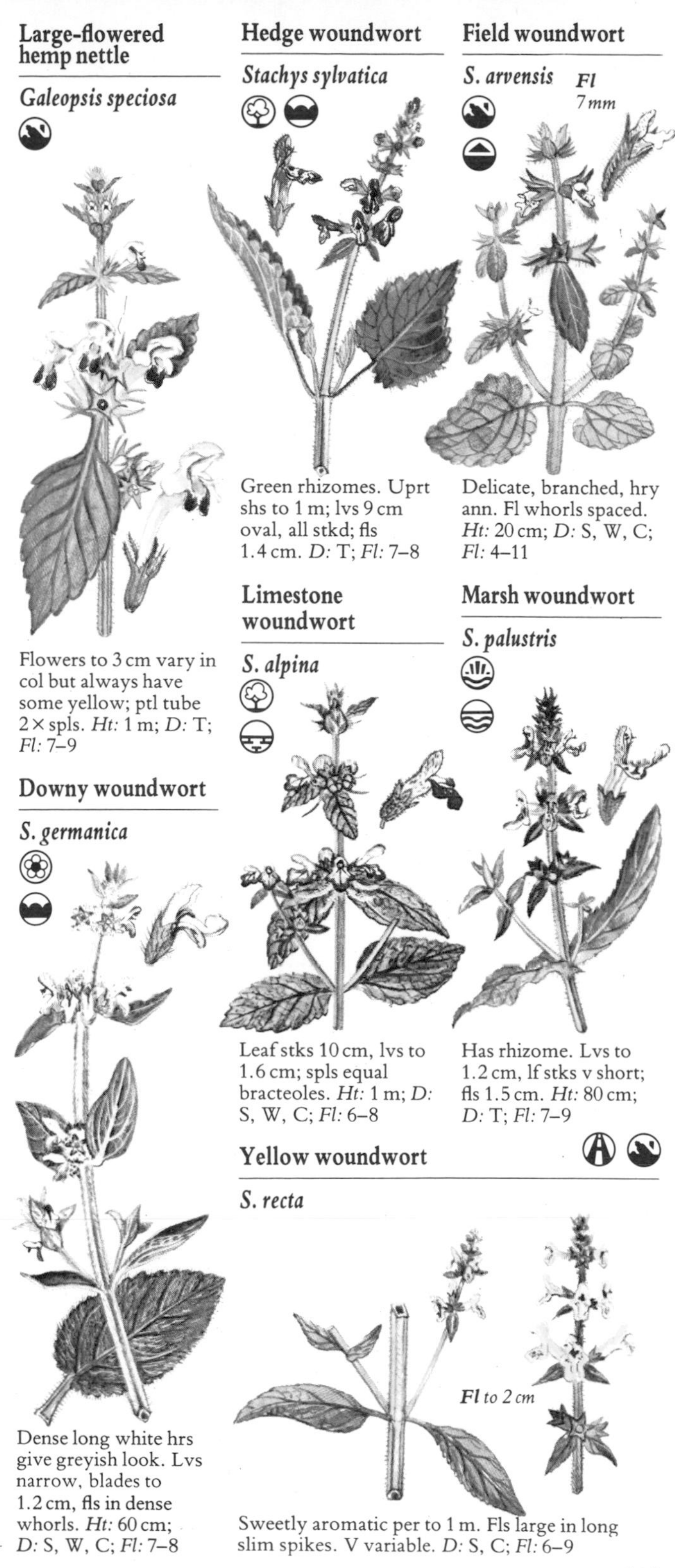

Flowers to 3 cm vary in col but always have some yellow; ptl tube 2× spls. *Ht:* 1 m; *D:* T; *Fl:* 7–9

Hedge woundwort

Stachys sylvatica

Green rhizomes. Uprt shs to 1 m; lvs 9 cm oval, all stkd; fls 1.4 cm. *D:* T; *Fl:* 7–8

Field woundwort

S. arvensis

Fl *7 mm*

Delicate, branched, hry ann. Fl whorls spaced. *Ht:* 20 cm; *D:* S, W, C; *Fl:* 4–11

Downy woundwort

S. germanica

Dense long white hrs give greyish look. Lvs narrow, blades to 1.2 cm, fls in dense whorls. *Ht:* 60 cm; *D:* S, W, C; *Fl:* 7–8

Limestone woundwort

S. alpina

Leaf stks 10 cm, lvs to 1.6 cm; spls equal bracteoles. *Ht:* 1 m; *D:* S, W, C; *Fl:* 6–8

Marsh woundwort

S. palustris

Has rhizome. Lvs to 1.2 cm, lf stks v short; fls 1.5 cm. *Ht:* 80 cm; *D:* T; *Fl:* 7–9

Yellow woundwort

S. recta

Fl *to 2 cm*

Sweetly aromatic per to 1 m. Fls large in long slim spikes. V variable. *D:* S, C; *Fl:* 6–9

Bugle

Ajuga reptans

Blue bugle

A. genevensis

Ground pine

A. chamaepitys

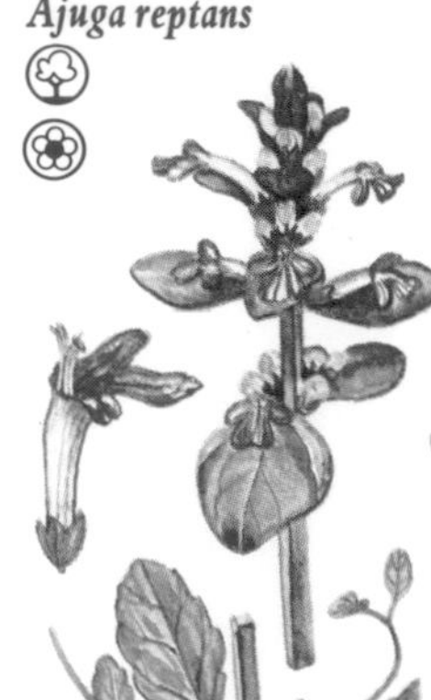

Has stolons; lvs in basal rosette hry on opp faces; top ptl lip short. *Ht:* 20 cm; *D:* T (not far N); *Fl:* 5–7

Erect shs to 30 cm. Lf blades hry, long-stkd; fls appear after basal lvs have died. *D:* T (not N); *Fl:* 5–7

Aromatic hry ann; lvs cut into 3 narrow lobes. Paired fls shorter than lvs. *Ht:* 10 cm; *D:* T (not N); *Fl:* 5–9

Motherwort

Leonurus cardiaca

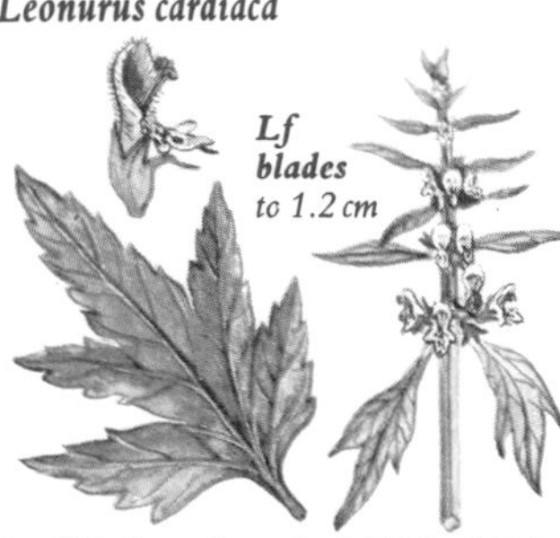

Leaf blades palmately 5–7 lobed. Ptl tube shorter than spls. *Ht:* 1 m; *D:* T (not far N); *Fl:* 7–9

Gypsywort

Lycopus europaeus

Leaves elliptic, deeply toothed. Fls 3 mm, dense whorls, only 2 stms. *Ht:* 80 cm; *D:* T; *Fl:* 6–9

Watermint

Mentha aquatica

Smells of mint. Infl dense, terminal, ptl tube 4 equal lobes. *Ht:* 70 cm; *D:* T (not far N); *Fl:* 7–10

Cornmint

M. arvensis

No strong smell. Fls in dense whorls in axils of bracts, spl tube hry. *Ht:* 45 cm; *D:* T; *Fl:* 5–10

Spearmint

M. spicata

Strong smelling per to 90 cm. Stem hrlss, branched, lvs unstkd to 9 cm; fl whorls in dense spike, spl tube hrlss. *D:* T; *Fl:* 8–9

Catmint

Nepeta cataria

Strong smelling herb to 1 m. Inflorescence dense, terminal, ptl tube bent half way down. *D:* S, E; *Fl:* 7–9

Common calamint

Calamintha sylvatica

***Fl** to 2.2 cm*

Has creeping rhizome. Uprt shs to 60 cm, lvs round, serrate; fls stkd in loose clusters in lf axils. *D:* S, W; *Fl:* 8–9

Marjoram

Origanum vulgare

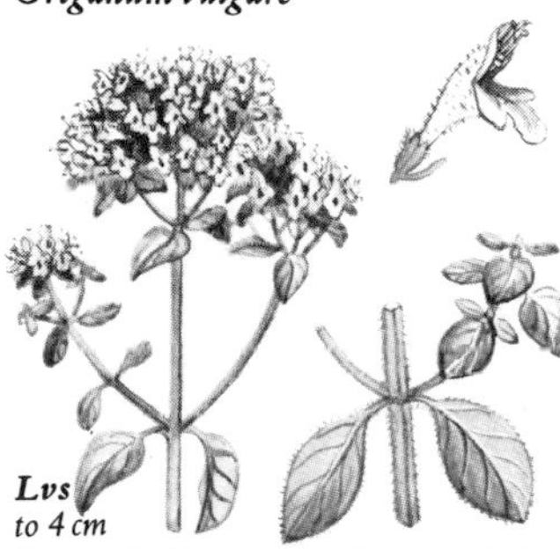

***Lvs** to 4 cm*

Aromatic. Stems uprt, branched; fls 7 mm in dense head, protruding stamens. *Ht:* 60 cm; *D:* T; *Fl:* 7–9

Wild thyme

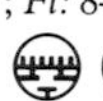

Thymus serpyllum

***Plant** woody, aromatic*

Flower stks round, evenly spaced hrs. Spl tube 2-lipped, top lip 3-lobed. *Ht:* 20 cm; *D:* N; *Fl:* 7–8

Large wild thyme

T. pulegioides

Like *T. serpyllum* but stems square, hry at angles. Infl long. *Ht:* 20 cm; *D:* T; *Fl:* 7–8

Wild thyme

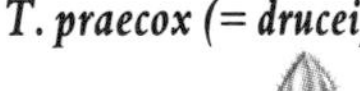

T. praecox (= drucei)

As *T. serpyllum* but stems square, hry on opp faces. Infl short. *Ht:* 10 cm; *D:* S, W, C; *Fl:* 5–8

Wild basil

Clinopodium vulgare

Hairy per. Lvs just toothed; fls in dense terminal and axillary whorls. *Ht:* 60 cm; *D:* T; *Fl:* 7–9

Basil thyme

Acinos arvensis ***Fl*** *to 1 cm*

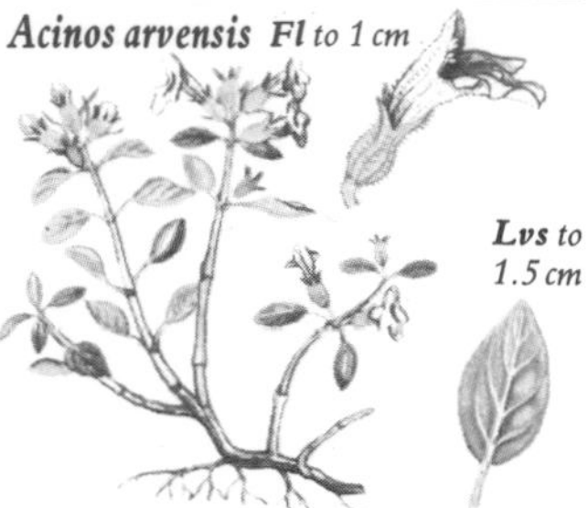

Branched hry ann; straggles to 20 cm. Fls in axillary whorls of 3–8. *D:* T (not far N); *Fl:* 5–9

Meadow clary

Salvia pratensis

Wild sage

S. nemorosa ***Fl*** *to 1.2 cm*

Wild clary

S. verbenaca ***Fl*** *to 1.5 cm*

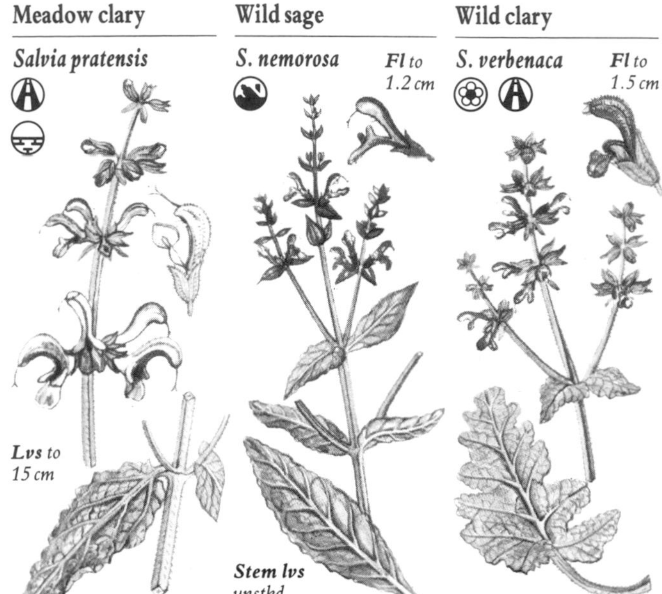

Meadow clary: Aromatic per to 1 m; hooded fls to 2.5 cm, 2 stamens, long style. *D:* T (not N); *Fl:* 6–7

Wild sage: Stems to 60 cm have flat hrs; fl bracts longer than spl tube. *D:* C, S, E; *Fl:* 6–8

Wild clary: Basal lvs broad; fl has 2 white spots on lower lip. *Ht:* 60 cm; *D:* S, W; *Fl:* 5–8

Wood sage

Teucrium scorodonia ***Fl*** *1.3 cm*

Flowers in whorled terminal spike, no upper lip as all *Teucrium* spp. *Ht:* 20 cm; *D:* S, W, C; *Fl:* 7–9

Mountain germander

T. montanum

Patch-forming shrub; prostrate stems 25 cm. Fls in terminal gp, bracts lf-like. *D:* C, S; *Fl:* 5–8

Wall germander

Teucrium chamaedrys

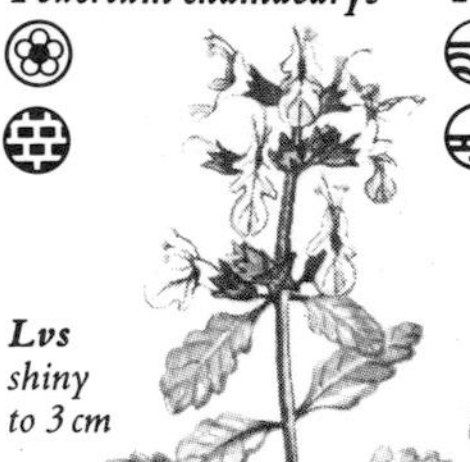

Tufted per to 30 cm. Lvs scalloped, fls in axils of lfy bracts. *D:* S, C; *Fl:* 7–9

Water germander

T. scordium

Serrate, unstkd lvs. Fls in axils of lfy bracts. *Ht:* 45 cm; *D:* T (not N); *Fl:* 7–10

Cut-leaved germander

T. botrys

Leaves and bracts pinnately lobed, segs narrow. *Ht:* to 30 cm; *D:* S, W, C; *Fl:* 7–9

Skull cap

Scutellaria galericulata

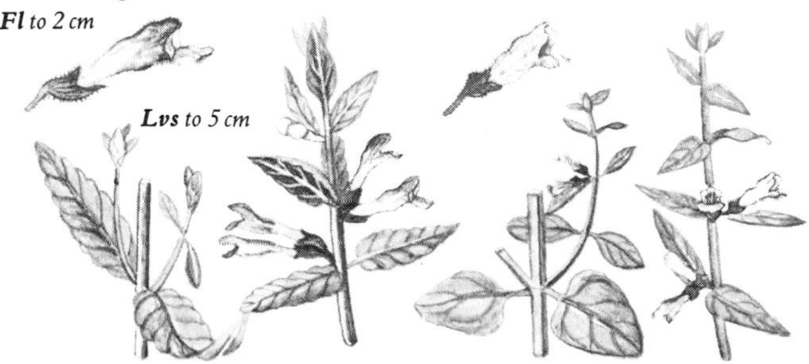

Hairy per to 50 cm. Lvs indented at edges. Fls in bract axils, infl 1-sided. *D:* T; *Fl:* 6–9

Lesser skull cap

S. minor

Like *S. galericulata* but to 15 cm, lvs unlobed to 3 cm, fls to 1 cm, spotted. *D:* W; *Fl:* 7–10

Dracocephalum

Dracocephalum ruyschiana

Near-hrlss per. Lvs linear; fls in dense spike with linear bracts. *Ht:* 50 cm; *D:* N, C; *Fl:* 7–8

Black horehound

Ballota nigra

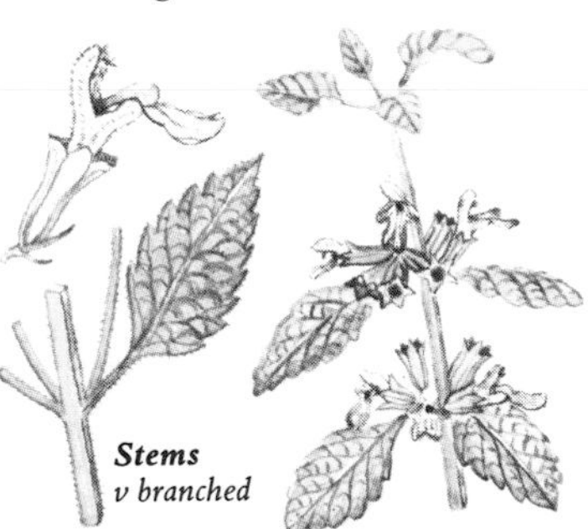

Fetid per to 1 m. Lvs to 4 cm; fls in dense whorls with big bracts, spl teeth bristly. *D:* T (not N); *Fl:* 6–10

White horehound

Marrubium vulgare

Woolly v branched per. Lf blades blunt-toothed to 4 cm. Many fls in whorls. *D:* T (not N); *Fl:* 6–11

Self heal

Prunella vulgaris

Stems and oval lvs often purplish, spl tube 2-lipped. *Ht:* 20 cm; *D:* T; *Fl:* 6–9

Cut-leaved self heal

P. laciniata

Like *P. vulgaris* but hairier leaves deeply lobed. *Ht:* 20 cm; *D:* S, W, C; *Fl:* 6–8

Bastard balm

Melittis melissophyllum

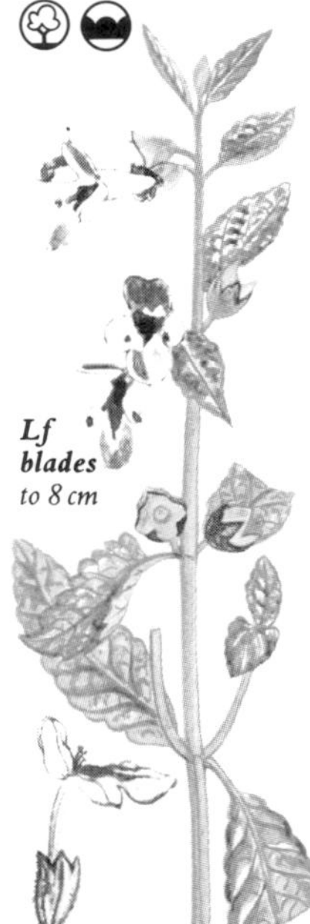

Aromatic hry per to 50 cm. Fls to 4 cm, spl tube 2-lipped, lower lip 2-lobed. *D:* W, C, S; *Fl:* 5–7

Yellow archangel

Lamiastrum galeobdolon

Has stolons. Leaves serrate. Fl 2 cm, top lip hooded. *Ht:* 40 cm; *D:* T; *Fl:* 5–6

Betony

Stachys officinalis

Long-stkd lvs, edges scalloped, in basal rosette. *Ht:* 45 cm; *D:* T (not far N); *Fl:* 6–9

Ground ivy

Glechoma hederacea

Stems creeping, erect fl shs to 30 cm, lvs kidney-shaped; few fls in whorl. *D:* T; *Fl:* 3–5

Nightshade family Solanaceae

Alternate-leaved herbs and shrubs. Tubular symmetrical flowers are 5-lobed with stamens joining the petal tube.

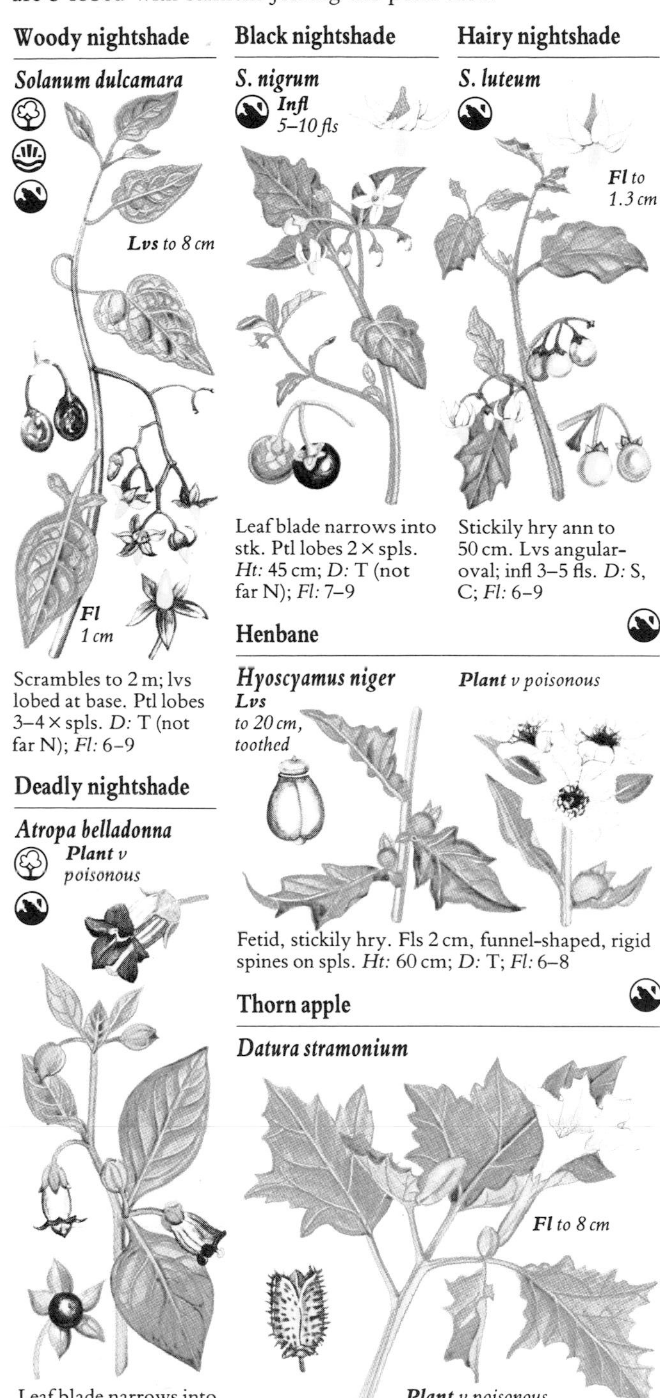

Woody nightshade

Solanum dulcamara

Scrambles to 2 m; lvs lobed at base. Ptl lobes 3–4 × spls. *D:* T (not far N); *Fl:* 6–9

Black nightshade

S. nigrum

Leaf blade narrows into stk. Ptl lobes 2 × spls. *Ht:* 45 cm; *D:* T (not far N); *Fl:* 7–9

Hairy nightshade

S. luteum

Stickily hry ann to 50 cm. Lvs angular-oval; infl 3–5 fls. *D:* S, C; *Fl:* 6–9

Deadly nightshade

Atropa belladonna

Leaf blade narrows into stk; fls drooping, bell-shaped. *Ht:* 1 m; *D:* S, W, C; *Fl:* 6–8

Henbane

Hyoscyamus niger

Fetid, stickily hry. Fls 2 cm, funnel-shaped, rigid spines on spls. *Ht:* 60 cm; *D:* T; *Fl:* 6–8

Thorn apple

Datura stramonium

Stems bifurcating to 1 m. Fls sol, spls long, tubular; fr spiny. *D:* T (not far N); *Fl:* 7–10

Figwort family Scrophulariaceae

Herbs, some of them partially parasitic. Two-lipped asymmetrical flowers have 5 petals and sepals joined at least at their base and usually 4 stamens (but sometimes 5 or 2). The ovary is two-celled and superior, the fruit is usually a capsule.

Great mullein

Verbascum thapsus

Robust bi to 2 m, dense woolly covering. Fls in tall dense spike, 5 stamens as all *Verbascum* spp. *D:* T (not far N); *Fl:* 6–8

Orange mullein

V. phlomoides

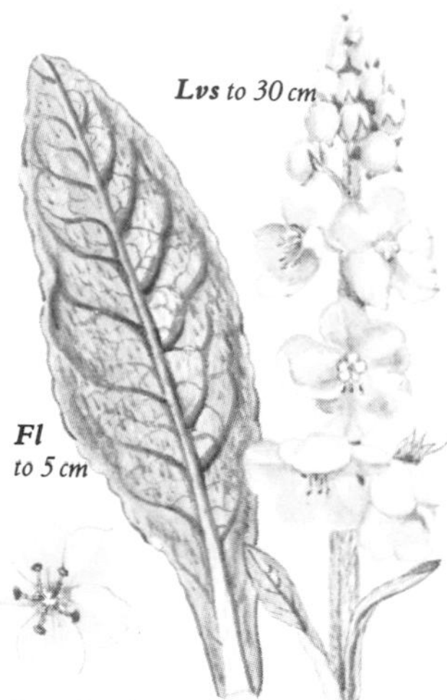

Stem lvs do not run down stem at junction. Ptls hry on outside. *Ht:* 1 m; *D:* T (not N, UK); *Fl:* 6–8

Dark mullein

V. nigrum

Ridged stems to 1.2 m, star-shaped hrs. Hrs on stamens purple. *D:* T (not N); *Fl:* 6–10

Hoary mullein

V. pulverulentum

Fl 2 cm

Has easily detached white woolly covering. Stamen hrs white. *Ht:* 1 m; *D:* W, S; *Fl:* 7–8

Moth mullein

V. blattaria

Leaves hrlss; 1 fl per bract in infl; stamen hrs purple. *Ht:* 80 cm; *D:* S, C; *Fl:* 6–10

White mullein

Verbascum lychnitis

Ridged stems to 1.5 m, short star-shaped hrs. Lvs hrlss above. *D:* S, C; *Fl:* 7–8

Germander speedwell

Veronica chamaedrys

Stems to 40 cm, rooting prostrate, with 2 lines of hrs. Infl loose from lf axils, fls 2 stamens as all *Veronica* spp. *D:* T; *Fl:* 3–7

Large speedwell

V. austriaca

Erect per to 1 m. Infl axillary, 5 spl lobes (1 may be small). *D:* T (not N); *Fl:* 6–8

Common field speedwell

V. persica

Much branched ann to 40 cm, stems hry. Fls to 1.2 cm, sol in lf axils. Lvs to 3 cm shorter than fl stks; fr lobes diverge. *D:* T; *Fl:* 1–12

Ivy-leaved speedwell

V. hederifolia

Prostrate ann, hry stems to 60 cm. Lvs to 1.5 cm, prominent lobes. Fls sol in lf axils, stks shorter than lvs. *D:* T; *Fl:* 3–8

Heath speedwell

V. officinalis

Infl dense

Prostrate perennial, hry stems to 40 cm; infl in lf axils, 15–25 fls. *D:* T; *Fl:* 5–8

Spiked speedwell

Veronica spicata

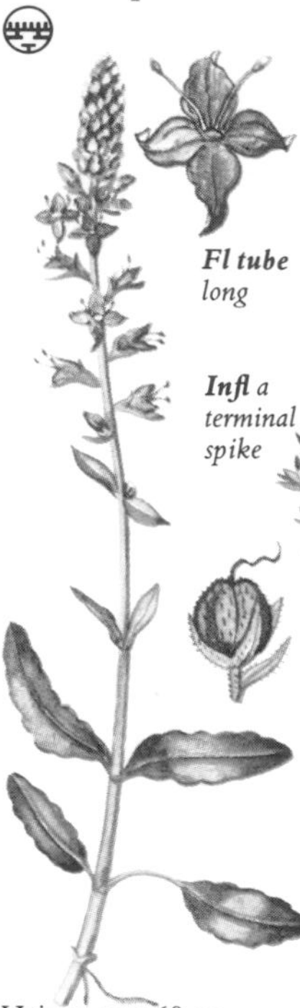

Fl tube long

Infl a terminal spike

Hairy per to 60 cm. Lower lvs oval, top lvs linear; infl dense. *D:* T (not W); *Fl:* 7–9

Spring speedwell

V. verna

Erect ann to 15 cm; lvs pinnate, 3–7 lobes; fl stks shorter than spls, fr broad. *D:* T (not far N, W); *Fl:* 5–6

Water speedwell

V. anagallis-aquatica

Lvs to 12 cm

Hairless per to 30 cm. Lvs long; infl in opp prs. *D:* T (not far N); *Fl:* 6–8. *V. catenata* sim but pink fls

Wall speedwell

V. arvensis

Thyme-leaved speedwell

V. serpyllifolia

Erect to 25 cm. Lvs coarsely toothed; fl stks shorter than spls, top bracts longer than fls. *D:* T; *Fl:* 3–10

Prostrate per, creeps to 30 cm. Infl long, terminal up to 30 fls. Bracts longer than fl stks. *D:* T; *Fl:* 3–10

Rock speedwell

V. fruticans

Lvs hrlss. Infl terminal, fl stks longer than bracts. Large fl *c.* 1 cm. *Ht:* 15 cm; *D:* C mts, NW; *Fl:* 7–8

Brooklime

V. beccabunga

Hairless per to 60 cm. Lvs round, blunt; infls axillary in opp prs. *D:* T (not far N); *Fl:* 5–9

Marsh speedwell

V. scutellata

Hairless per to 50 cm; lvs serrate to 4 cm. Infls alt, loose in lf axils, fl stks 2 × bracts. *D:* T; *Fl:* 6–8

Wood speedwell

V. montana

Creeping per, uprt shs to 40 cm, hry all round; lvs stkd *c.* 1 cm. Infl axillary, 4–5 fls. *D:* W, C, S; *Fl:* 4–7

Slender speedwell

V. filiformis

Mat-forming per, shs creep to 40 cm. Lvs kidney-shaped; fls sol, long-stkd in fl axils. *D:* NW, C; *Fl:* 4–6

Eyebright

Euphrasia spp

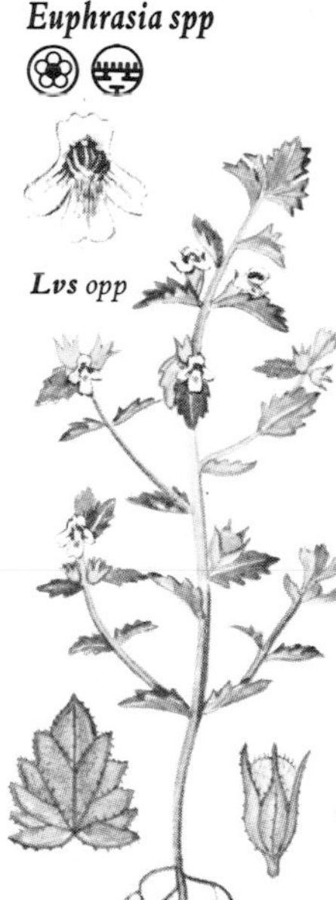

A gp of variable semi-parasitic anns; fls stklss in bract axils, 2-lipped, lower lip 3-lobed. *Ht:* 25 cm; *D:* T; *Fl:* 7–9

Fairy foxglove

Erinus alpinus

Tufted per to 15 cm. Lvs alt, obovate; spl tube narrow, 5-lobed, ptl tube slim, 5-lobed. *D:* C, S mts; *Fl:* 5–10

Foxglove  

Digitalis purpurea

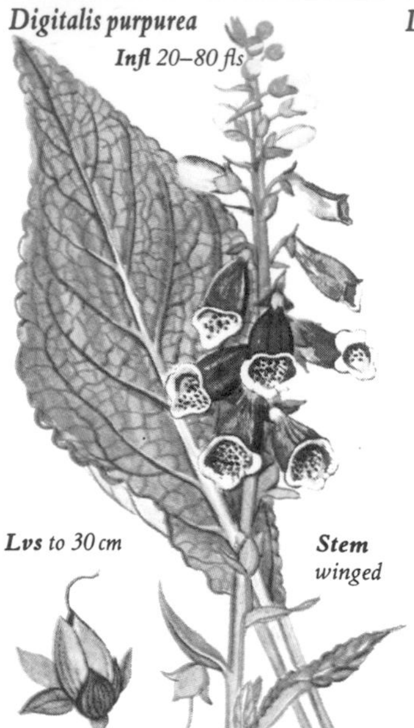

Erect bi to 1.5 m. Felty hrs all over. Fls to 5 cm spotted on lower part of tube. *D:* W; *Fl:* 6–9

Large yellow foxglove  

D. grandiflora

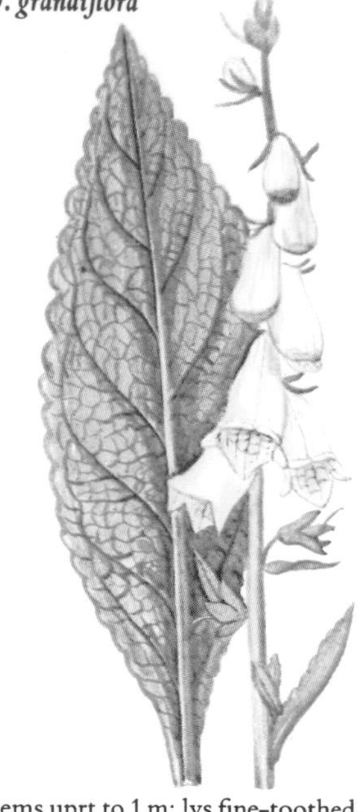

Stems uprt to 1 m; lvs fine-toothed. Fl to 5 cm, yellow-brown network in tube. *D:* E, C; *Fl:* 6–9

Common figwort

Scrophularia nodosa

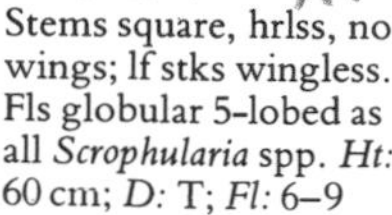

Stems square, hrlss, no wings; lf stks wingless. Fls globular 5-lobed as all *Scrophularia* spp. *Ht:* 60 cm; *D:* T; *Fl:* 6–9

Water figwort

S. auriculata

Hairless per to 1 m like *S. nodosa* but winged stems and lf stks. Lvs scalloped at edge. *D:* W; *Fl:* 6–9

Yellow figwort

S. vernalis

Hairy bi or per to 80 cm. Lvs serrate. Infl in upper lf axils, fls flask-shaped, 7 mm. *D:* S, C; *Fl:* 4–6

Balm-leaved figwort

Scrophularia scorodonia

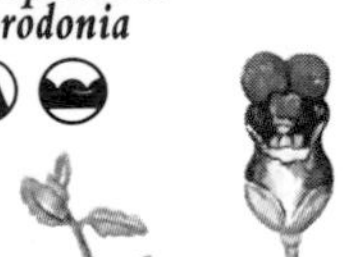

Grey, hry per to 1 m, stem square, no wings. Lvs serrate, oval to 10 cm. *D:* W; *Fl:* 6–8

French figwort

S. canina

Much branched per to 60 cm. Lvs pinnately lobed. Fls to 5 mm. *D:* S, C; *Fl:* 5–8

Common toadflax

Linaria vulgaris

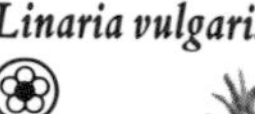

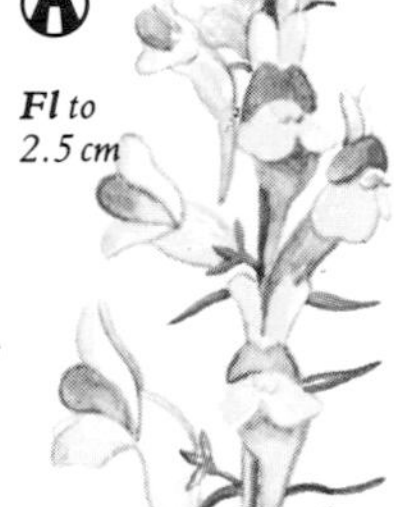

Flowers as *Antirrhinum* (p 124) but with spur. *Ht:* 60 cm; *D:* T (not far N); *Fl:* 7–10

Pale toadflax

L. repens

Hairless creeping per, uprt shs to 80 cm. Fls pale, dark-veined, spur short. *D:* S, W, C; *Fl:* 6–9

Alpine toadflax

L. alpina

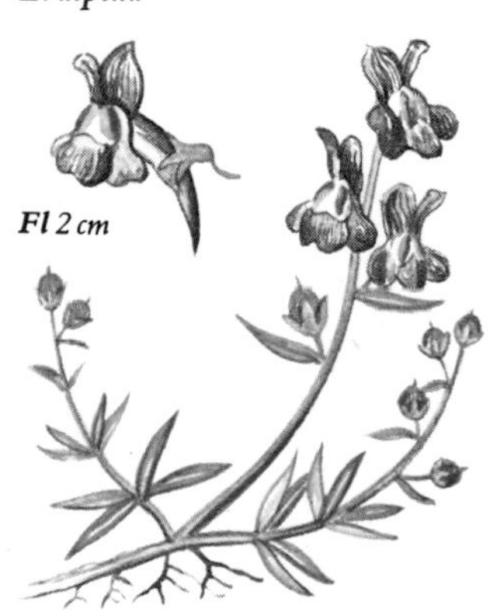

Prostrate, glaucous. Lvs in whorls, fls long-spurred, 3–15 per gp. *Ht:* 20 cm; *D:* C, E; *Fl:* 6–9

Ivy-leaved toadflax

Cymbalaria muralis

Stems hrlss, trail to 80 cm. Lvs alt, round, 5-lobed, long-stkd. Fls to 1 cm, sol in lf axils, yellow patch at mouth. *D:* S, W, C; *Fl:* 5–11

Daisy-leaved toadflax

Anarrhinum bellidifolium

Fl to 5 mm

Plant hrlss

Basal lvs to 8 cm, oval, serrate, stem lvs v cut, 3–5 narrow segs. Infl a spike. *Ht:* 60 cm; *D:* SW; *Fl:* 3–8

Leafy lousewort

P. foliosa

Leafy per to 50 cm, shs hry. Infl dense spike of yellow fls, lfy bracts longer than fls. *D:* S, C; *Fl:* 6–8

Snapdragon

Antirrhinum majus

Woody per to 80 cm, brs from base. Infl terminal, fls to 4 cm, variable colour, no spur. *D:* SW; *Fl:* 7–9

Marsh lousewort

P. palustris

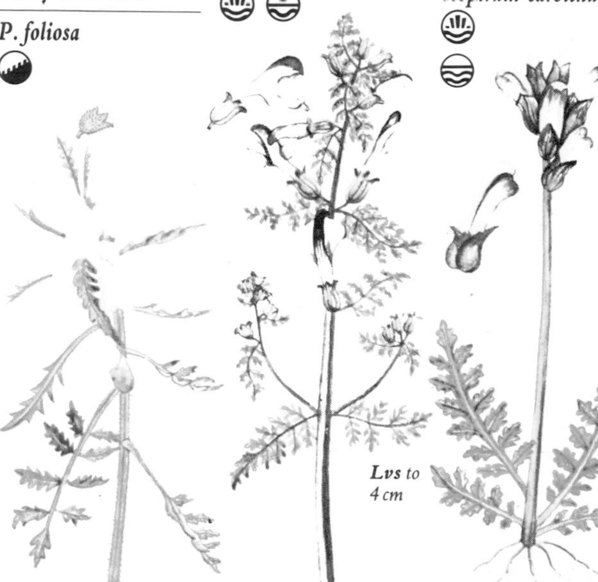

Lvs to 4 cm

Annual, 1 main uprt stem, spls 2-lipped, hry, top ptl lip has tooth on each side. *Ht:* 45 cm; *D:* T; *Fl:* 5–9

Lousewort

Pedicularis sylvatica

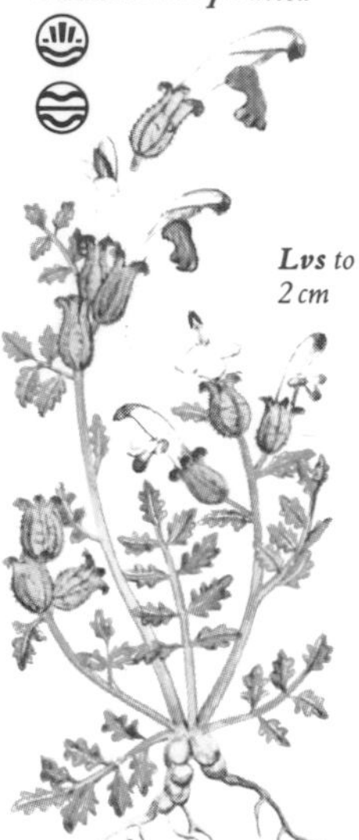

Lvs to 2 cm

Perennial, trails to 25 cm. Spls hrlss, not 2-lipped, no lateral teeth on top ptl lip. *D:* W, C; *Fl:* 4–7

Moor king

Pedicularis sceptrum-carolinum

Erect per. Lvs to 2 cm, most in basal rosette, few stem lvs; infl a spike, fl 3 cm. *Ht:* 60 cm; *D:* N, C; *Fl:* 7– 8

Gratiola

Gratiola officinalis

Hairless per, stems hollow, 4-angled; fls long-stkd, sol in lf axils. *Ht:* to 50 cm; *D:* S, C; *Fl:* 5–10

Yellow rattle

Rhinanthus minor

Semi-parasitic per to 50 cm, lvs green, opp; spl tube flat, inflated in fr. A variable sp. *D:* T; *Fl:* 5–8

Red bartsia

Odontites verna

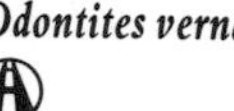

Hairy v branched ann to 50 cm. Infl dense spike, fls 1 cm, 2-lipped, no teeth on top lip. *D:* T; *Fl:* 6–8

Mudwort

Limosella aquatica

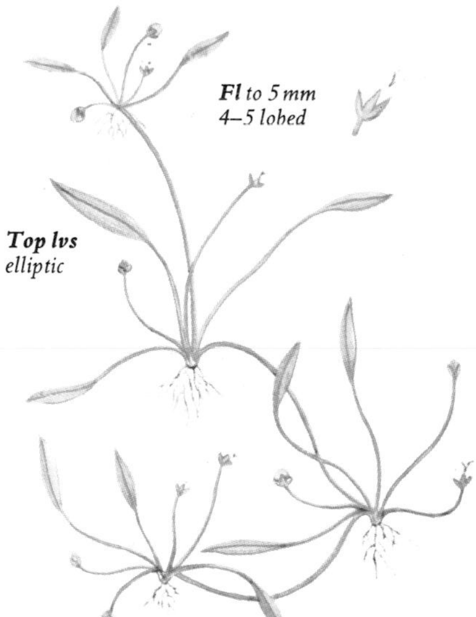

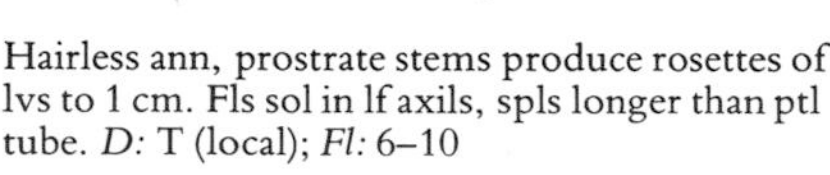

Hairless ann, prostrate stems produce rosettes of lvs to 1 cm. Fls sol in lf axils, spls longer than ptl tube. *D:* T (local); *Fl:* 6–10

Yellow odontites

O. lutea

Erect hrlss ann to 40 cm, many brs; infl loose, linear bracts, fls hry, stamens protrude. *D:* S, C; *Fl:* 7–9

Sharp-leaved fluellen

Kickxia elatine

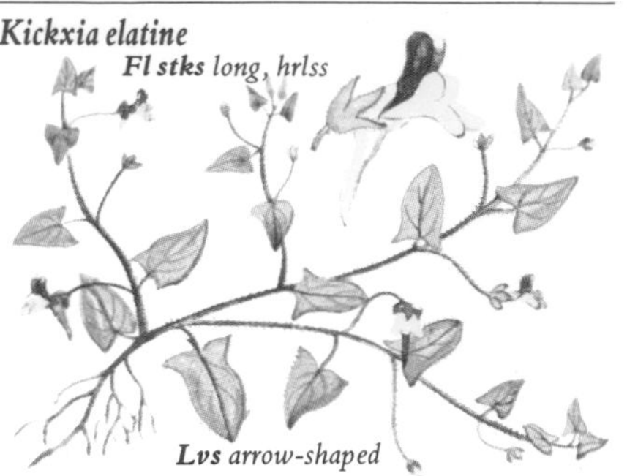

Slim prostrate shs to 50 cm. Fls as *Linaria* (p 123), sol, axillary. *D:* S, W, C; *Fl:* 7–10

Round-leaved fluellen

K. spuria

Like *K. elatine* but hry and more robust. Lvs round, fls 1 cm, stks hry. *D:* S, W, C; *Fl:* 7–10

Common cow-wheat

M. pratense

Leaves unstkd. Fls in axils of lfy bracts, ptls 2 × spls. *Ht:* to 60 cm; *D:* T; *Fl:* 5–10

Wood cow-wheat

M. sylvaticum

Very like *M. pratense* but spl lobes spread and about same length as ptls. *Ht:* 25 cm; *D:* S mts, N; *Fl:* 6–8

Field cow-wheat

Melampyrum arvense

Hairy ann to 60 cm, lvs unstkd. Infl dense spike, bracts narrow, toothed, uprt, pink. *D:* T (not far N); *Fl:* 6–9

Crested cow-wheat

M. cristatum

Little branched ann to 50 cm. Infl dense 4-angled spike, bracts toothed, curl back. *D:* T (rare in N); *Fl:* 6–9

Melampyrum

M. nemorosum

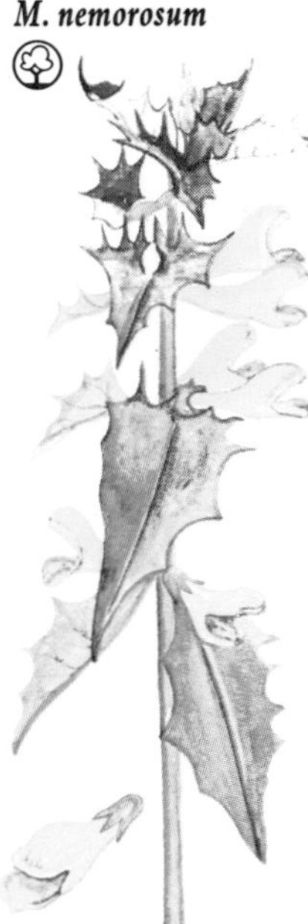

Hairy uprt ann to 50 cm. Lvs oval to 4 cm wide; fl 2 cm, bracts bluish-violet, infl lfy. *D:* N, C; *Fl:* 6–8

Yellow bartsia

Parentucellia viscosa

Erect stickily hry ann to 50 cm. Lvs not lobed. Fls 2 cm, top lip shorter than lower. *D:* S, W; *Fl:* 6–10

Alpine bartsia

Bartsia alpina

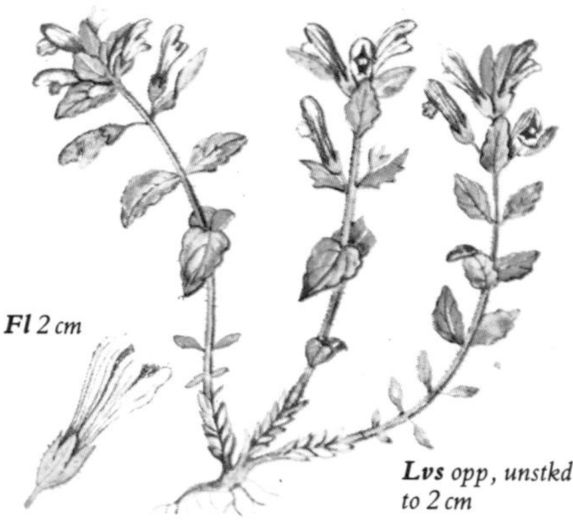

Hairy per to 20 cm. Purple bracts in infl, top fl lip longer than lower. *D:* S mts, N; *Fl:* 6–8

Cornish moneywort

Sibthorpia europaea

Creeps to 40 cm. Lvs rounded, 5–7 lobed; fls 2 mm, sol, short-stkd in lf axils. *D:* W; *Fl:* 7–10

Monkey flower

Mimulus guttatus

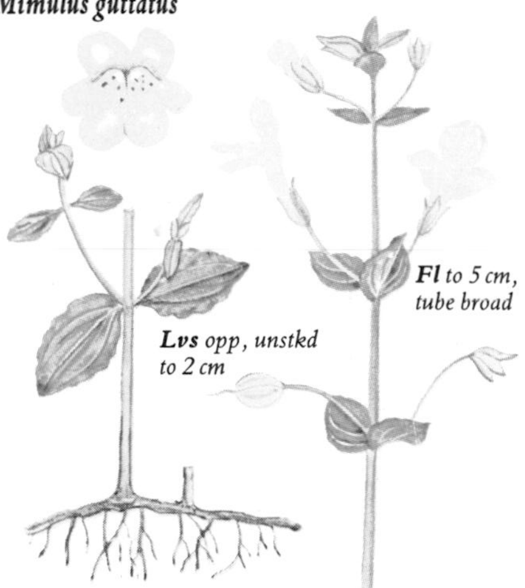

Perennial to 50 cm. Lvs rounded, toothed to 7 cm. Fls sol in bract axils. *D:* T; *Fl:* 7–9

Globularia family Globulariaceae

Simple-leaved perennials. Flowers in very dense heads have 5 sepals and petals, 4 stamens and a one-celled ovary.

Globularia

Globularia vulgaris

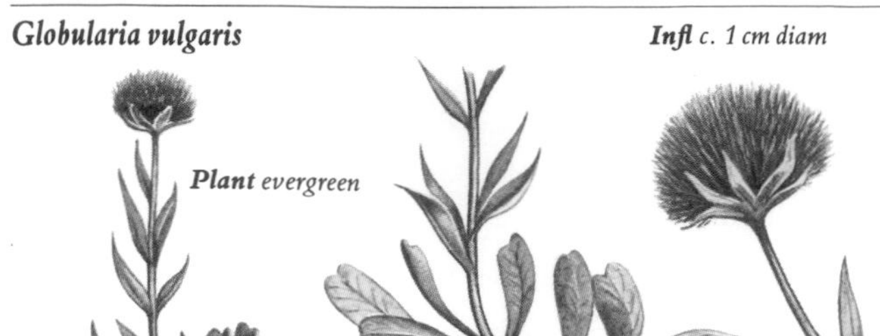

Rosette lvs have 3 teeth at tip and narrow gradually, stem lvs unlobed, unstkd. Fls 2-lipped, lower lip 3-lobed. *Ht:* 20 cm; *D:* S, Swed; *Fl:* 4–6

Broomrape family Orobanchaceae

Parasites on plant roots and lacking green pigment. Leaves are scales, flowers two-lipped with a bent petal tube.

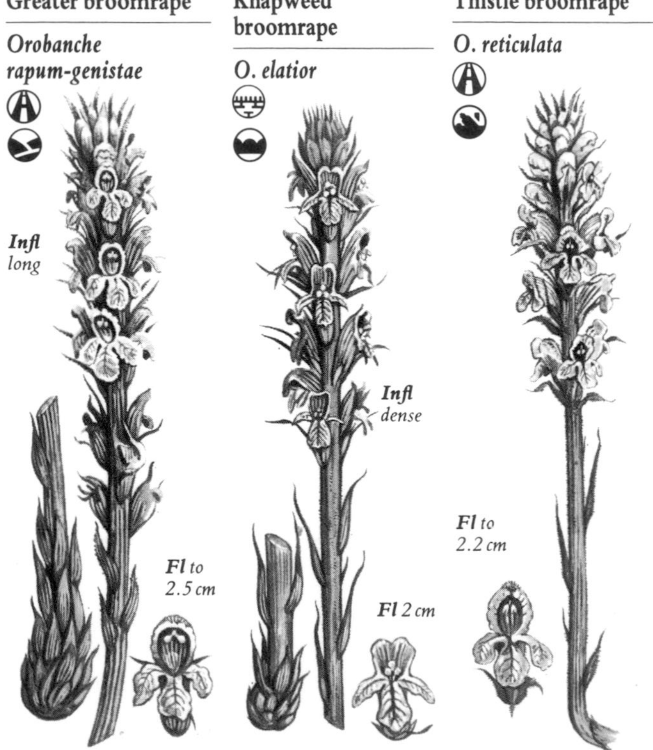

Greater broomrape — Parasite on gorse, broom. Top ptl tube lip unlobed, stamens join ptl tube, yellow stigmas. *Ht:* to 80 cm; *D:* W; *Fl:* 5–7

Knapweed broomrape — Parasite on greater knapweed. Stigmas yellow, stms attached 5 mm above ptl tube base. *Ht:* 50 cm; *D:* T (not N); *Fl:* 6–7

Thistle broomrape — Parasite on thistles. Fls v curved at base, have small black glands at edges and purple stigmas. *Ht:* 35 cm; *D:* T (not N); *Fl:* 6–8

Common broomrape

Orobanche minor

Parasite on clover, catsear. Ptl tube curved. *Ht:* 35 cm; *D:* W, S, C; *Fl:* 6–9

Purple broomrape

O. purpurea

Spike *loose*

Stems *bluish*

Parasite of yarrow. Each 3 cm fl has 3 bracts. *Ht:* 30 cm; *D:* T (not N); *Fl:* 6–7

Toothwort

Lathraea squamaria

Infl *1-sided*

Ptl tube *2 lipped*

Parasite of hazel, elm. Spl tube 4-lobed. *Ht:* 20 cm; *D:* T (not N); *Fl:* 4–5

Butterwort family Lentibulariaceae

Insectivorous plants with sticky leaves or bladder traps. Flowers have 5-lobed or two-lipped sepal tubes, spurred two-lipped petal tubes, two stamens and two carpels.

Common butterwort  

Pinguicula vulgaris

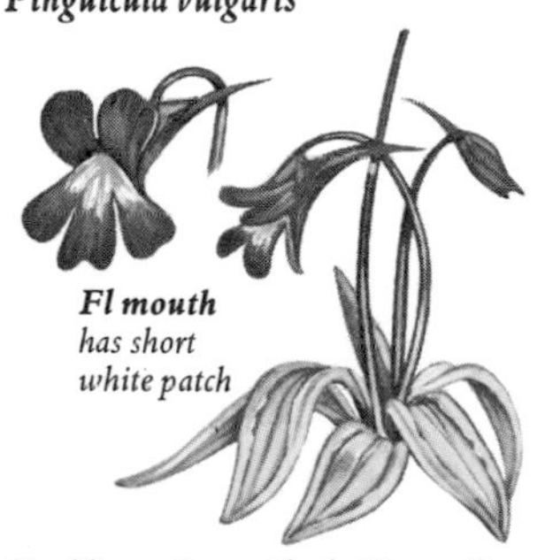

Oval lvs to 8 cm. Fl stk 10 cm, fls to 1.5 cm, lower lip v cleft, spur 6 mm. *D:* N, W, C; *Fl:* 5–7

Pale butterwort

P. lusitanica

Leaves to 2 cm. Fl stks 10 cm, fls to 7 mm, spur 3 mm, cylindrical, pointed tip. *D:* W; *Fl:* 6–10

Large-flowered butterwort 

P. grandiflora

Oval lvs to 20 cm. Fl stk 15 cm, fls 2 cm, shallow cleft in lower lip, 1 cm spur. *D:* SW; *Fl:* 5–6

Alpine butterwort  

P. alpina

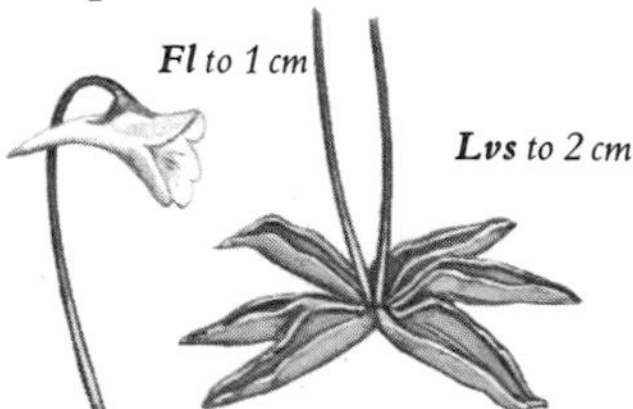

One or 2 yellow spots at fl mouth, spur conical, downcurved, to 3 mm. *Ht:* 7 cm; *D:* C, Arct; *Fl:* 5–8

Hairy butterwort

Pinguicula villosa

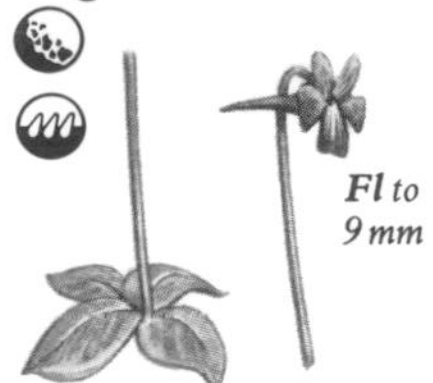

Very like *P. alpina* (p 129) but fl stks stickily hry. *Ht:* 7 cm; *D:* Fennoscand; *Fl:* 5–8

Lesser bladderwort

Utricularia minor

Slender stems to 25 cm have bladders, some stems green, some colourless in mud. Lvs lobed, palmate. *D:* T; *Fl:* 6–9

Greater bladderwort

U. vulgaris

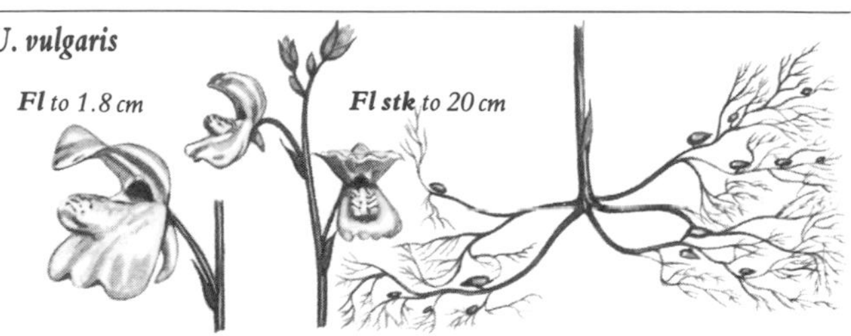

Free-floating aquatic. Stems to 45 cm all green with bladders. Lvs pinnately cut into fine-toothed segs. *D:* T; *Fl:* 7–8

Plantain family Plantaginaceae

Herbs with leaves in basal rosettes. Tiny flowers in dense heads have petal and sepal tubes with 4 fused parts and 4 stamens joining the petal tube. The fruit is a capsule.

Ribwort plantain

Plantago lanceolata

Greater plantain

P. major

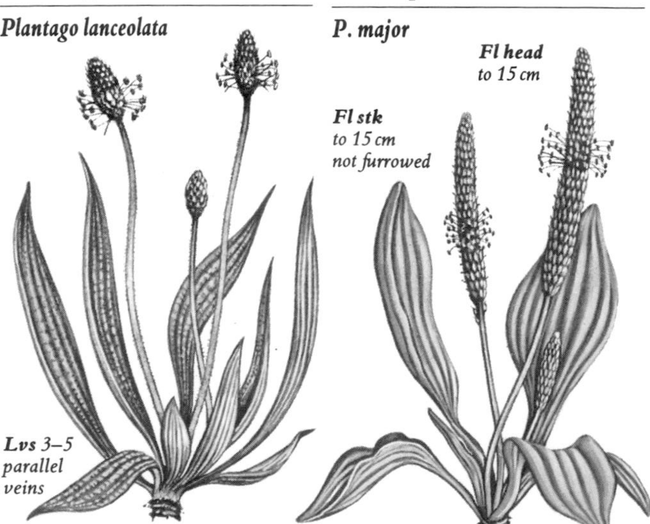

Perennial. Lvs long, narrow to 15 cm. Infl head to 2 cm long on deeply furrowed stk to 40 cm. *D:* T (not far N); *Fl:* 4–8

Leaves to 15 cm long and almost as broad, narrow abruptly to long stk. *Ht:* 20 cm; *D:* T; *Fl:* 5–9

Hoary plantain  

P. media

Buckshorn plantain 

P. coronopus

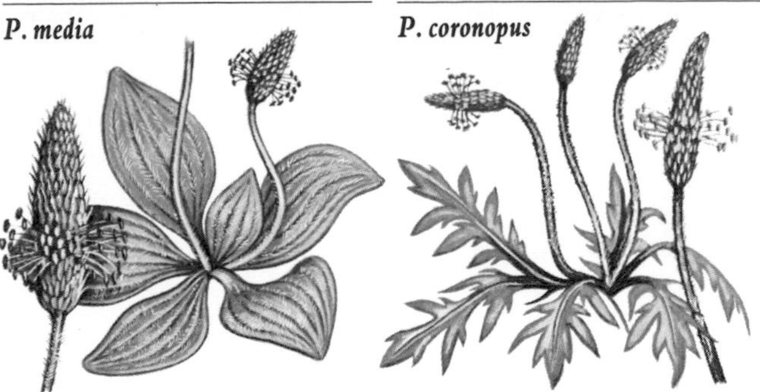

Softly hry lvs to 6 cm v short-stkd. Infl head to 6 cm on long stk to 30 cm. *D:* T; *Fl:* 5–8

Leaves to 6 cm pinnately cut into narrow segs. Infl head to 4 cm on 5 cm stk. *Ht:* 10 cm *D:* T; *Fl:* 5–7

Branched plantain

P. arenaria

Scrambles to 30 cm. Lvs narrow, lower lvs have axillary shs; infl 1 cm. *D:* T; *Fl:* 7–8

Sea plantain

P. maritima

Tuft of succ narrow lvs with 3–5 veins. Infl head 4 cm. *Ht:* 13 cm; *D:* T; *Fl:* 6–8

Shoreweed

Littorella uniflora

Fine lvd, has stolons. ♂, ♀ fls sep in same or diff heads. *Ht:* 7 cm; *D:* W, C; *Fl:* 6–8

Moschatel family Adoxaceae

Uppermost flower has two joined sepals, 4 petals and stamens, side flowers have three sepals, 5 petals and stamens.

Moschatel

Adoxa moschatellina

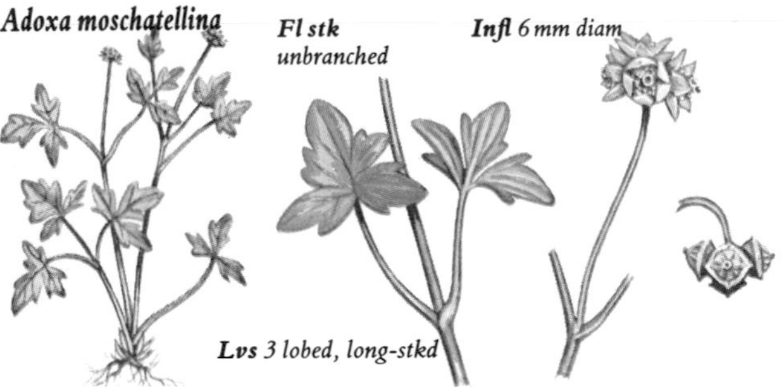

The only species in the family, a delicate herb to 10 cm with creeping rhizome. Infl of 5 fls has cubic form. *D:* T; *Fl:* 4–5

Honeysuckle family Caprifoliaceae

Woody or herbaceous plants with opposite leaves. Flowers have 5 petals and sepals and 5 stamens attached to the petal tube which may be two-lipped.

Honeysuckle

Lonicera periclymenum

Woody climber to 6 m. Fls to 5 cm in terminal infl are 2-lipped, top lip 4-lobed, lower unlobed. *D:* W, C, S; *Fl:* 6–9

Perfoliate honeysuckle

L. caprifolium

As *L. periclymenum* but glaucous lf prs fused below, some fls in lf axils. *Ht:* 5 m; *D:* S, EC; *Fl:* 5–6

Twin flower

Linnaea borealis

Mat-forming evergreen. Fls 8 mm, nodding, fl stks delicate to 7 cm. *D:* S mts, N; *Fl:* 6–8

Valerian family Valerianaceae

Opposite-leaved herbs. Small 5-lobed funnel-shaped flowers have sepals indistinct from feathery attachment to fruit.

Common valerian

Valeriana officinalis

Erect per to 1.5 m. Lvs pinnate, lobed, basal lvs stkd. Fls 5 mm, 3 stamens. *D:* T; *Fl:* 6–8

Red valerian

Centranthus ruber

Leaves oval. Fls white or red, narrow, spurred, 1 protruding stamen. *Ht:* 60 cm; *D:* S; *Fl:* 6–8

Marsh valerian 

Valeriana dioica

Cornsalad   

Valerianella locusta

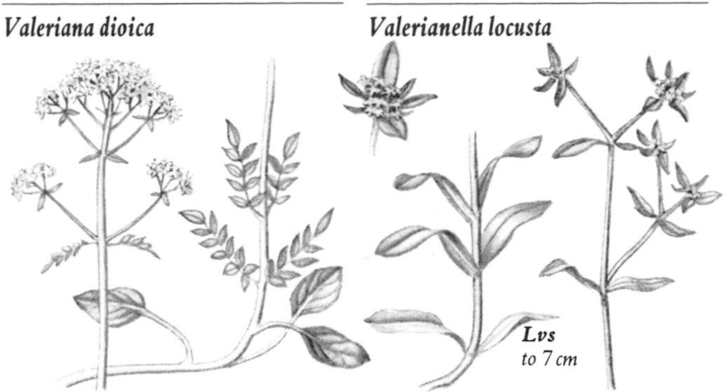

Marsh valerian: Has stolons. Lf blades to 3 cm, basal unlobed, stkd, upper unstkd, pinnate. ♂, ♀ parts in sep fls. *Ht:* 20 cm; *D:* W, C; *Fl:* 5–6

Cornsalad: Erect branched ann to 40 cm. Lvs unlobed. Fls in small dense heads surrounded by narrow bracts, spls indistinct. *D:* T; *Fl:* 4–6

Scabious family Dipsacaceae

Opposite-leaved herbs with dense round flower heads. Sepals are inconspicuous but each 4–5 lobed flower is surrounded by bracts. There are 2 or 4 stamens.

Field scabious

Knautia arvensis

Lvs in basal rosette

Robust per to 1 m; lvs lobed, hry; infl 4 cm diam, outer fls larger than inner, bristly spls. *D:* T; *Fl:* 7–9

Wood scabious

K. dipsacifolia

Like *K. arvensis* but taller. Stem lvs not lobed, serrate. Infl 3 cm diam. *Ht:* 1.2 m; *D:* C mts; *Fl:* 6–9

Devilsbit scabious

Succisa pratensis

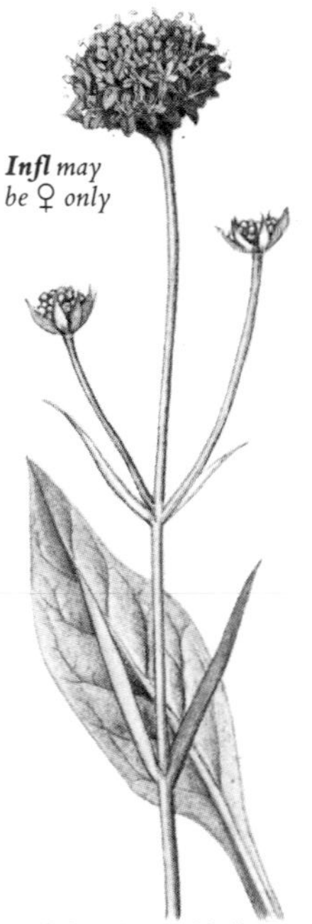

Infl may be ♀ only

Unlobed lvs, midribs white. Infl 2 cm diam, all fls same size. Ptl tube to 7 mm. *Ht:* 80 cm; *D:* T; *Fl:* 6–10

Small scabious

Scabiosa columbaria

Teasel

Dipsacus fullonum

Small teasel

D. pilosus

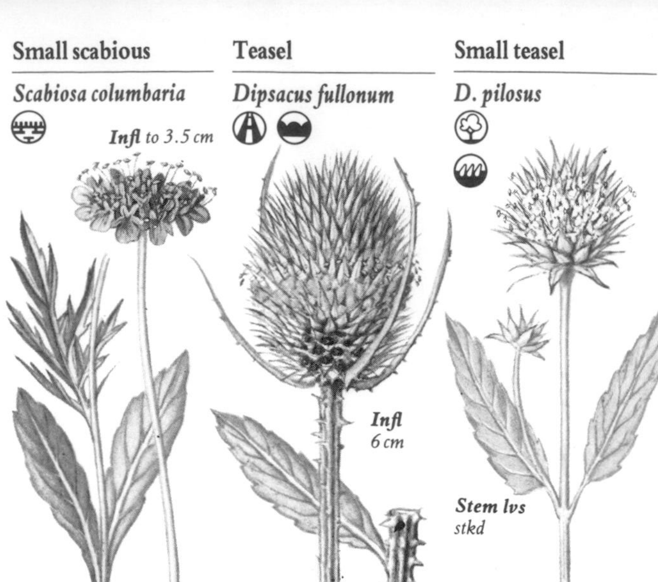

Basal lvs just lobed, mid lvs v lobed, top lvs finely cut; outer fls largest. *Ht:* 55 cm; *D:* T (not N); *Fl:* 7–8

Prickly bi to 2 m. Narrow stem lvs encircle stem; infl has long spiny bracts. *D:* S, W, C; *Fl:* 7–8

Weakly prickly bi, ridged stems to 1.2 m. Infl *c.* 2 cm, round, drooping in bud. *D:* W, C; *Fl:* 8

Bellflower family Campanulaceae

Herbs with a milky sap and simple, alternate leaves. Bell-shaped, symmetrical flowers have 5 stamens. The family includes the lobelias with asymmetrical two-lipped flowers.

Harebell

Campanula rotundifolia

Spreading bellflower

C. patula

Clustered bellflower

C. glomerata

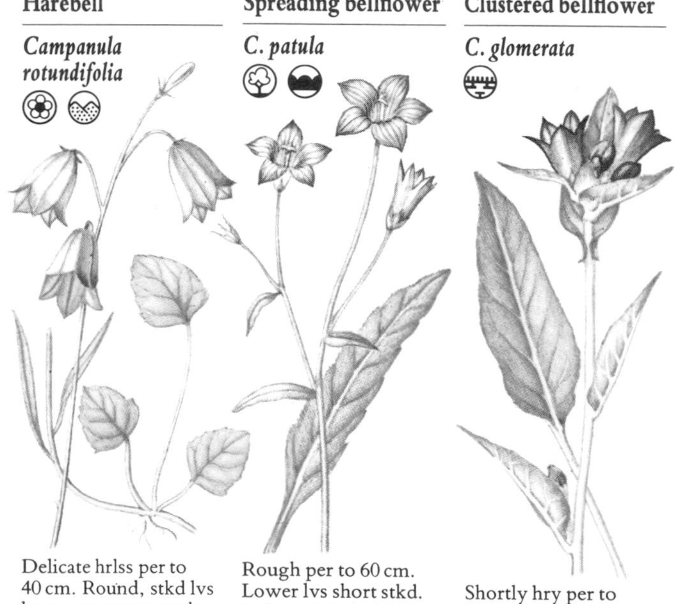

Delicate hrlss per to 40 cm. Round, stkd lvs borne on prostrate shs, narrow unstkd lvs on fl shs. Fls nodding, 1.5 cm. *D:* T; *Fl:* 7–9

Rough per to 60 cm. Lower lvs short stkd. Infl much branched, bracts in middle of fl stks, fls erect, 2 cm. *D:* T; *Fl:* 7–9

Shortly hry per to 20 cm. Basal lvs long stkd. Fls uprt, unstkd in dense clusters. *D:* T (not N); *Fl:* 5–9

Bearded bellflower

C. barbata

***Fl** to 3 cm*

Drooping fls in 1-sided infl, white hrs in ptl tube. *Ht:* 20 cm; *D:* Nwy, Alps; *Fl:* 6–8

Creeping bellflower

C. rapunculoides

***Fl** 3 cm, nodding*

***Spls** spread*

Basal lvs abruptly rounded at stk, stem lvs unstkd. *Ht:* 45 cm; *D:* T; *Fl:* 7–9

Giant bellflower

C. latifolia

***Top lvs** unstkd*

Robust softly hry per to 1.2 m. Stem lvs to 20 cm, blades narrow gradually to stks; fls to 5 cm long, spls not spreading. *D:* T (not N); *Fl:* 7–8

Nettle-leaved bellflower

C. trachelium

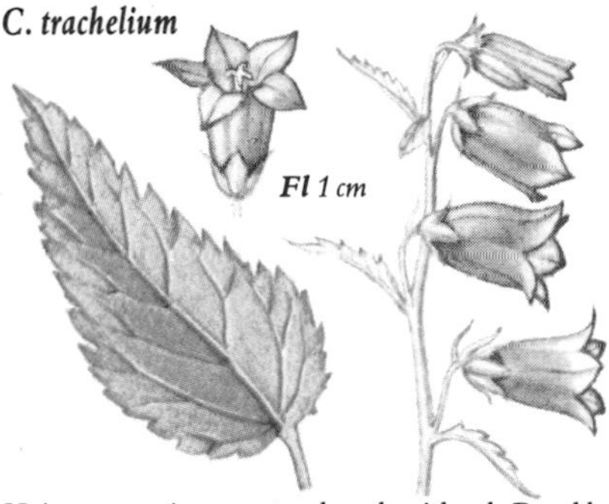

***Fl** 1 cm*

Hairy per to 1 m, stems sharply ridged. Basal lvs contracted at stk, stem lvs short-stkd; fls erect, spls not spread. *D:* T (not N); *Fl:* 7–9

Ivy-leaved bellflower

Wahlenbergia hederacea

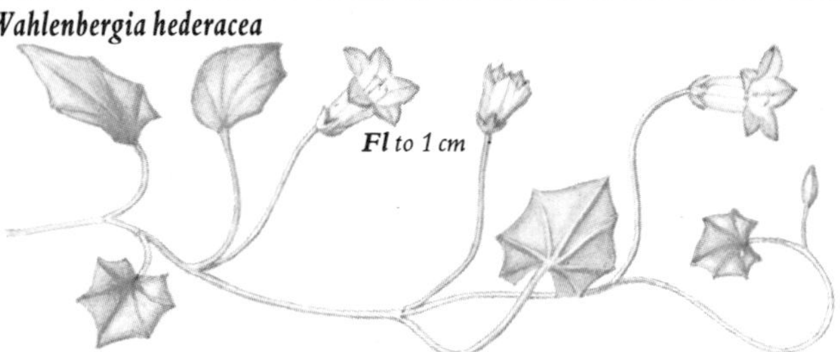

Delicate creeping per, sprawling stems to 30 cm. Lvs ivy-shaped, long stkd. Slim fl stks to 4 cm, fls nodding. *D:* W; *Fl:* 7–8

Sheepsbit scabious

Jasione montana

Small fls in dense head surrounded by short bracts. *Ht:* 35 cm; *D:* T; *Fl:* 5–8

Round-headed rampion

Phyteuma orbiculare

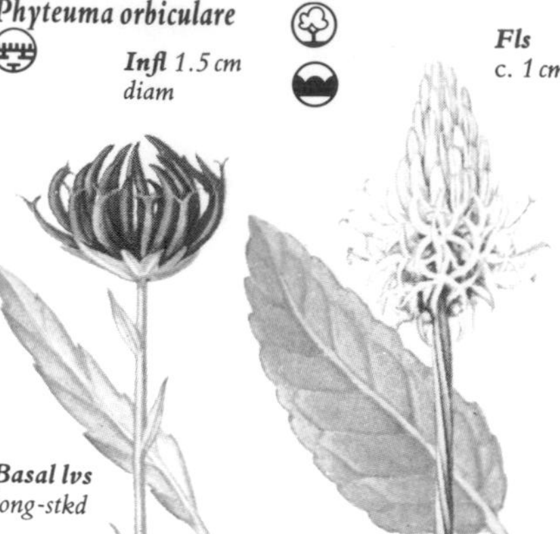

Spherical infl, ptl lobes tubular below, then spread. *Ht:* 35 cm; *D:* T (not N); *Fl:* 7–8

Spiked rampion

P. spicatum

Flowers in 6 cm spike, ptl lobes spread as fl ages. *Ht:* 60 cm; *D:* T (not N); *Fl:* 7–8

Heath lobelia

Lobelia urens

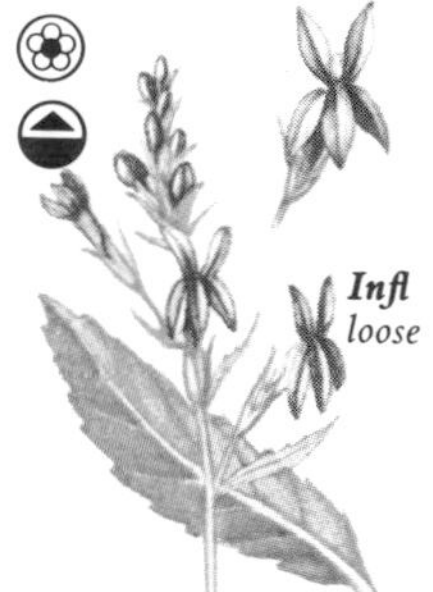

Many serrate lvs to 7 cm. Ptl tube to 1.5 cm, 2-lipped. *Ht:* 45 cm; *D:* W; *Fl:* 8–9

Water lobelia

L. dortmanna

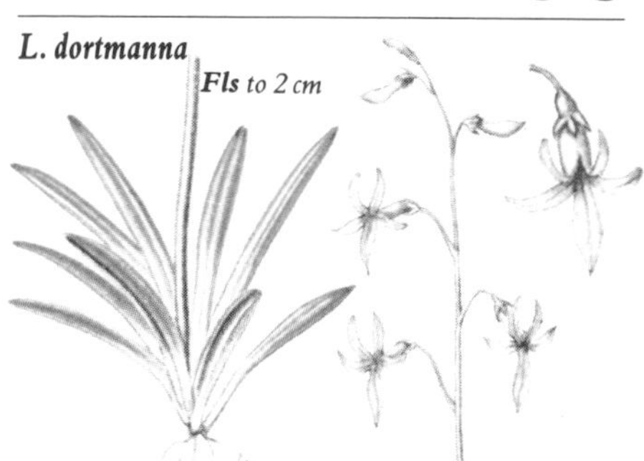

Spreads by stolons. Tuft of narrow lvs to 4 cm. Fl stems to 60 cm emerge from water. Infl loose, fls 2-lipped, nodding. *D:* N, NC; *Fl:* 7–8

Venus' looking glass

Legousia hybrida

Has stiff hrs. Lf edges wavy. Fls uprt, ovary elongate, spls 2 × ptls. *Ht:* 20 cm; *D:* W, S; *Fl:* 5–8

Large Venus' looking glass

L. speculum-veneris

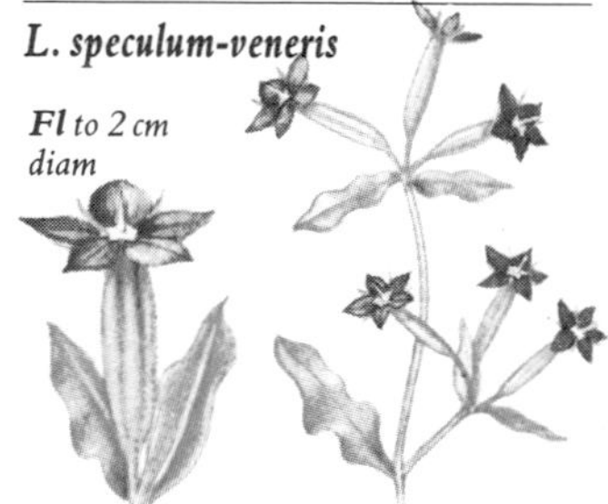

Much branched ann to 40 cm. Ptls as long as spls and ovary, spls spread in fr. *D:* SW, SC; *Fl:* 5–7

Daisy family Compositae

Usually herbs, but a huge and variable family. Leaves have no stipules. Small flowers (florets) are in dense heads on the flat top of the inflorescence stalk and surrounded by one or more rows of sepal-like bracts. Florets may be all alike (as thistles) or the outer ones longer (as daisies) and either tubular (disc florets) or strap-shaped (ray florets). Each ovary has one cell.

Daisy

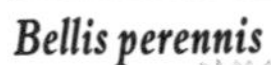

Bellis perennis

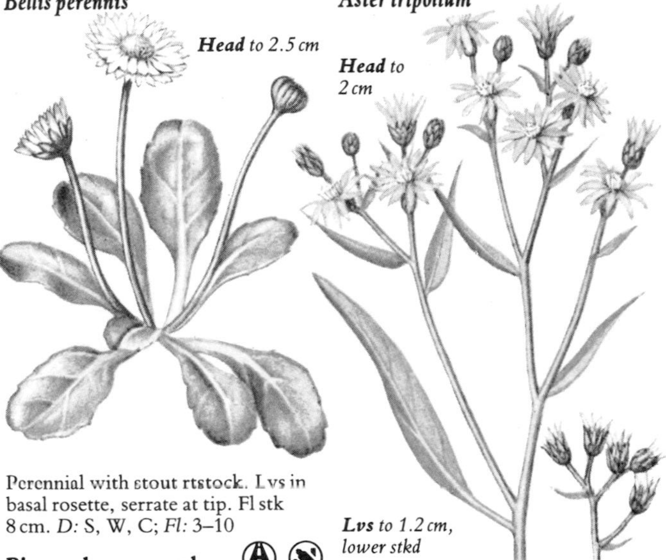

Perennial with stout rtstock. Lvs in basal rosette, serrate at tip. Fl stk 8 cm. *D:* S, W, C; *Fl:* 3–10

Pineapple mayweed

  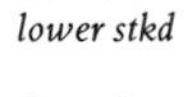

Chamomilla suaveolens (= Matricaria matricarioides)

Aromatic herb to 30 cm. Lvs 2–3 pinnate, fine segs. Heads have disc florets only. *D:* T; *Fl:* 6–7

Sea aster

Aster tripolium

Succulent per, hrlss lfy stems to 1 m. Outer ray florets may be absent. *D:* T; *Fl:* 7–10

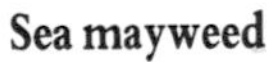

Sea mayweed

M. maritima

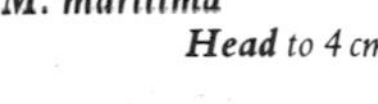

Head to 4 cm

Lvs 2–3 pinnate, fine segs

Biennial or per, stout rtstock. Common weed *M. perforata* sim but ann. *Ht:* 50 cm; *D:* W, N; *Fl:* 7–9

Golden rod

Solidago virgaurea

Erect, few brs. Fl heads to 1 cm in terminal clusters. *Ht:* 55 cm; *D:* T; *Fl:* 7–9

Blue fleabane

Erigeron acer

Dense, long hrs on stem and lvs. Many ray florets in 2 or more rows. *Ht:* 30 cm; *D:* T; *Fl:* 7–8

Canadian fleabane

Conyza canadensis

Stems branched to 1 m, many narrow lvs to 4 cm. Heads 4 mm, sev rows ray florets. *D:* T; *Fl:* 8–9

Gallant soldier

Galinsoga parviflora

Many brs; serrate lvs in opp prs. Oval bracts round 5-rayed heads. *Ht:* 60 cm; *D:* T (not N); *Fl:* 5–11

Ploughman's spikenard

Inula conyza

Robust bi or per, red stems to 1.3 m; heads in loose terminal gps, no rays, narrow bracts. *D:* W, S, C; *Fl:* 7–9

Fleabane

I. britannica

Erect per to 60 cm, usually v hry. Heads to 4 cm, usually sol, bracts narrow, hry. *D:* S, C; *Fl:* 7–8

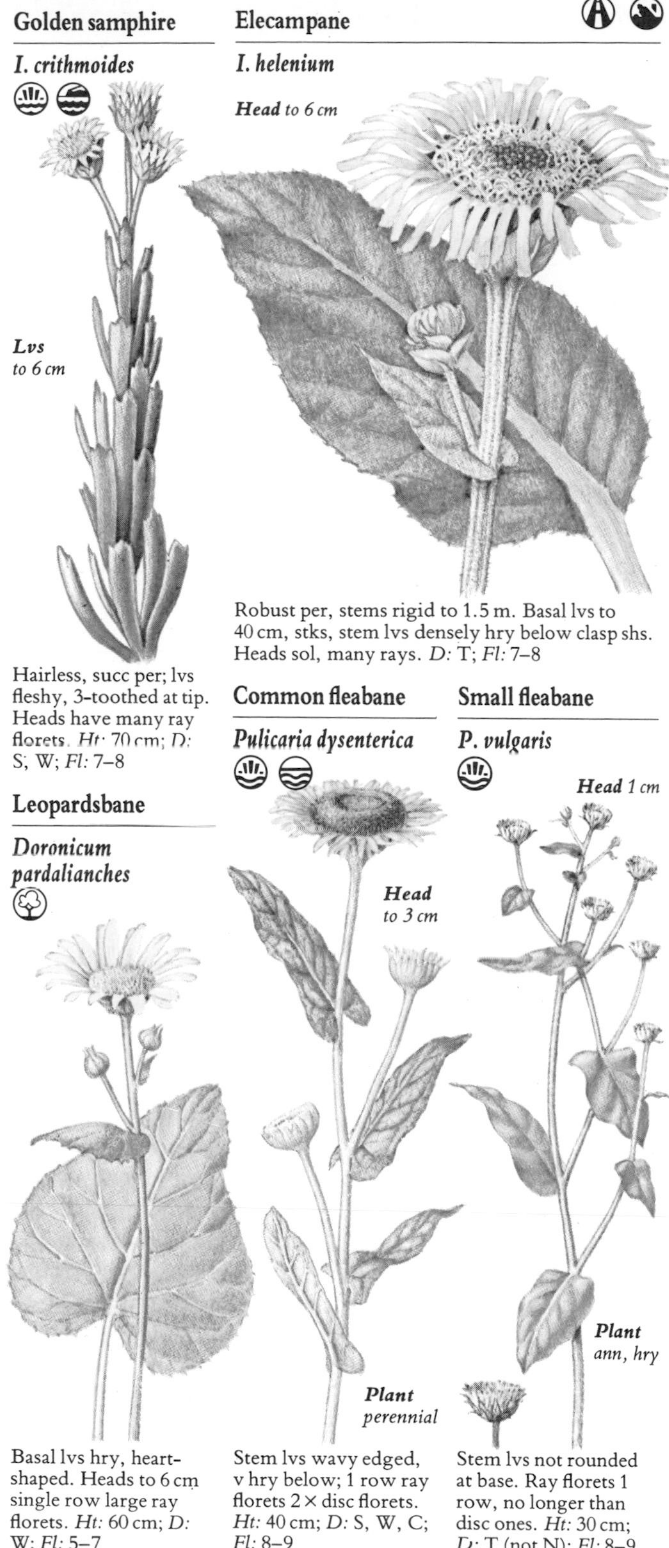

Golden samphire

I. crithmoides

Hairless, succ per; lvs fleshy, 3-toothed at tip. Heads have many ray florets. *Ht:* 70 cm; *D:* S; W; *Fl:* 7–8

Elecampane

I. helenium

Robust per, stems rigid to 1.5 m. Basal lvs to 40 cm, stks, stem lvs densely hry below clasp shs. Heads sol, many rays. *D:* T; *Fl:* 7–8

Leopardsbane

Doronicum pardalianches

Basal lvs hry, heart-shaped. Heads to 6 cm single row large ray florets. *Ht:* 60 cm; *D:* W; *Fl:* 5–7

Common fleabane

Pulicaria dysenterica

Stem lvs wavy edged, v hry below; 1 row ray florets 2 × disc florets. *Ht:* 40 cm; *D:* S, W, C; *Fl:* 8–9

Small fleabane

P. vulgaris

Stem lvs not rounded at base. Ray florets 1 row, no longer than disc ones. *Ht:* 30 cm; *D:* T (not N); *Fl:* 8–9

Corn chamomile

Anthemis arvensis

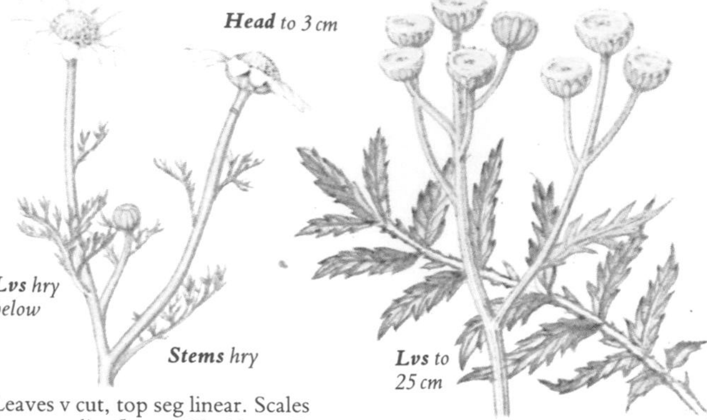

Leaves v cut, top seg linear. Scales between disc florets. *Ht:* 40 cm; *D:* T (not far N); *Fl:* 6–7

Ox-eye daisy

Leucanthemum vulgare

Erect stems to 70 cm plus non-flowering lfy rosettes. Heads sol, long rays to 5 cm. *D:* T; *Fl:* 6–8

Coltsfoot

Tussilago farfara

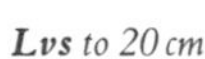

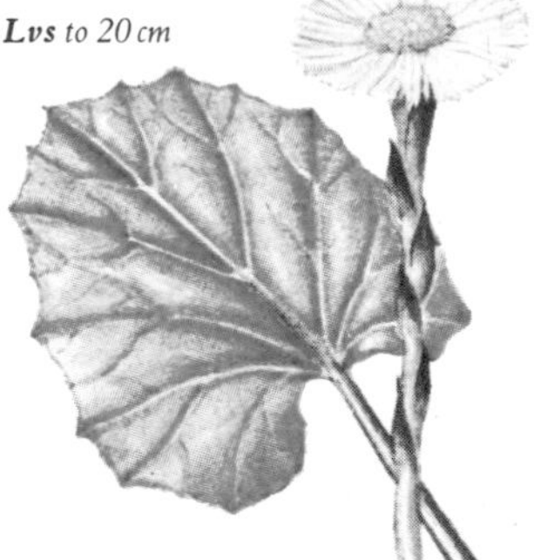

Round, toothed lvs appear after fls. All florets have strap-shaped ligule. *Ht:* 10 cm; *D:* T; *Fl:* 3–4

Tansy

Tanacetum vulgare

Strong-smelling per. Lvs pinnate, lobes toothed, no ray florets. *Ht:* 80 cm; *D:* T; *Fl:* 7–9

Corn marigold

Chrysanthemum segetum

Erect hrlss ann to 50 cm; lvs succ, coarsely toothed. Heads to 6.5 cm, sol, long-stkd. *D:* W; *Fl:* 6–8

Purple coltsfoot

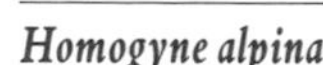

Homogyne alpina

Basal lvs kidney-shaped, toothed, purple below. Heads sol to 1.5 cm. *Ht:* 20 cm; *D:* W, C, S; *Fl:* 5–8

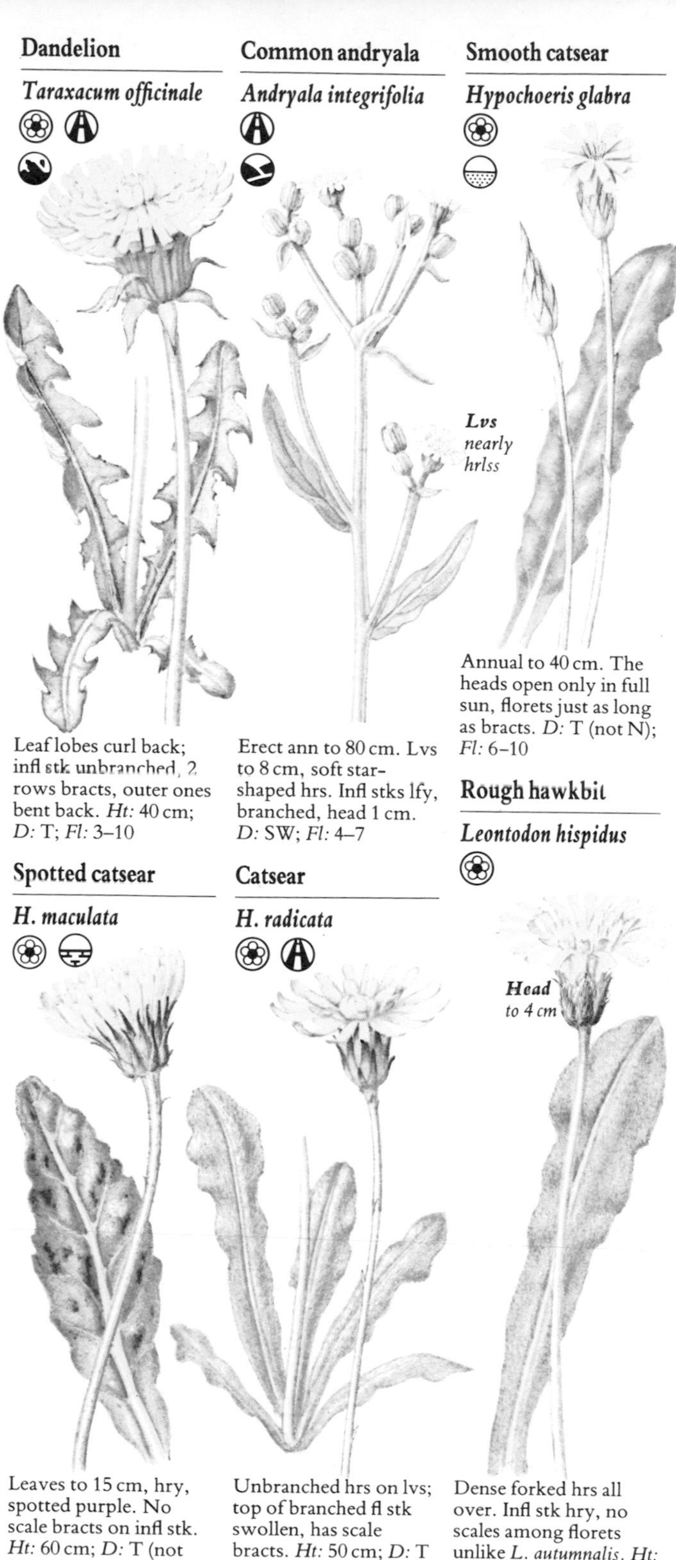

Dandelion

Taraxacum officinale

Leaf lobes curl back; infl stk unbranched, 2 rows bracts, outer ones bent back. *Ht:* 40 cm; *D:* T; *Fl:* 3–10

Common andryala

Andryala integrifolia

Erect ann to 80 cm. Lvs to 8 cm, soft star-shaped hrs. Infl stks lfy, branched, head 1 cm. *D:* SW; *Fl:* 4–7

Smooth catsear

Hypochoeris glabra

Annual to 40 cm. The heads open only in full sun, florets just as long as bracts. *D:* T (not N); *Fl:* 6–10

Spotted catsear

H. maculata

Leaves to 15 cm, hry, spotted purple. No scale bracts on infl stk. *Ht:* 60 cm; *D:* T (not N, NW); *Fl:* 6–8

Catsear

H. radicata

Unbranched hrs on lvs; top of branched fl stk swollen, has scale bracts. *Ht:* 50 cm; *D:* T (not NE); *Fl:* 6–9

Rough hawkbit

Leontodon hispidus

Dense forked hrs all over. Infl stk hry, no scales among florets unlike *L. autumnalis*. *Ht:* 45 cm; *D:* T; *Fl:* 6–9

Ragwort  

Senecio jacobaea

Alpine ragwort  

S. nemorensis

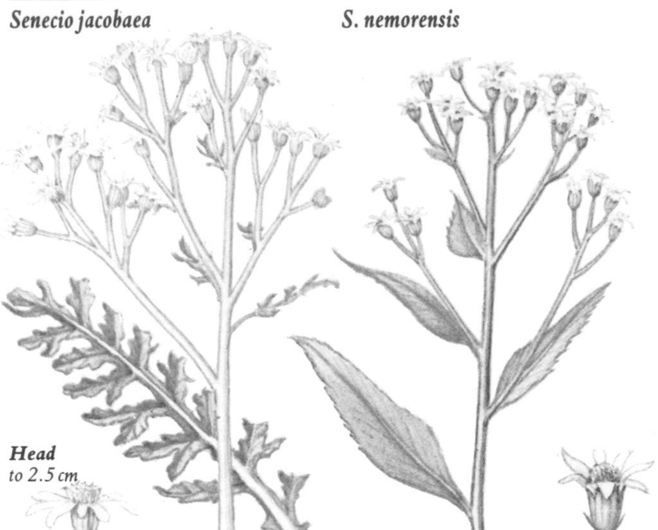

Head
to 2.5 cm

Erect bi or per to 1.5 m. Stem ridged, often with long hrs; basal lvs deeply lobed in rosette, stem lvs pinnate. *D:* T; *Fl:* 6–10

Robust lfy per to 2 m. Lvs toothed, hry below. Heads 3 cm, densely gpd, bracts in 1 row as most *Senecio* spp. *D:* C, S; *Fl:* 7–9

Groundsel

S. vulgaris

Erect ann to 45 cm. Lvs lobed, clasping, may have woolly hrs. Heads to 1 cm, rarely with ray florets. *D:* T; *Fl:* 1–12. *S. sylvaticus* sim but always with rays.

Oxford ragwort

S. squalidus

***Stks** of lower lvs winged*

Hairless erect ann to 30 cm. Heads to 2 cm in irregular gps have ray florets. *Ht:* 25 cm; *D:* C, S; *Fl:* 5–12

Broad-leaved ragwort

S. fluviatilis

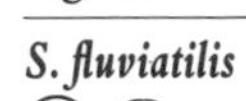

Has stolons. Uprt shs to 1.5 m. Lvs hrlss, serrate to 20 cm. Heads 3 cm have rays. *D:* C, E; *Fl:* 7–9

Marsh ragwort

Senecio aquaticus

Field fleawort

S. integrifolius

Marsh fleawort

S. congestus

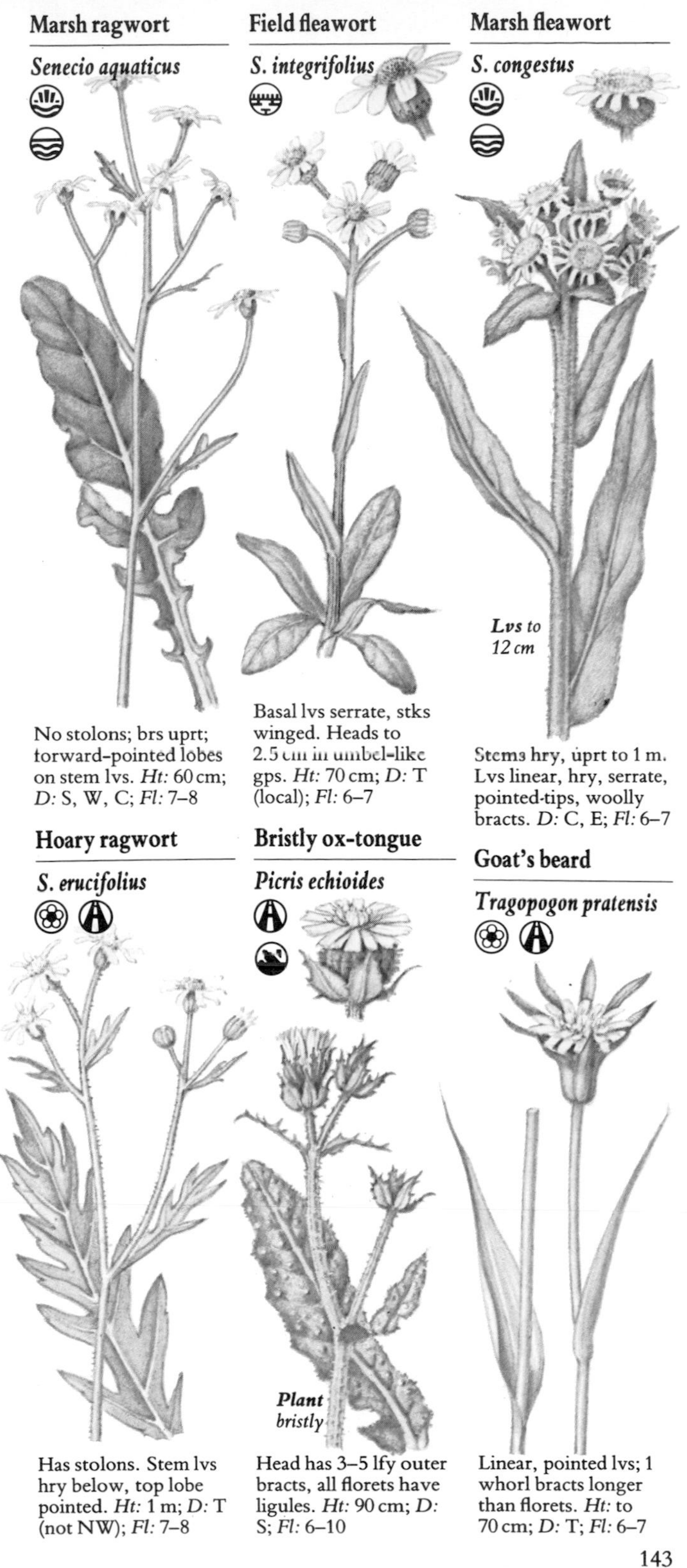

No stolons; brs uprt; forward-pointed lobes on stem lvs. *Ht:* 60 cm; *D:* S, W, C; *Fl:* 7–8

Basal lvs serrate, stks winged. Heads to 2.5 cm in umbel-like gps. *Ht:* 70 cm; *D:* T (local); *Fl:* 6–7

Stems hry, uprt to 1 m. Lvs linear, hry, serrate, pointed-tips, woolly bracts. *D:* C, E; *Fl:* 6–7

Hoary ragwort

S. erucifolius

Has stolons. Stem lvs hry below, top lobe pointed. *Ht:* 1 m; *D:* T (not NW); *Fl:* 7–8

Bristly ox-tongue

Picris echioides

Head has 3–5 lfy outer bracts, all florets have ligules. *Ht:* 90 cm; *D:* S; *Fl:* 6–10

Goat's beard

Tragopogon pratensis

Linear, pointed lvs; 1 whorl bracts longer than florets. *Ht:* to 70 cm; *D:* T; *Fl:* 6–7

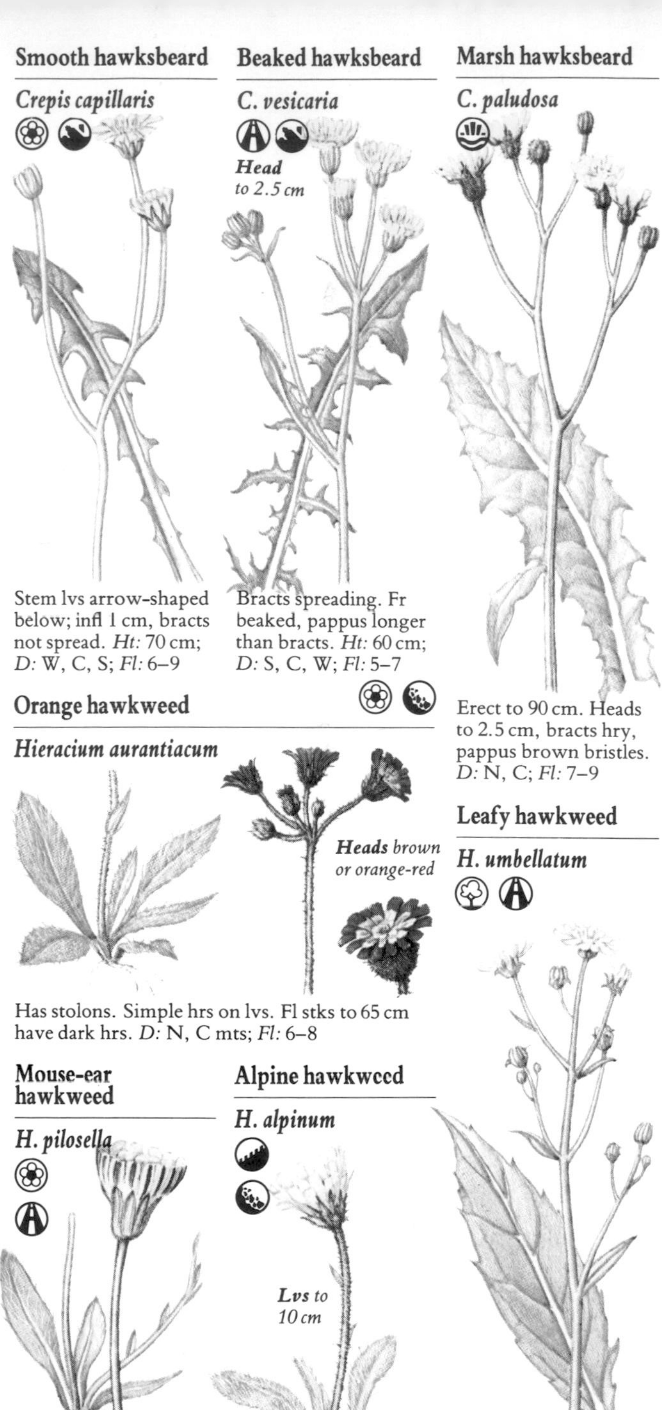

Smooth hawksbeard

Crepis capillaris

Stem lvs arrow-shaped below; infl 1 cm, bracts not spread. *Ht:* 70 cm; *D:* W, C, S; *Fl:* 6–9

Beaked hawksbeard

C. vesicaria

Bracts spreading. Fr beaked, pappus longer than bracts. *Ht:* 60 cm; *D:* S, C, W; *Fl:* 5–7

Marsh hawksbeard

C. paludosa

Erect to 90 cm. Heads to 2.5 cm, bracts hry, pappus brown bristles. *D:* N, C; *Fl:* 7–9

Orange hawkweed

Hieracium aurantiacum

Has stolons. Simple hrs on lvs. Fl stks to 65 cm have dark hrs. *D:* N, C mts; *Fl:* 6–8

Leafy hawkweed

H. umbellatum

Stems uprt lfy to 1 m. Crowded stem lvs to 15 cm below, smaller above. *D:* T; *Fl:* 8–9

Mouse-ear hawkweed

H. pilosella

Leaf hrs sparse above, dense below. Red stripe on ligule back *Ht:* 20 cm; *D:* T; *Fl:* 5–8

Alpine hawkweed

H. alpinum

Stems hry to 15 cm; lf hrs long, simple. Large heads to 3 cm. *D:* N, C; *Fl:* 7–8

Perennial sow thistle  

Sonchus arvensis

Marsh sow thistle  

S. palustris

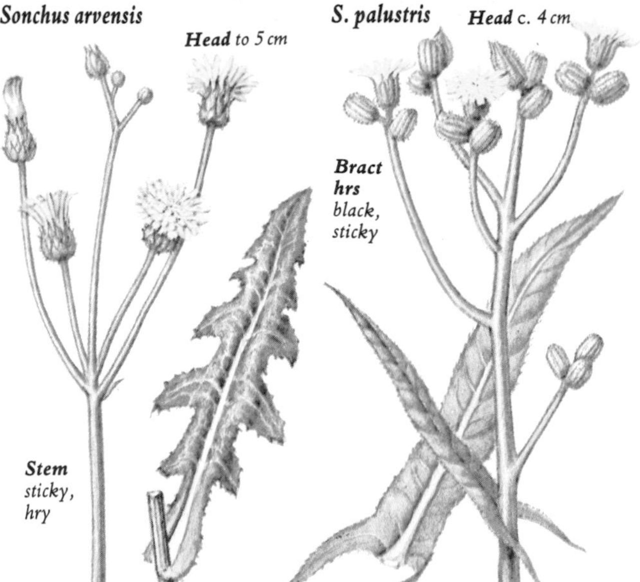

Robust per to 1.5 m. Round lobes on stem lvs encircle stem. Bract hrs yellow, sticky. *D:* T; *Fl:* 7–10

Ridged stems to 3 m. Lf lobes long, lance-shaped, spread, bases pointed. *D:* T (not N); *Fl:* 7–9

Smooth sow thistle

S. oleraceus

Stems ridged

Hairless ann to 1.5 m. Lvs spiny, pointed lobes encircle stem. Heads to 2.5 cm, fr rough. *D:* T; *Fl:* 6–8

Prickly sow thistle

S. asper

Like *S. oleraceus* but prickly lvs have round lobes encircling stem. Fr smooth. *Ht:* 1 m; *D:* T; *Fl:* 6–8

Scorzonera

Scorzonera laciniata

Scrambles to 60 cm; lvs pinnate, lobes narrow or round. Sev rows of bracts; fr base tubular. *D:* C, S; *Fl:* 4–7

Chicory

Cichorium intybus

Lamb's succory

Arnoseris minima

Nipplewort

Lapsana communis

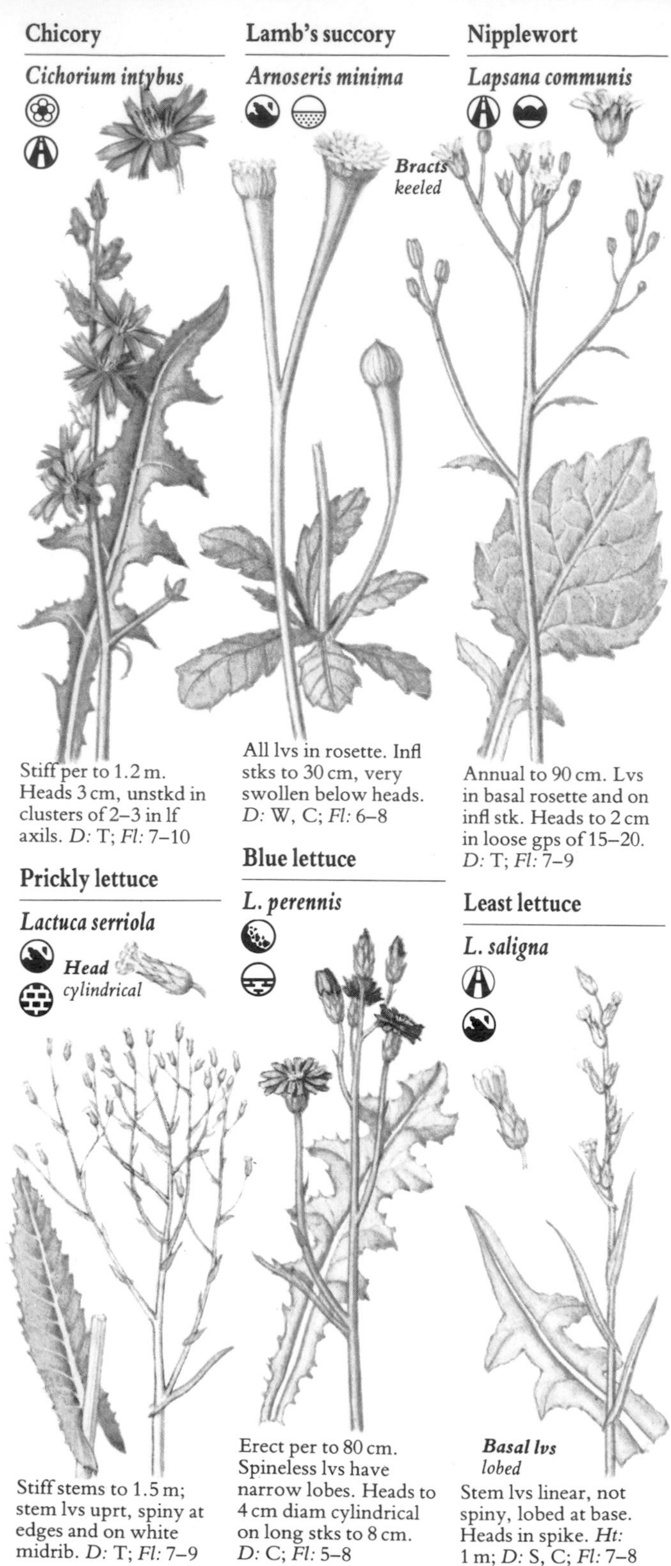

Stiff per to 1.2 m. Heads 3 cm, unstkd in clusters of 2–3 in lf axils. *D:* T; *Fl:* 7–10

All lvs in rosette. Infl stks to 30 cm, very swollen below heads. *D:* W, C; *Fl:* 6–8

Annual to 90 cm. Lvs in basal rosette and on infl stk. Heads to 2 cm in loose gps of 15–20. *D:* T; *Fl:* 7–9

Prickly lettuce

Lactuca serriola

Stiff stems to 1.5 m; stem lvs uprt, spiny at edges and on white midrib. *D:* T; *Fl:* 7–9

Blue lettuce

L. perennis

Erect per to 80 cm. Spineless lvs have narrow lobes. Heads to 4 cm diam cylindrical on long stks to 8 cm. *D:* C; *Fl:* 5–8

Least lettuce

L. saligna

Stem lvs linear, not spiny, lobed at base. Heads in spike. *Ht:* 1 m; *D:* S, C; *Fl:* 7–8

Wall lettuce

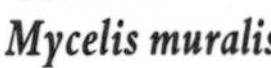

Mycelis muralis

Erect per to 1 m. Lower lvs have big top lobe itself 3-lobed; head of 5 ligulate fls. *D:* T; *Fl:* 7–9

Globe thistle

Echinops sphaerocephalus

Leaves pinnately lobed, hry esp below. Spherical head to 6 cm diam. *D:* S, C; *Fl:* 6–9

Lesser burdock

Arctium minus

Bushy bi to 1.3 m. Lvs unlobed, lower lf stks hollow. Many hooked bracts in heads. *D:* T; *Fl:* 7–9

Purple lettuce

Prenanthes purpurea

Leaves elliptical, glaucous to 80 cm. Heads 2–5 narrow cylindric fls. *Ht:* 1 m; *D:* C, S mts; *Fl:* 7–9

Milk thistle

Silybum marianum

Stems ridged, woolly, unwinged to 1.2 m. White patches on veins of spiny lvs. *D:* S, W; *Fl:* 6–8

Greater burdock

A. lappa

As *A. minus* but basal lvs broader, lf stks solid. Fls fewer, long-stkd heads 3 cm. *Ht:* 1.2 m; *D:* T (not far N); *Fl:* 7–9. *A. tomentosum* sim, cobweb-like hrs in fl head

Stemless carline thistle  

Carlina acaulis

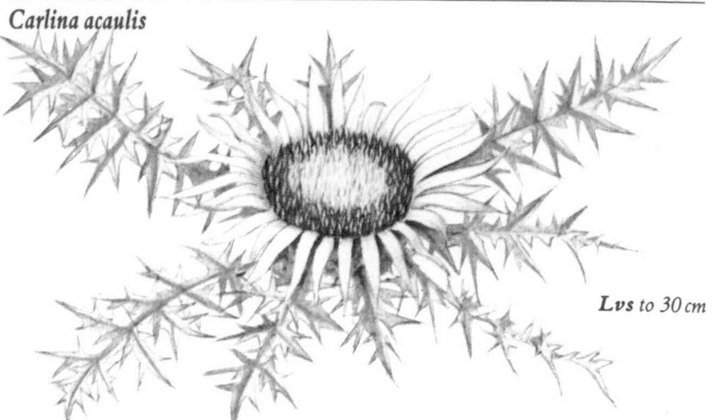

Unstalked heads to 5 cm in centre of rosette of spiny lvs. Inner bracts silvery white, spread. Fls white to brown. *Ht:* 30 cm; *D:* S; *Fl:* 5–9

Carline thistle 

Carlina vulgaris

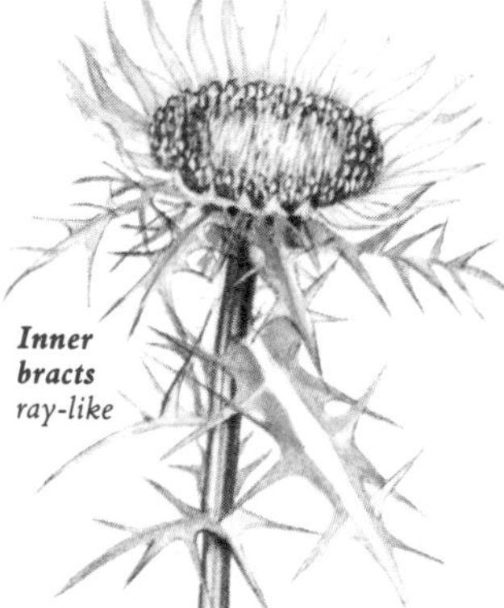

Erect bi to 60 cm. Rosette of woolly lvs in 1st year lost before 4 cm fls arise in 2nd. *D:* T; *Fl:* 7–10

Spear thistle  

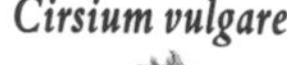

Cirsium vulgare

Basal lvs prickly, hry to 30 cm

Stems to 1.5 m, spiny wings discontinuous in broken patches. Globular heads to 5 cm. *D:* T; *Fl:* 7–10

Stemless thistle

C. acaule ***Head*** *to 4 cm*

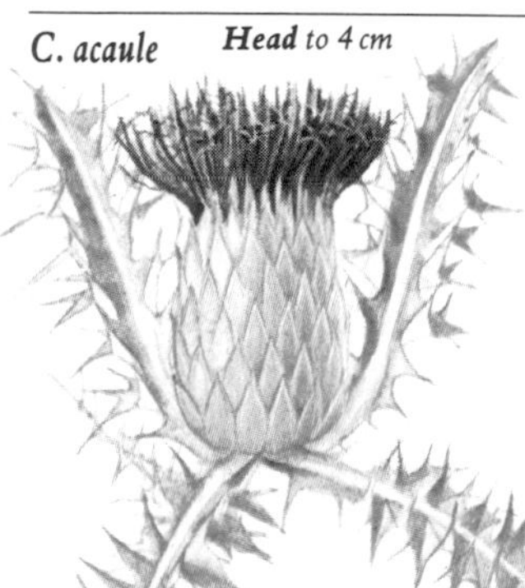

Rosette of spiny lvs to 15 cm. Sev central fl heads on v short stks. *Ht:* 20 cm; *D:* C, W, S; *Fl:* 7–9

Cabbage thistle  

C. oleraceum

Head *to 4 cm*

Stems uprt, grooved, unwinged to 1.2 m. Stem lvs unlobed, top lvs extend over heads. *D:* T; *Fl:* 7–9

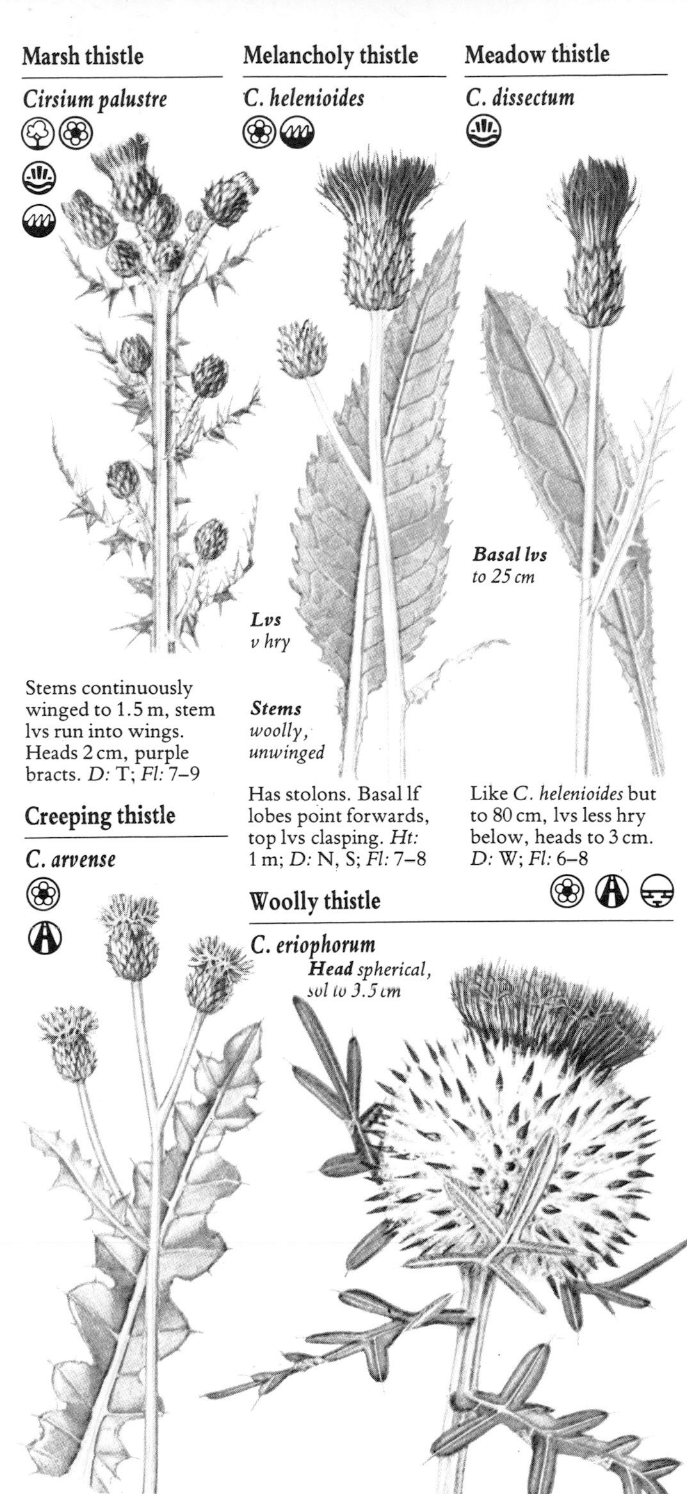

Marsh thistle

Cirsium palustre

Stems continuously winged to 1.5 m, stem lvs run into wings. Heads 2 cm, purple bracts. *D:* T; *Fl:* 7–9

Melancholy thistle

C. helenioides

Has stolons. Basal lf lobes point forwards, top lvs clasping. *Ht:* 1 m; *D:* N, S; *Fl:* 7–8

Meadow thistle

C. dissectum

Like *C. helenioides* but to 80 cm, lvs less hry below, heads to 3 cm. *D:* W; *Fl:* 6–8

Creeping thistle

C. arvense

Patch-forming per to 1 m. Stems lfy, not winged. Heads may be sol. *D:* T; *Fl:* 7–9

Woolly thistle

C. eriophorum

Robust bi. Stems ridged, unwinged to 1.5 m. Basal lvs 60 cm, pinnate lobed, cottony below. Dense woolly hrs on bracts. *D:* W, C; *Fl:* 7–9

Welted thistle

Carduus acanthoides

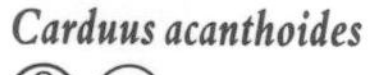

Plant *covered with cottony white hrs*

Winged stems to 1.5 m, wings stop well below unstkd fl heads to 2.5 cm. *D:* T; *Fl:* 6–8

Musk thistle

C. nutans

Heads *nodding to 5 cm*

Stems woolly, winged except below heads. Bracts spiny, spread. *Ht:* 80 cm; *D:* W, C; *Fl:* 5–8

Winged thistle

C. crispus

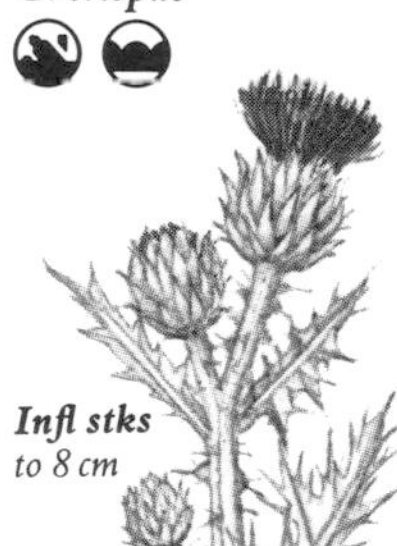

Infl stks *to 8 cm*

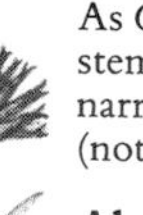

As *C. acanthoides* but stems near hrlss, wings narrow. *Ht:* 1 m; *D:* T (not UK); *Fl:* 6–10

Cotton thistle

Onopordum acanthium

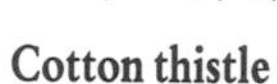

Head *to 5 cm*

Stems winged, woolly to 1.5 m. Globular heads, woolly bracts. *D:* C, S; *Fl:* 7–9

Alpine saw wort

Saussurea alpina

Lvs *woolly below*

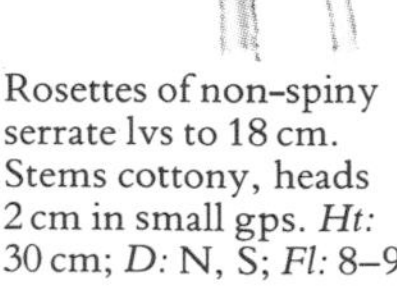

Rosettes of non-spiny serrate lvs to 18 cm. Stems cottony, heads 2 cm in small gps. *Ht:* 30 cm; *D:* N, S; *Fl:* 8–9

Alpine sow thistle

Cicerbita alpina

Ridged stem to 2 m, reddish hrs above. Heads 2 cm, stickily hry in loose gps. *D:* N, S; *Fl:* 7–9

Greater knapweed   

Centaurea scabiosa

Basal lvs pinnate. Outer florets big, spread. *Ht:* 70 cm; *D:* T; *Fl:* 7–9. *C. jacea* sim, brown bracts

Perennial cornflower  

C. montana

Creeping, rhizomatous. Winged stems to 80 cm. Outer florets blue, inner purple. *D:* C mts; *Fl:* 5–7

Cornflower 

C. cyanus

Stiff, cottony stems to 90 cm. Basal lvs pinnate lobed, hry; heads to 3 cm. *D:* T; *Fl:* 6–8

Black knapweed  

C. nigra

Tough, branching per, stems uprt, grooved, hry to 90 cm. Basal lvs unlobed. Heads to 4 cm diam, no spreading florets. Bracts dark at tips. *D:* W, C, S; *Fl:* 6–9

Rough star thistle  

C. aspera

Erect to 90 cm. Heads sol, 2.5 cm, bracts have finger-like spines spread at tips. *D:* SW; *Fl:* 7–9

Red star thistle 

C. calcitrapa

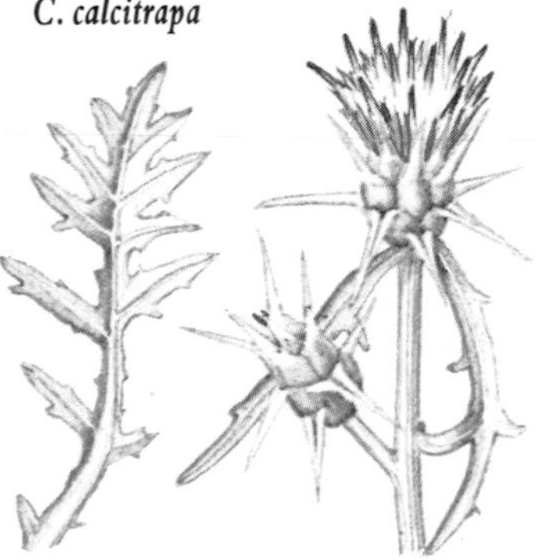

Pinnate lvs, lobes spined. Bracts spreading to 2.5 cm with 1 spine. *Ht:* 45 cm; *D:* S, W, C; *Fl:* 7–9

Saw wort

Serratula tinctoria

Hemp agrimony  

Eupatorium cannabinum

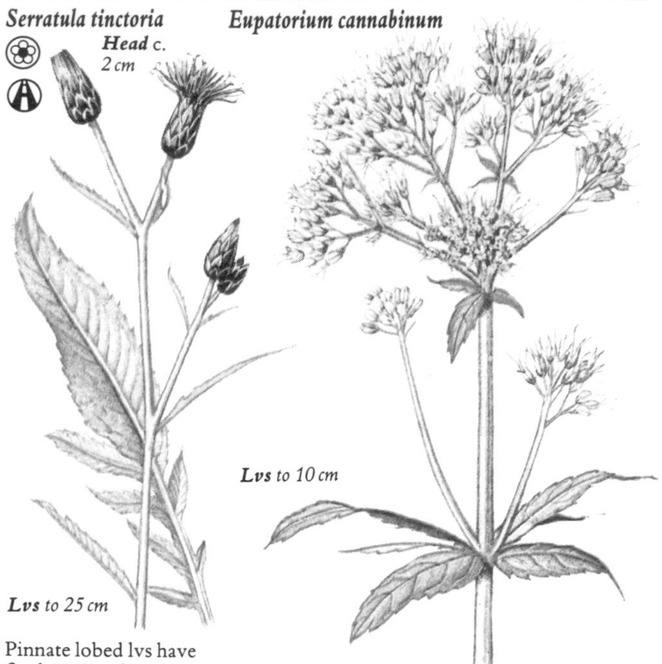

Pinnate lobed lvs have finely pointed teeth. ♂, ♀ fls separate. *Ht:* 65 cm; *D:* T (not NE); *Fl:* 7–9

Robust, uprt per to 1.2 m. Lvs opp, 3-lobed, lobes toothed. Heads in dense terminal gps each with *c.* 6 tubular florets. *D:* T; *Fl:* 7–9

Mountain everlasting  

Antennaria dioica

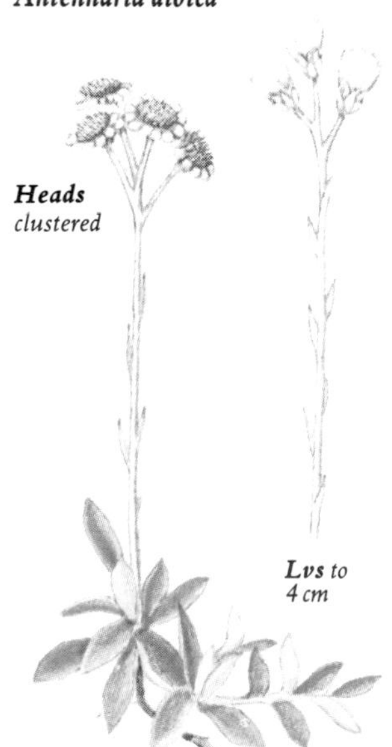

Has stolons. Lvs in rosettes have dense white hrs below. Bracts dense, woolly. *Ht:* 15 cm; *D:* T; *Fl:* 6–7

Common cudweed  

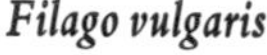

Filago vulgaris

Woolly uprt ann to 35 cm. Lvs uprt, wavy, white hrs; 20–40 heads form dense group. *D:* S, W, C; *Fl:* 7–8

Small cudweed

Logfia minima

Delicate ann to 15 cm; lvs to 1 cm. Heads, 3 mm, 3–6 in a cluster. *D:* T (not NE); *Fl:* 6–9

Heath cudweed

Omalotheca sylvatica

Head *2 mm*

Basal lvs to 8 cm. Axillary heads in loose spikes. *Ht:* 45 cm; *D:* T; *Fl:* 7–9

Helichrysum

H. arenarium

Basal lvs *to 7 cm, obovate*

Hairy per, stem lvs short, linear. Heads globular, bracts orange-yellow. *Ht:* 20 cm; *D:* S, C; *Fl:* 7–9

Dwarf cudweed

O. supina

Heads *form short spike*

Prostrate per, forms small tussocks. Lvs woolly. Fl shs to 12 cm. *D:* N, S, C; *Fl:* 7

Micropus

Bombycilaena erecta

Lvs *all narrow*

Heads in dense terminal gps to 1 cm diam; some lvs overtop fl clusters. *Ht:* 10 cm; *D:* S, C; *Fl:* 6–7

Marsh cudweed

Filaginella uliginosa

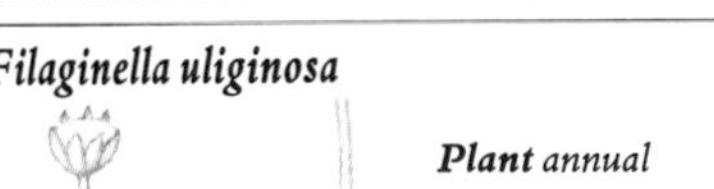

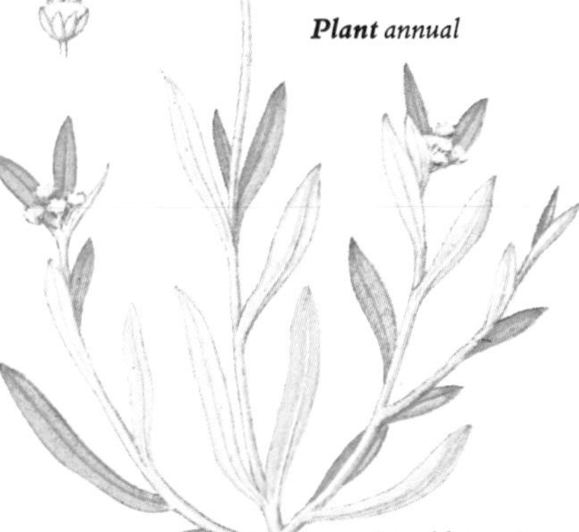

Plant *annual*

Basal lvs *to 5 cm*

Many brs from base; 3–10 heads in dense group, v long lvs at infl bse. *Ht:* 10 cm; *D:* T; *Fl:* 7–8

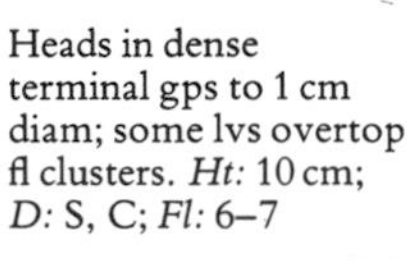

Yarrow

Achillea millefolium

Sneezewort

A. ptarmica

Aromatic per. Stems uprt to 45 cm, Lvs v cut. Heads *c.* 5 mm, 5-rayed in dense clusters. *D:* T; *Fl:* 6–8

Ridged shs to 60 cm. Lvs linear, serrate, unlobed. Heads *c.* 1.5 cm in loose cluster. *D:* T; *Fl:* 7–8

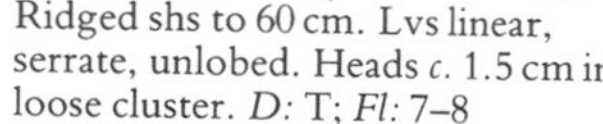

Nodding bur marigold

Bidens cernua

Trifid bur marigold

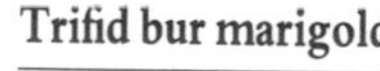

B. tripartita

Erect ann to 60 cm. Lvs unlobed, unstkd. Heads to 2.5 cm, drooping, no rays. *D:* T (not far N); *Fl:* 7–9

Many brs. Lvs to 15 cm, stkd, 3-lobed, serrate. Heads erect. *Ht:* 45 cm; *D:* T (not far N); *Fl:* 7–9

Butterbur

Petastites hybridus

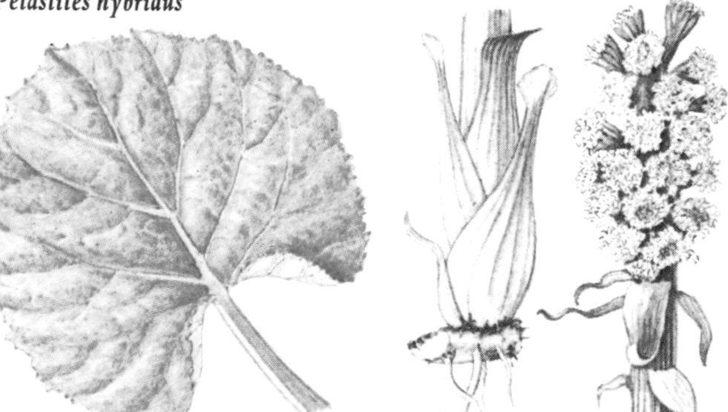

Rhizomatous per. Lvs to 90 cm. Fl shs to 40 cm. Serrate lvs appear after fl shs. Heads in dense gps, ♂, ♀ separate. *D:* T (not N); *Fl:* 3–5

Mugwort

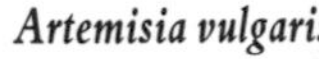

Artemisia vulgaris

Tufted aromatic per to 1.2 m. Lvs pinnate lobed, pointed, dark and hrlss above, white, woolly below. Heads oval. *D:* T; *Fl:* 7–9

Field wormwood

A. campestris

Unscented creeping per to 60 cm. Lvs v cut into narrow linear segs, hry at first then hrlss. Heads globular. *D:* T (not NW); *Fl:* 8–9

Wormwood

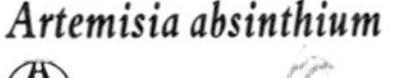

Artemisia absinthium

Aromatic per to 90 cm. Like *A. vulgaris* but lf segs more rounded, silky hrs on both sides. Heads globular or bell-shaped. *D:* T; *Fl:* 7–8

Sea wormwood

A. maritima

Very aromatic per to 50 cm. White woolly hrs all over lvs and stems; heads drooping. *D:* W, N; *Fl:* 8–9

Cotton weed

Otanthus maritimus

Woody-based per to 30 cm, stems densely woolly, white. Lvs not lobed, felty. Heads to 9 mm have felty white bracts. *D:* W; *Fl:* 8–9

Water plantain family Alismataceae

Aquatic or wetland herbs with unlobed, stalked, sometimes floating leaves. Flowers have three sepals and petals and 6 or 3 stamens. There are usually many free carpels.

Common water plantain

Alisma plantago-aquatica

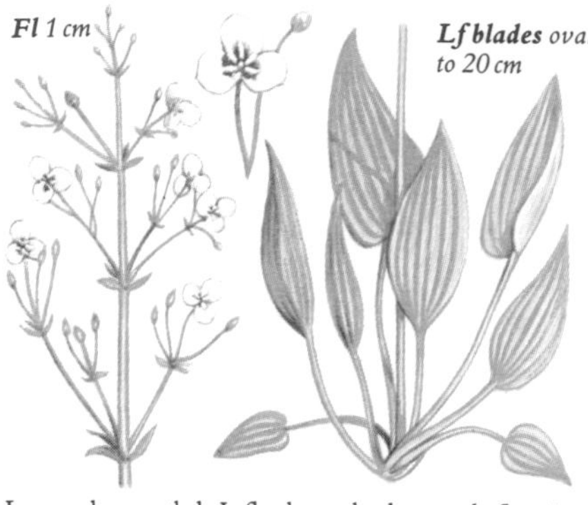

Leaves long-stkd. Infl v branched, carpels flat, 1 whorl. *Ht:* 80 cm; *D:* T (not far N); *Fl:* 6–8

Floating water plantain

Luronium natans *Lvs 8 cm*

Slim floating shs to 50 cm. Lvs long-stkd, fls sol, long-stkd in lf axils. *D:* W, C; *Fl:* 7–8

Star-fruit

Damasonium alisma

Stems to 30 cm; 6–10 carpels in 1 whorl make spread star when ripe. *D:* SW; *Fl:* 6–8

Parnassus-leaved water plantain

Caldesia parnassifolia

Erect per to 80 cm. Lf blades cleft at base, infl whorled. *D:* S, C, E; *Fl:* 7–9

Arrowhead

Sagittaria sagittifolia

Floating lvs oval, uprt arrow-shaped. ♂, ♀ separate, ♂ fls many stamens. *Ht:* 70 cm; *D:* T (not far N); *Fl:* 7–8

Lesser water plantain

Baldellia ranunculoides

Erect herb to 20 cm. Lf blades 3 cm. Fls 1.5 cm diam in umbel or 2 whorls, fl stks vary in length up to 10 cm; fr curved. *D:* W; *Fl:* 5–8

Flowering rush family Butomaceae
Frogbit family Hydrocharitaceae

Aquatic or wetland herbs. Flowering rushes have three-petalled and sepalled flowers in umbels and 6–9 unjoined stamens and carpels. Frogbit flowers have three petals, three or no sepals, one to many stamens and 2–5 fused carpels.

Flowering rush

Butomus umbellatus

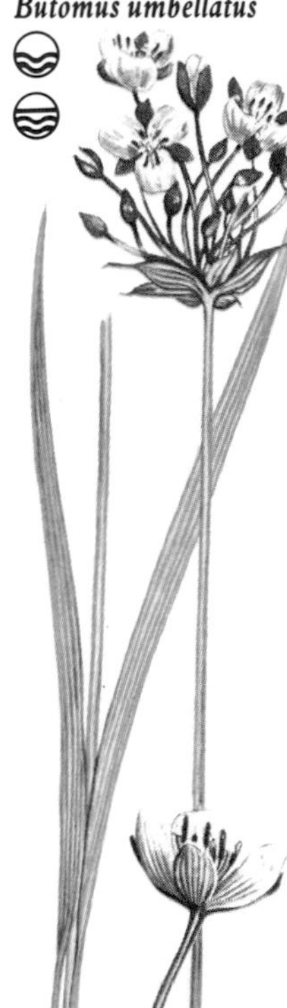

Hairless per. Lvs long, narrow, twisted. Fls *c.* 3 cm diam in an umbel with pointed bracts. *Ht:* 1 m; *D:* T (not NW); *Fl:* 7–9

Water soldier

Stratiotes aloides

Dense lfy clusters, new plants develop on stolons. Lvs stiff, spiny-toothed. Fls to 4 cm on short shs. *Ht:* 40 cm; *D:* C, E; *Fl:* 6–8

Canadian pondweed

Elodea canadensis

Submerged stems to 3 m. Lvs 3 per whorl have tiny teeth. Fls 5 mm. *D:* T (not N); *Fl:* 5–10

Frogbit

Hydrocharis morsus-ranae

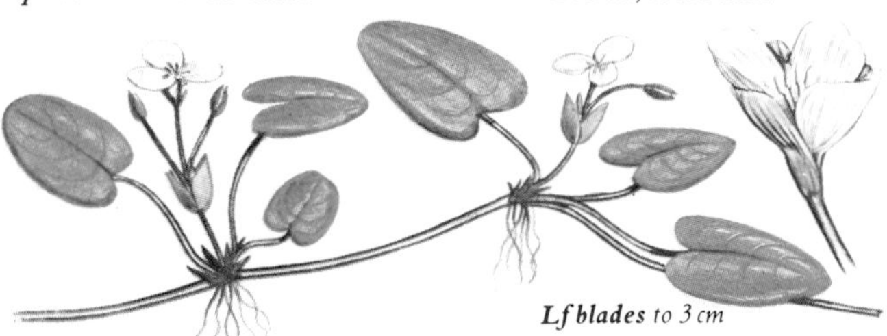

Floating herb to 3 m; rts in bunches with lvs. Floating lvs heart-shaped. Opp pair of bracts at fl stk base. *D:* T (not N); *Fl:* 7–8

Eel grass family Zosteraceae

Marine grass-like herbs with creeping rhizomes. Flowers in dense spike are alternately male and female.

Eel grass 

Zostera marina

Rhizomatous per to 60 cm. Lvs to 50 cm long by 1 cm broad, rounded at tips, sheathed at base. *Z. noltii* sim but lvs to 12 cm. *D:* T; *Fl:* 6–9

Pondweed family Potamogetonaceae

Flexible-stemmed aquatics. Floating leaves are broad, submerged ones narrow. Flowers have 4 bracts and 4 stamens.

Broad-leaved pondweed 

Potamogeton natans

Stems to 5 m. Floating lf blades to 1.3 cm, joint at stk attachment. Lf stks winged. *D:* T; *Fl:* 5–9

Shining pondweed  

P. lucens

Stems to 6 m. Submerged lvs to 20 cm, wavy edges, no floating lvs. *D:* T (not N); *Fl:* 6–9

Bog pondweed 

P. polygonifolius

Stems to 60 cm. Floating lvs to 6 cm with large blunt stipules to 4 cm at base. *D:* W; *Fl:* 5–10

Opposite-leaved pondweed 

Groenlandia densa

Much branched stems to 30 cm; lvs in opp prs, toothed edges, all submerged. *D:* W; *Fl:* 5–9

Tasselweed family Ruppiaceae

Naiad family Najadaceae

Submerged aquatic herbs. Tasselweeds have hair-like leaves and flowers in umbels without sepals or petals. Naiads have whorled leaves and separate male and female flowers, the male with one stamen and a bract, female with 2–4 stigmas.

Beakeded tasselweed *Ruppia maritima* — **Slender naiad** *Najas flexilis* — **Holly-leaved naiad** *N. marina*

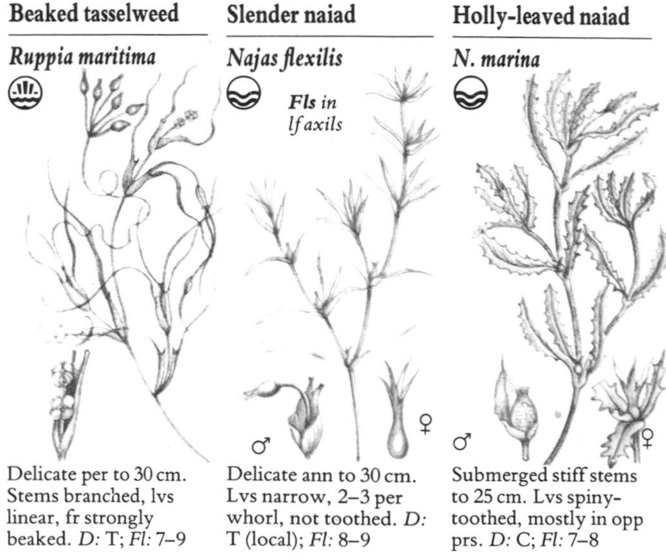

Beaked tasselweed — *Ruppia maritima*: Delicate per to 30 cm. Stems branched, lvs linear, fr strongly beaked. *D:* T; *Fl:* 7–9

Slender naiad — *Najas flexilis*: Delicate ann to 30 cm. Lvs narrow, 2–3 per whorl, not toothed. *D:* T (local); *Fl:* 8–9

Holly-leaved naiad — *N. marina*: Submerged stiff stems to 25 cm. Lvs spiny-toothed, mostly in opp prs. *D:* C; *Fl:* 7–8

Lily family Liliaceae

A diverse family of herbs. Flowers have two whorls of three petal-like parts which may be fused or free and 6 stamens. The ovary of three fused carpels is below other flower parts.

Orange lily *Lilium bulbiferum* — **Martagon lily** *L. martagon*

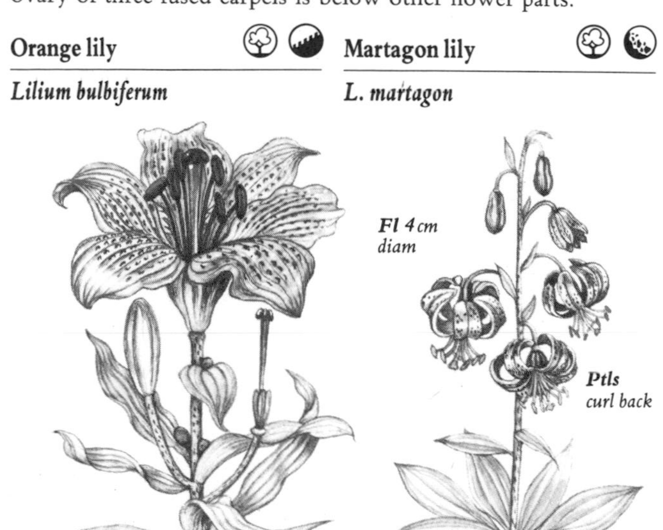

Orange lily — *Lilium bulbiferum*: Leaves linear, often bulbils in axils; 1–5 fls per gp, curled ptls. *Ht:* 50 cm; *D:* C; *Fl:* 6–7

Martagon lily — *L. martagon*: Erect stems to 1 m. Lvs linear in widely separated whorls. Fls nodding. *D:* S, C, E; *Fl:* 8–9

Kerry lily

Simethis planifolia

All lvs basal, linear to 45 cm. Infl loose with short bracts, infl stk to 45 cm, fl 2 cm. *Ht:* 1 m; *D:* W; *Fl:* 5–7

Snowdon lily

Lloydia serotina

Bulbous per; stems to 15 cm with 2–4 linear lvs. Fls 2 cm, 1–2 per sh, ptls veined. *D:* C, S, Wales; *Fl:* 6

May lily

Maianthemum bifolium

Rhizomatous per to 20 cm. Lvs to 6 cm, heart-shaped. Infl dense, terminal, 8–15 fls with 4 ptls, 4 stamens, fr red. *D:* T; *Fl:* 5–7

St Bernard's lily

Anthericum liliago

Delicate per to 60 cm. Lvs all basal, flat, 5 mm broad. Infl terminal, fls to 5 cm divided into 6 spread segs. *D:* C; *Fl:* 5–6

Wild tulip

Tulipa sylvestris

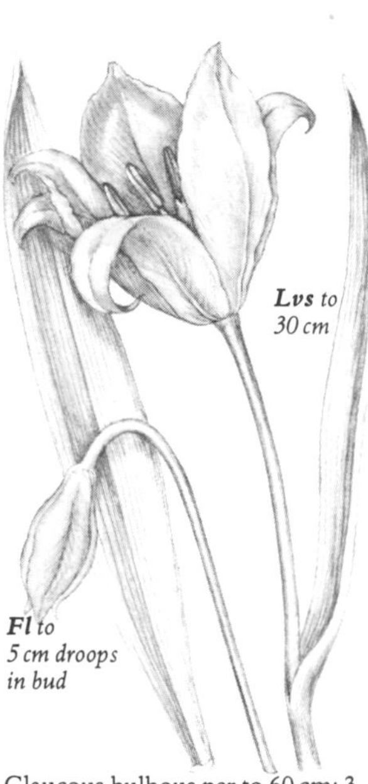

Glaucous bulbous per to 60 cm; 3 basal linear lvs. Fl erect, spreading, bell-shaped. *D:* C, S; *Fl:* 4–5

Spring squill

Scilla verna

Bulbous per; infl 2–5 fls, bracts longer than fl stks. *Ht:* 20 cm; *D:* W coasts; *Fl:* 4–5

Bluebell

Hyacinthoides non-scripta

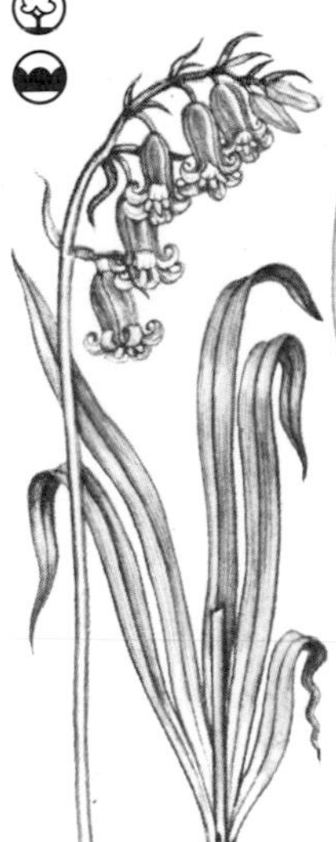

Bulbous per, narrow channelled lvs. Fl stk to 50 cm, 1-sided infl droops slightly. Fl bell-shaped to 2 cm. *D:* W; *Fl:* 4–6

Autumn squill

S. autumnalis

Leaves to 15 cm appear after fls; infl 4–20 fls no bracts. *Ht:* 20 cm; *D:* W; *Fl:* 7–9

Lily of the valley

Convallaria majalis

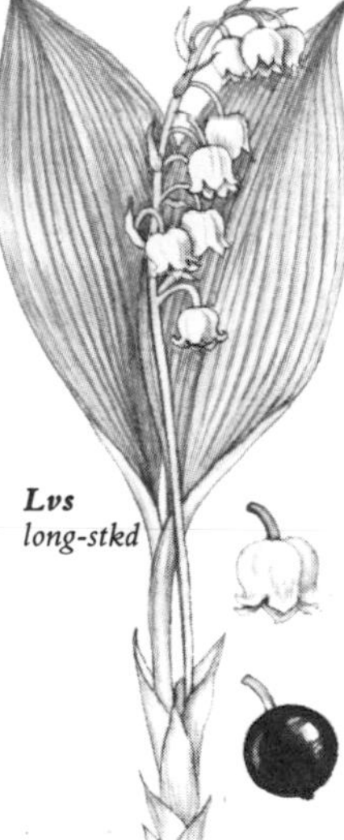

Rhizomatous per; lvs to 20 cm, elliptic. Infl 1-sided, 6–12 nodding fls. Fr a red, poisonous berry. *Ht:* 20 cm; *D:* T; *Fl:* 5–6

Alpine squill

S. bifolia

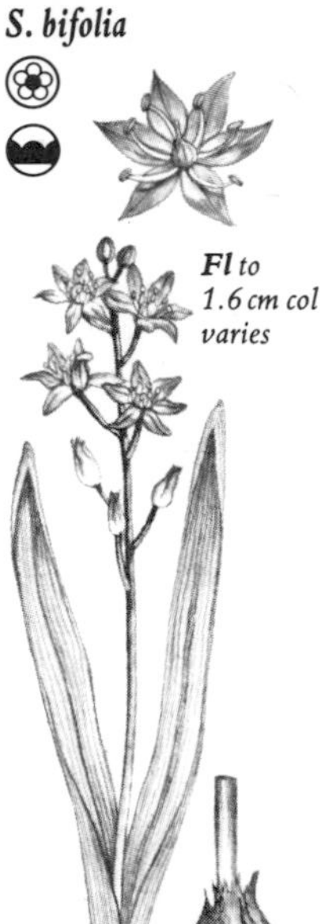

Usually only 2 glossy linear lvs. Infl loose 2–8 fls. *Ht:* to 20 cm; *D:* C, S; *Fl:* 3–6

Fritillary

Fritillaria meleagris

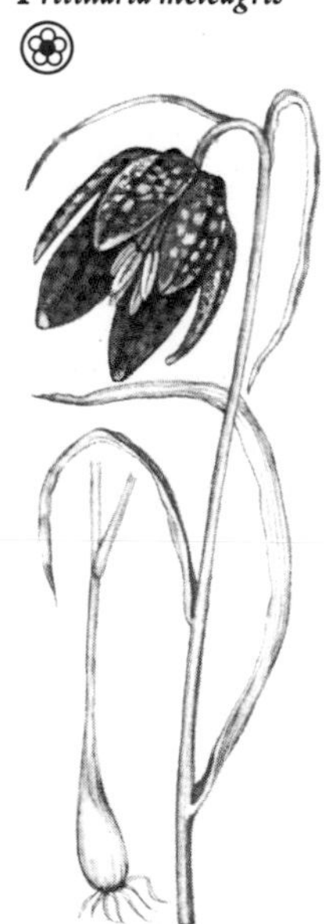

Bulbous per to 50 cm; 3–6 narrow stem lvs; 1 or 2 nodding fls to 5 cm. *D:* C, W; *Fl:* 4–5

Ramsons

Allium ursinum

Garlic smell as all *Allium* spp; 2 broad lvs; ridged fl stk to 45 cm, no bulbils. *D:* T (not far N); *Fl:* 4–6

Round-headed leek

A. sphaerocephalon

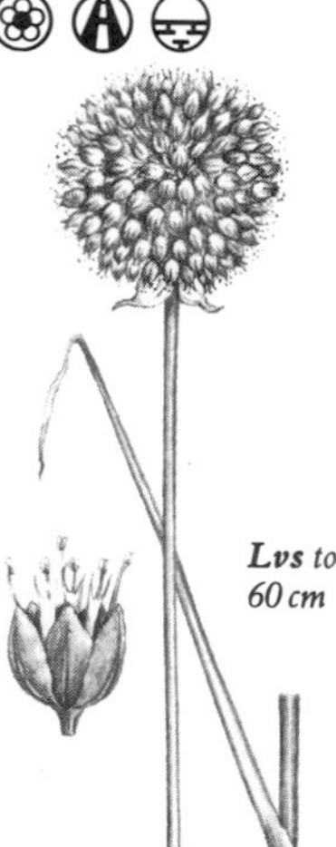

Hollow lvs; dense infl no bulbils, 2 bracts, fls short-stkd. *Ht:* 60 cm; *D:* S; *Fl:* 6–8

Field garlic

A. oleraceum

Leaves hollow below. Infl of few fls, many bulbils and 2 bracts longer than fls. *Ht:* 60 cm; *D:* T; *Fl:* 7–8

Sand leek

A. scordoprasum

Flat linear lvs have rough edges. Infl has 2 bracts shorter than few fls, many bulbils. *Ht:* 60 cm; *D:* T (not N, SW); *Fl:* 5–8

Crow garlic

A. vineale

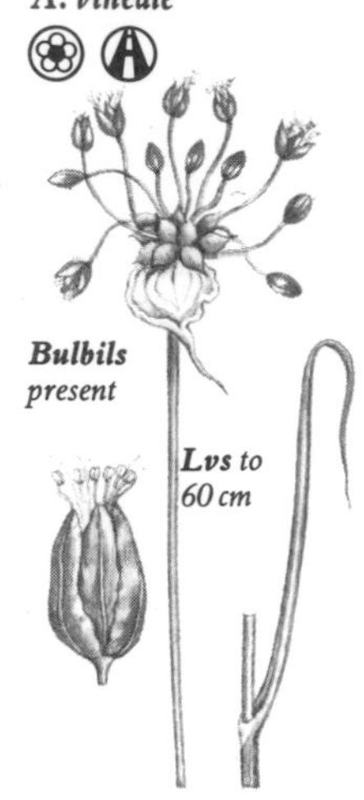

Hollow lvs; stamens protrude; 1 infl bract equals fls. *Ht:* 60 cm; *D:* T (not N); *Fl:* 6–7

Wild leek

A. ampeloprasum

Strong ridge on lf underside, infl dense, few bulbils, 1 bract soon falling. *Ht:* 1.5 m; *D:* W; *Fl:* 7–8

Chives

A. schoenoprasum

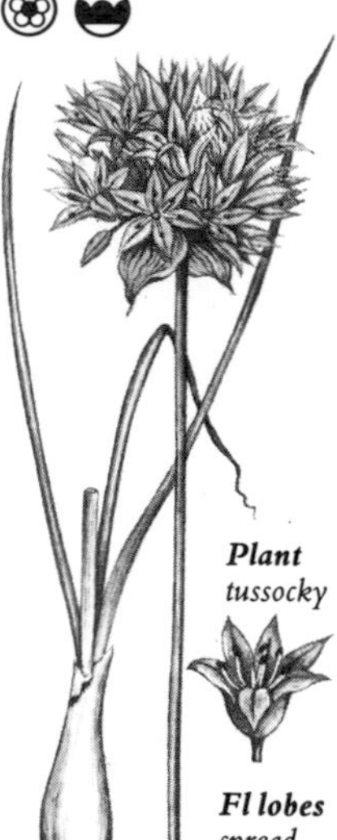

Leaves v narrow; infl dense, 2 bracts, no bulbils. *Ht:* 30 cm; *D:* T (local); *Fl:* 6–7

Small grape hyacinth

Muscari botryoides

Linear lvs broader above, 2–4 per plant. Infl dense. *Ht:* 20 cm; *D:* S, C; *Fl:* 3–5

Wild leek

A. scordoprasum subsp rotundum

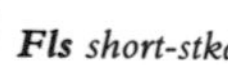

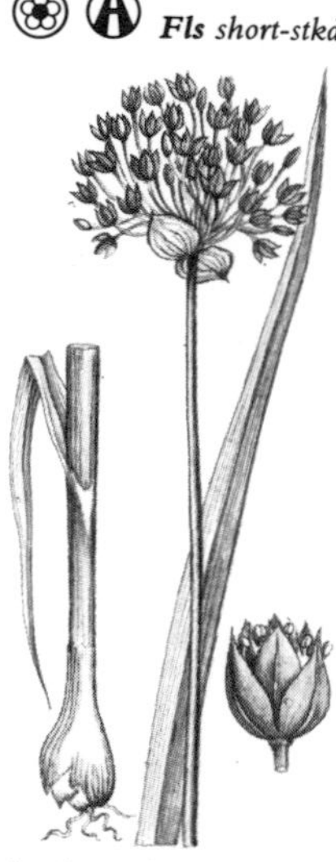

As *A. scordoprasum* (p. 162) but lf edges not rough or toothed. *Ht:* 30 cm; *D:* C, E; *Fl:* 6–8

Grape hyacinth

M. neglectum

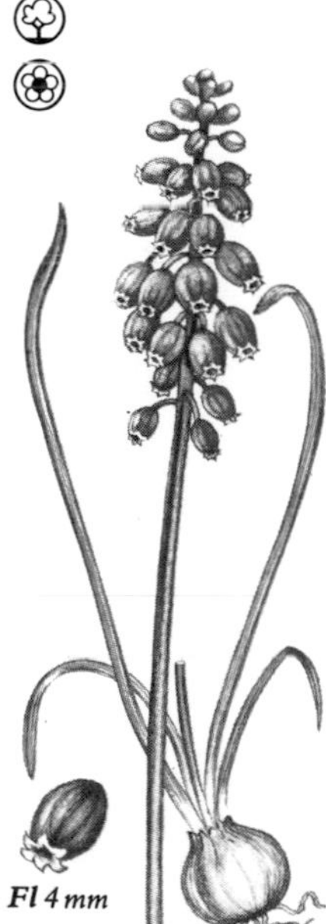

Leaves fine to 3 mm broad, 3–5 per plant. Infl long, dense, fls short-stkd. *Ht:* 17 cm; *D:* SW; *Fl:* 4–5

German garlic

A. senescens

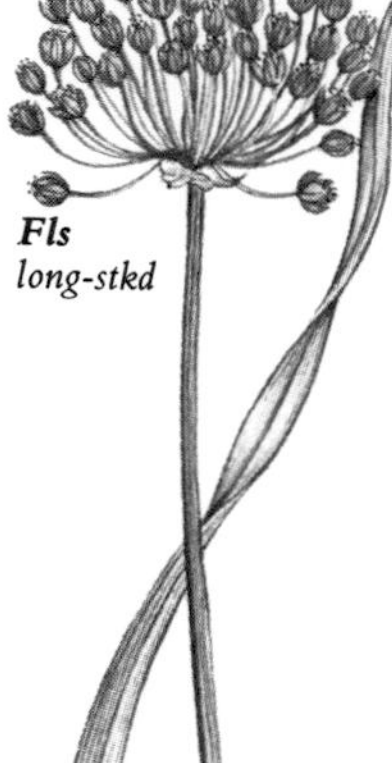

Flat lvs; infl dense, stk ridged, 2 short bracts, no bulbils. *Ht:* 25 cm; *D:* SE; *Fl:* 6–7

Tassel hyacinth

M. comosum

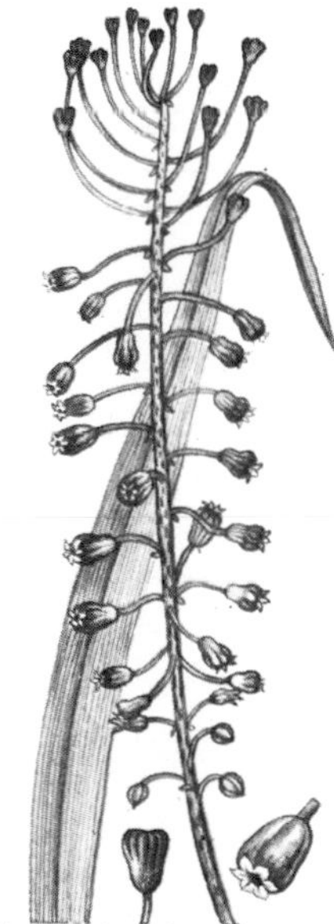

Leaves 1 cm broad; infl loose fl stks v long, fls erect. *Ht:* 35 cm; *D:* S, C; *Fl:* 4–7

Meadow saffron

Colchicum autumnale

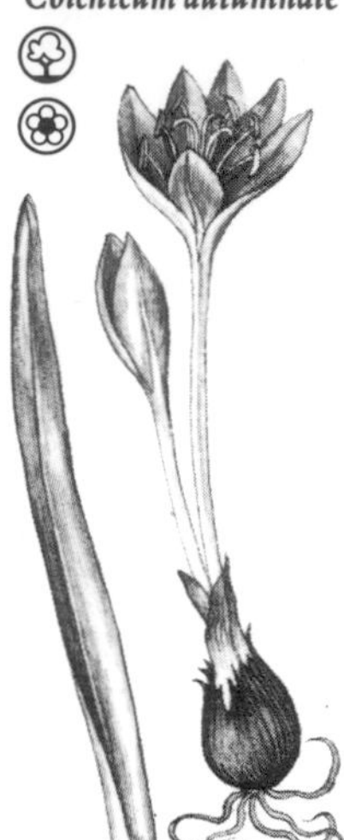

Linear lvs appear in spring, long-tubed fls in autumn. *Ht:* 25 cm; *D:* S, C; *Fl:* 8–10

Spiked star of Bethlehem

O. pyrenaicum

Linear lvs to 60 cm; infl of many fls all less than 1 cm, all fl stks equal length. *Ht:* to 1 m; *D:* SW; *Fl:* 6–7

Common star of Bethlehem

Ornithogalum umbellatum

***Fl** to 2 cm*

Narrow lvs; loose infl, 5–15 fls, longest stks on lowest fls, ptls free. *Ht:* 20 cm; *D:* T (not N); *Fl:* 4–6

Yellow star of Bethlehem

Gagea lutea

Single hooded lf to 45 cm. Infl an umbel, 2–3 bracts at base, 1–5 fls. *Ht:* 45 cm; *D:* T (not N, W); *Fl:* 3–5

Drooping star of Bethlehem

O. nutans

Leaves to 60 cm channelled. Infl 1-sided, 2–12 large fls to 3 cm, stks all equal. *Ht:* 45 cm; *D:* S; *Fl:* 4–5

Gagea

G. arvensis

Two linear basal lvs; infl a loose umbel, 2 large hry bracts at base, fl stks hry, fls 3 cm diam. *Ht:* 25 cm; *D:* C, W; *Fl:* 2–4

Meadow gagea

Gagea pratensis

***Bracts** equal fl stks*

One v keeled basal lf; infl 1–5 fls, 2 bracts at base equal fl stks. *Ht:* 15 cm; *D:* E; *Fl:* 3–4

Belgian gagea

G. spathaca

***Fl stks** hrlss*

Has 2 v narrow basal lvs. Infl 2–5 fls, 2 bracts. *Ht:* to 15 cm; *D:* C, E; *Fl:* 4–5

Least gagea

G. minima

Has single v narrow basal lf. Infl 1–7 fls with 2 basal bracts, slim fl stks. *Ht:* to 45 cm; *D:* E; *Fl:* 3–5

Scottish asphodel

Tofieldia pusilla

Rhizomatous herb to 20 cm; lvs 3–5 veins, stiff, erect; infl dense, fl stks lflss, fls 2 mm. *D:* N. S; *Fl:* 6–8

German asphodel

T. calyculata

As *T. pusilla* but infl stk lfy, each fl has unlobed and 3-lobed bract. Plant robust. *Ht:* 20 cm; *D:* C, E; *Fl:* 7–8

Bog asphodel

Narthecium ossifragum

Rhizomatous, mat-forming. Lvs strongly flattened as *Iris* spp (p 168). Fl stk to 1 cm, 1 bract. *Ht:* 30 cm; *D:* W; *Fl:* 7–9

Wild asparagus

Asparagus officinalis

Hairless herb to 1.5 m. Stems die back in winter. Brs lf-like, narrow, clustered. ♂, ♀ fls separate, 1 or 2 in lf axils. *D:* W coasts; *Fl:* 6–7

Whorled Solomon's seal

Polygonatum verticillatum

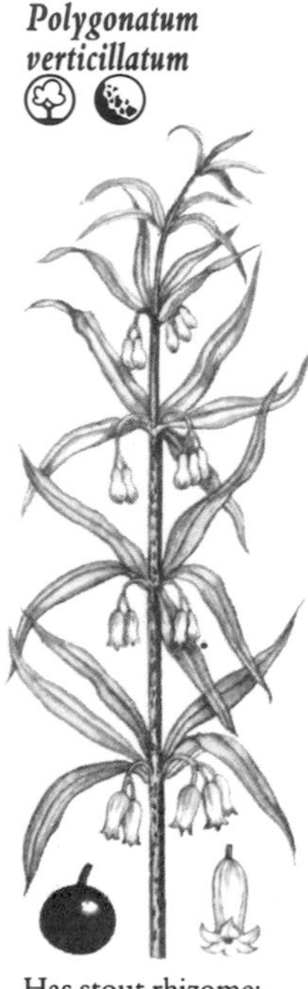

Has stout rhizome; stems v ridged, lvs linear, 3–6 per whorl. Fls 1–4 per stk. *Ht:* 60 cm; *D:* T; *Fl:* 6–7

Herb Paris

Paris quadrifolia

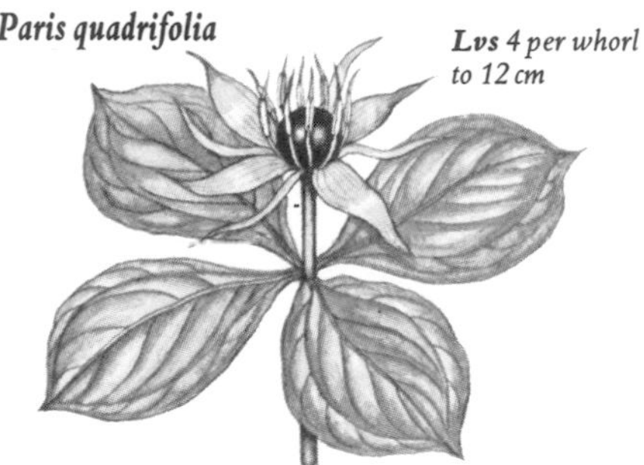

Rhizomatous, hrlss per to 40 cm. Fls 4 equal ptls and spls. Fr a black berry. *D:* T; *Fl:* 5–8

Solomon's seal

P. multiflorum

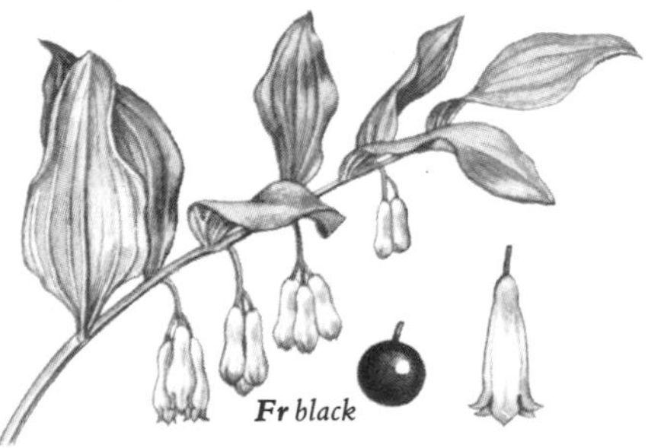

Stems unridged to 80 cm. Lvs alt, unstkd. Fls to 1.5 cm, 2–5 per gp. *D:* T (not N); *Fl.* 5–6

Butcher's broom

Ruscus aculeatus

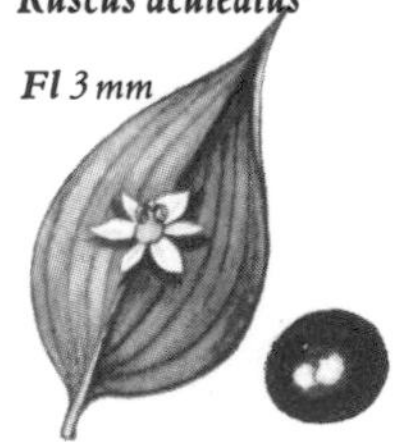

Erect, stiff evergreen to 80 cm. Shs lf-like, leathery, sharp points. ♂, ♀ fls separate on flat shs in axil of small bract. *D:* W; *Fl:* 1–4

Daffodil family Amaryllidaceae

Bulbous herbs. Flowers surrounded by a non-green bract (spathe) have petals in two whorls, the inner ones often trumpet shaped. The ovary lies below other flower parts.

Wild daffodil

Narcissus pseudonarcissus

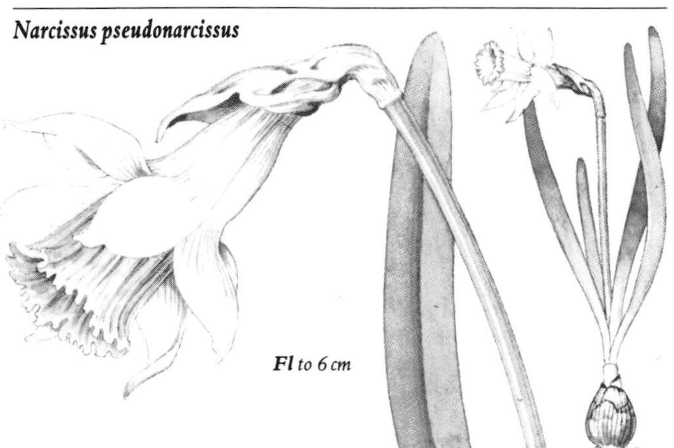

Erect glaucous lvs narrow, ridged. Fl stk to 35 cm, 2 ridges. Fl has trumpet equal in length to spread outer ptl whorl. *D:* W; *Fl:* 2–4

Summer snowflake

Leucojum aestivum

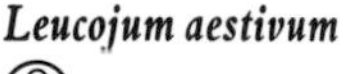

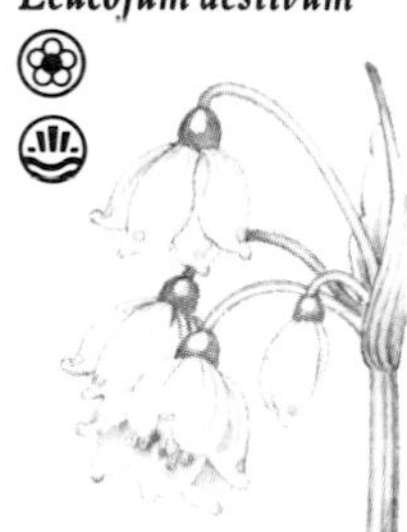

Linear lvs; infl 3–5 fls each 1.5 cm, bract green-tipped. *Ht:* 45 cm; *D:* C; *Fl:* 4–5

Spring snowflake

L. vernum

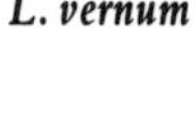

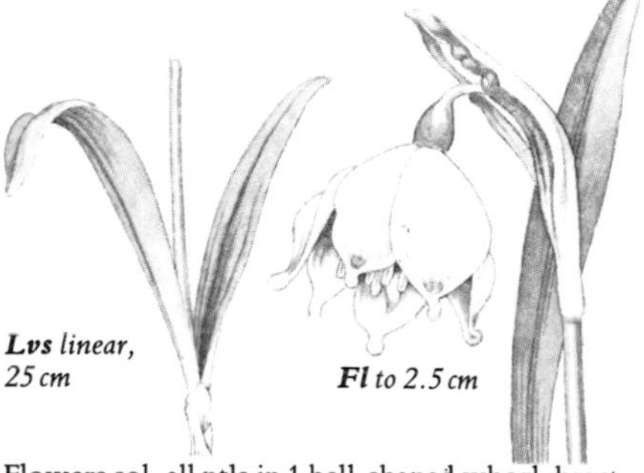

Flowers sol, all ptls in 1 bell-shaped whorl, bract green at centre. *Ht:* 25 cm; *D:* C; *Fl:* 2–4

Snowdrop

Galanthus nivalis

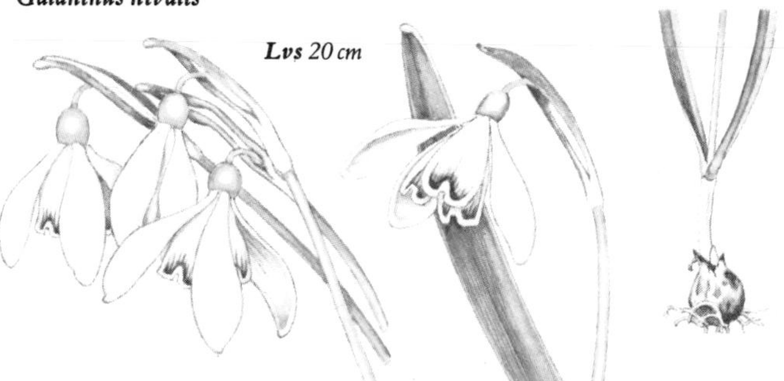

Linear lvs, outer ptl whorl to 1.7 cm, 2 × length of bell-shaped inner whorl. Bract 2-lobed, green at centre. *Ht:* 20 cm; *D:* C, S, W; *Fl:* 1–3

Iris family Iridaceae

Plants with linear sheathing leaves not divided into blades and stalks. Flowers have 6 petals in two whorls joined in a tube, three stamens and one or two bracts. The ovary is inferior.

Yellow iris

Iris pseudacorus

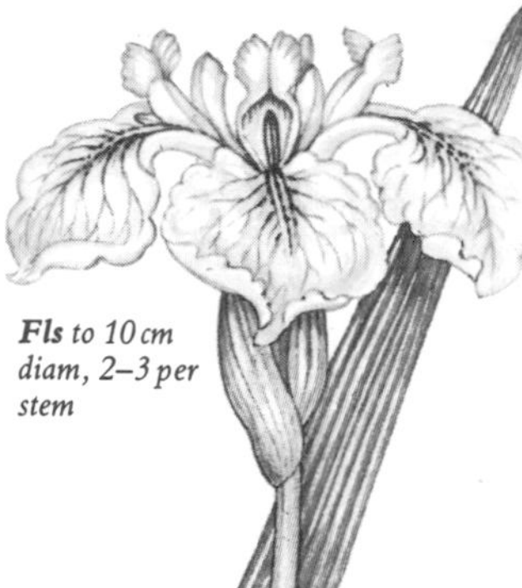

***Fls** to 10 cm diam, 2–3 per stem*

Tuberous rhizome. Infl stk flat, indiv fl stks as long as ovary. *Ht:* 1 m; *D:* T (not far N); *Fl:* 5–7

Butterfly iris

I. spuria

***Fls** to 5 cm diam, 1–3 per stem*

Rhizomatous per to 60 cm. Flat part of outer ptl whorl short compared with shaft. *D:* C, S; *Fl:* 5–6

Wild iris

I. aphylla

Leaves as long or longer than infl stk. Like garden iris (*I. germanica*). *Ht:* 70 cm; *D:* EC; *Fl:* 5–6

Siberian iris

I. sibirica

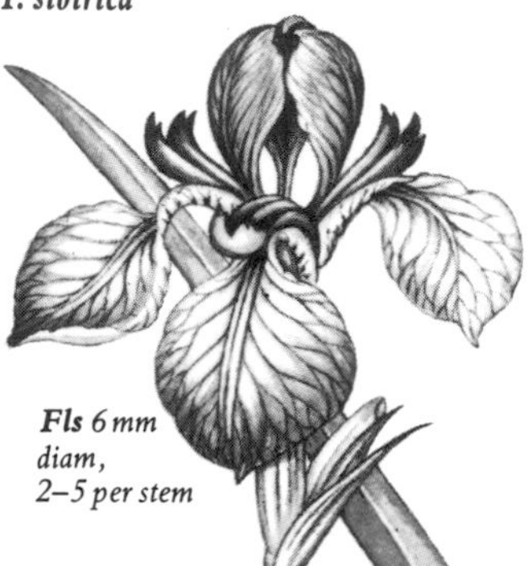

***Fls** 6 mm diam, 2–5 per stem*

Tussocky. Infl stk 70 cm, longer than lvs. Bracts brown, outer ptls rounded at tip. *D:* C, E; *Fl:* 5–6

Stinking iris

I. foetidissima

***Fl** 8 cm diam*

Strong-smelling erect per to 80 cm. Lvs evergreen; infl stk ridged on 1 side, indiv fl stks 4 × ovary length, 2–3 fls per stem. *D:* W; *Fl:* 5–7

Sand crocus

Romulea columnea

Very slim lvs longer than fl stk, 2 ptl whorls similar. *Ht:* 8 cm; *D:* W; *Fl:* 3–5

Spring crocus

Crocus vernus

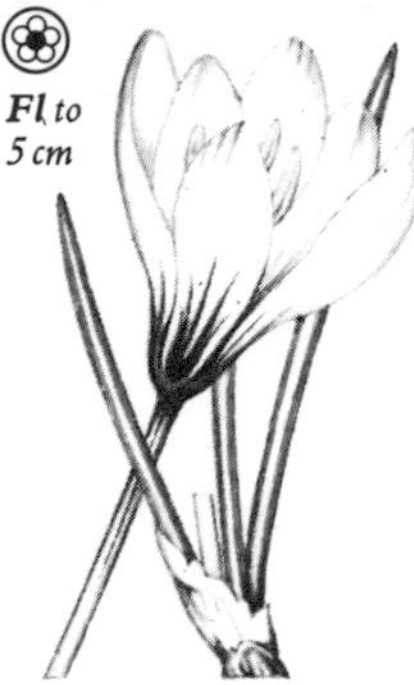

Channelled lvs, white line in groove, ptls all sim, joined below. *Ht:* 7 cm; *D:* W; *Fl:* 3–5

Blue-eyed grass

Sisyrinchium bermudianum

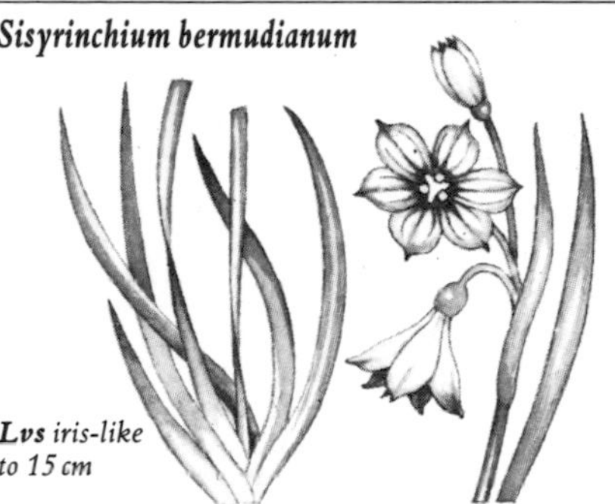

Erect per to 45 cm. Infl of 2–4 fls each 1.5 cm diam, all ptls sim. *D:* C, W; *Fl:* 7

Gladiolus

Gladiolus illyricus

Erect, hrlss to 90 cm. Lvs to 30 cm. Infl 1-sided spike, 2 lf-like bracts at base of each 3 cm fl, ptl tube short. *D:* W; *Fl:* 6–8

Yam family Dioscoreaceae

Herbaceous or woody climbers with rhizome tubers and spirally arranged leaves. Clustered bell-shaped flowers have 6 petals, 3 or 6 stamens and an inferior three-celled ovary.

Black bryony

Tamus communis

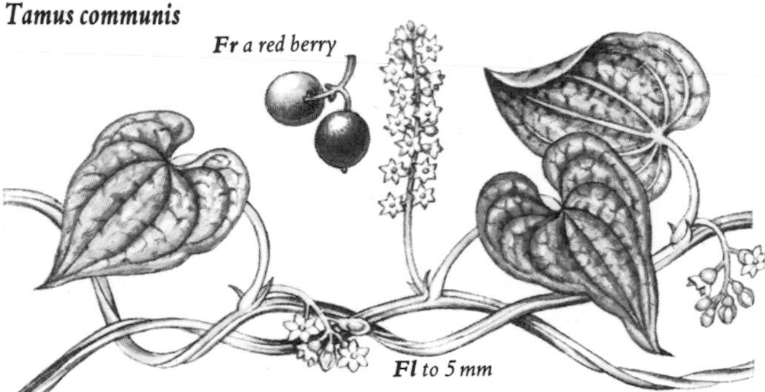

Clambers to 4 m. Lvs heart-shaped to 10 cm. ♂, ♀ fls axillary on separate plants, ♂ stkd, 6 stamens, ♀ unstkd. *D:* W; *Fl:* 5–7

Orchid family Orchidaceae

Rhizomatous perennials forming close associations with root fungi. Unlobed leaves have parallel veins. Asymmetrical flowers in spikes are often large and showy. Similar sepals and petals form six flower segments: one back and two side sepals, two erect petals and one large central lip.

Lady orchid 

Orchis purpurea

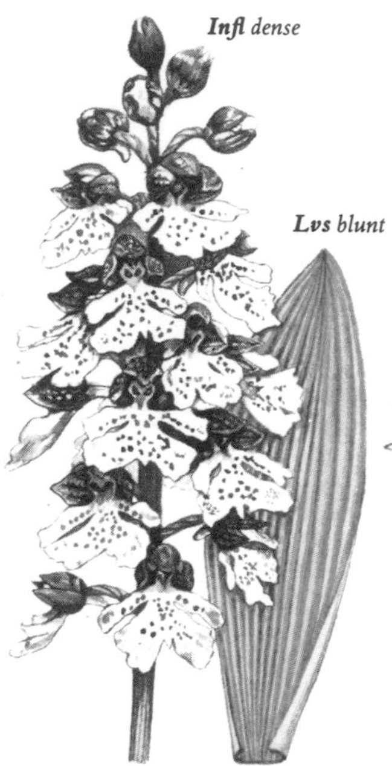

Leaves spotted. Fls have top lobes joined in helmet. Lip has 2 broad lobes. *Ht:* 30 cm; *D:* C, S; *Fl:* 5

Military orchid   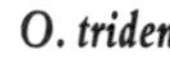

O. militaris

Helmet grey and pink; outer fl lobes v pointed, lip lobes spread. *Ht:* 35 cm; *D:* C, S; *Fl:* 5–6

Early purple orchid  

O. mascula

***Lip** 3-lobed*

***Lvs** to 20 cm*

Blunt lvs, round dark blotches. Fl spur upcurved, long, thick. *Ht:* 45 cm; *D:* T (not far N); *Fl:* 4–6

Toothed orchid   

O. tridentata

Dense globular infl. Prominent fl lip, lobes round with central tooth. *Ht:* 20 cm; *D:* E; *Fl:* 3–5

Monkey orchid

O. simia

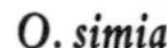

As *O. militaris* but slim stems *c.* 20 cm. Pale helmet, white veins. Lip lobes narrow, linear, outer lobes longest. *D:* S, W; *Fl:* 5–6

Loose-flowered orchid

O. laxiflora

Lvs to 18 cm

Robust stems to 50 cm. Lvs narrow, pointed, lance-shaped. Fl lip has 2 big round lobes. *D:* SW; *Fl:* 5–6

Burnt orchid

O. ustulata

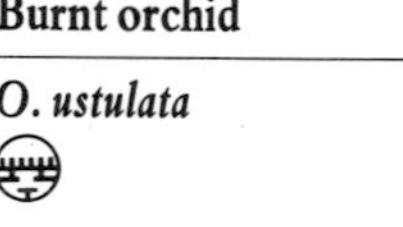

Spike dense, top buds dark purple, appearing burnt. Fl lip notched, spotted. *Ht:* to 20 cm; *D:* C, S; *Fl:* 5–6

Green-winged orchid

O. morio

Lvs to 9 cm

Helmet purple, green veins. Lip short, 3-lobed, spotted, spur straight. *Ht:* 25 cm; *D:* T (not N); *Fl:* 5–6

Bug orchid

O. coriophora

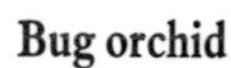

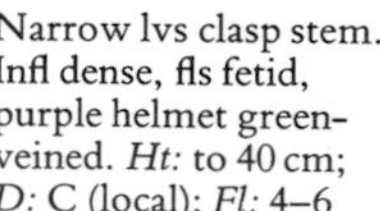

Lvs pointed

Narrow lvs clasp stem. Infl dense, fls fetid, purple helmet green-veined. *Ht:* to 40 cm; *D:* C (local); *Fl:* 4–6

Pale-flowered orchid

Orchis pallens

Leaves widest nr tip. Fls yellow, lip darker, 3-lobed. *Ht:* 20 cm; *D:* C, S; *Fl:* 5–6

Fly orchid

Ophrys insectifera

Side ptls narrow, brown, velvety. Lip 3-lobed, centre lobe v notched. *Ht:* 45 cm; *D:* T (not N); *Fl:* 5–7

Bog orchid

O. laxiflora subsp palustris

As *O. laxiflora* (p 171) but lip 3-lobed, centre lobe notched. *Ht:* 40 cm; *D:* SE, C; *Fl:* 5–6

Bee orchid

Ophrys apifera

Flower lip large, patterned, bee-like, curled tooth beneath, spls pink. *Ht:* 30 cm; *D:* W, S; *Fl:* 6–7

False musk orchid

Chamorchis alpina

Inconspicuous; lvs long, narrow. Lip not deeply lobed unlike *Herminium* (p 174). *Ht:* 10 cm; *D:* N, S; *Fl:* 7–8

Late spider orchid

Ophrys fuciflora

As *O. apifera* but lip flatter and broader than long, flat appendage at tip. *Ht:* 25 cm; *D:* C, S; *Fl:* 6–7

Early spider orchid

Ophrys sphegodes

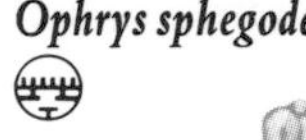

As *O. fuciflora* but lip velvety, no appendage. *Ht:* to 45 cm; *D:* C, W, S; *Fl:* 4–6

Black vanilla orchid

Nigritella nigra

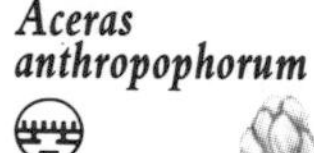

Ridged stem to 25 cm. Infl dense, conical, fls vanilla-scented. *D:* C, S; *Fl:* 6–8

Man orchid

Aceras anthropophorum

Narrow infl, fls have red margins, lip man-shaped. *Ht:* 30 cm; *D:* W, S; *Fl:* 6–7

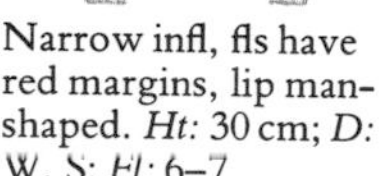

Lizard orchid

Himantoglossum hircinum

Fetid fls, lip to 5 cm, 3-lobed, side lobes *c.* 1 cm, centre lobe flexuous. *Ht:* 30 cm; *D:* W, S; *Fl:* 5–7

Pyramidal orchid

Anacamptis pyramidalis

Basal lvs to 15 cm, stem lvs smaller; spur long, thin. *Ht:* 35 cm; *D:* T (not N); *Fl:* 6–8

Frog orchid

Coeloglossum viride

Basal lvs rounded, blunt; lip oblong, tip 3-lobed, loose infl. *Ht:* 15 cm; *D:* T; *Fl:* 6–8

Lady's slipper orchid

Cypripedium calceolus

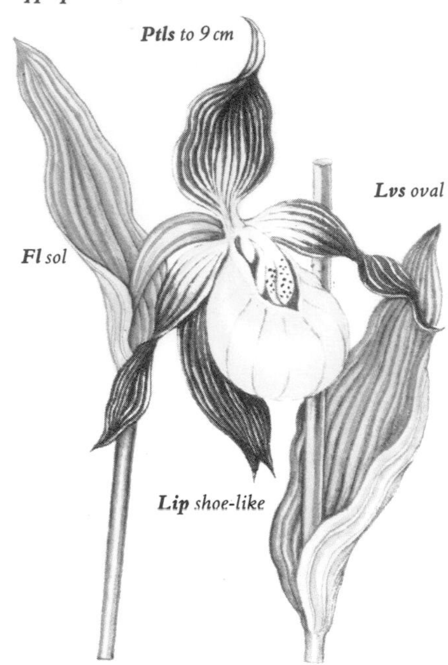

Two spls join into bifid lobe underneath curled, inflated lip. *Ht:* 35 cm; *D:* E, C; *Fl:* 5–6

Musk orchid

Herminium monorchis

Slim, inconspicuous; 3 short, spread lip lobes. *Ht:* 10 cm; *D:* T (not N); *Fl:* 6–7

White frog orchid

Pseudorchis albida

Glossy lvs; infl dense, columnar. Fls vanilla-scented, drooping, lip of 3 spread lobes. *Ht:* 20 cm; *D:* T; *Fl:* 5–7

Coralroot orchid

Corallorhiza trifida

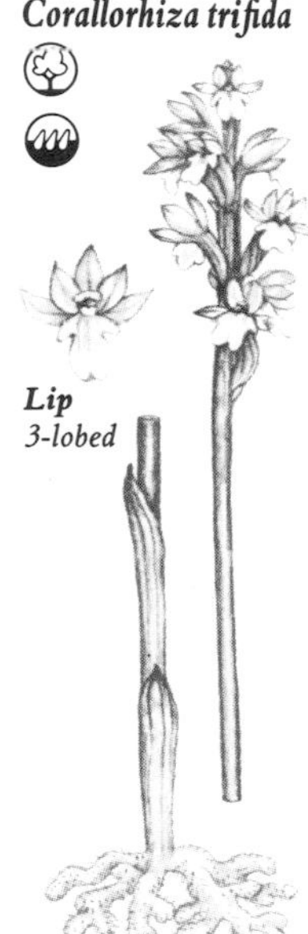

No green pigment, has coral-like rhizome; scale lvs on stem; infl loose. *Ht:* to 25 cm; *D:* N, E; *Fl:* 5–8

Common spotted orchid

Dactylorhiza fuchsii

Southern marsh orchid

D. majalis subsp praetermissa

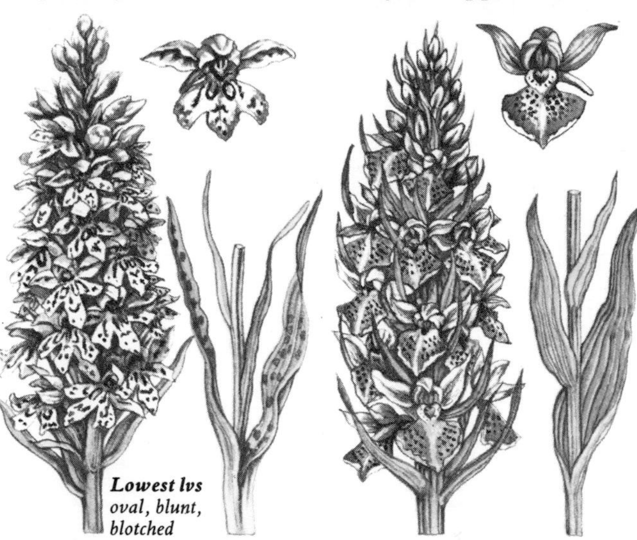

Lip has 3 almost equal lobes, centre lobe triangular, just largest. *Ht:* 17 cm; *D:* T (not NE); *Fl:* 6–8

Leaves unspotted. Infl dense, long bracts, lip slightly 3-lobed, spur robust. *Ht:* 45 cm; *D:* W; *Fl:* 6–8

Northern marsh orchid

D. majalis subsp purpurella

Dense infl, purplish bracts; lip unlobed, diamond-shaped. *Ht:* 20 cm; *D:* NW; *Fl:* 6–7

Early marsh orchid

D. incarnata

Hollow stems to 50 cm; infl dense, big bracts. Lip margins bend back making lip look slim. *D:* T; *Fl:* 5–7

Heath spotted orchid

D. maculata

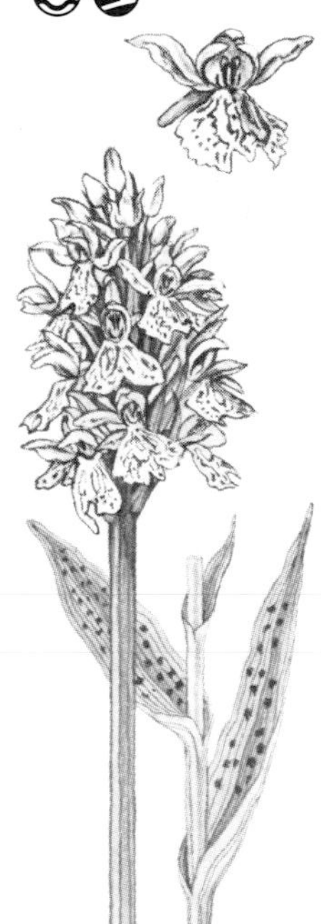

All lvs v pointed; 3-lobed lip, middle lobe smallest. *Ht:* to 50 cm; *D:* T; *Fl:* 6–8

Lesser butterfly orchid

Platanthera bifolia

Slim cylindrical infl; lip a narrow tongue, spur straight. *Ht:* 25 cm; *D:* T; *Fl:* 5–7

Ghost orchid

Epipogium aphyllum

No green col; twisted fls, lip uppermost, spur vertical. *Ht:* 15 cm; *D:* C, N; *Fl:* 6–8

Greater butterfly orchid

P. chlorantha

Loose, broad infl; lip narrow, spur long, curved. *Ht:* 30 cm; *D:* T (not far N); *Fl:* 5–7

Bog orchid

Hammarbya paludosa

Slender stems to 12 cm, basal lvs round, have bulbils at edge; loose infl. *D:* C, N; *Fl:* 7–9

Fragrant orchid

Gymnadenia conopsea

Slim, keeled lvs; fls frag, spur long, slim, curved. *Ht:* to 40 cm; *D:* T; *Fl:* 6–8

Fen orchid

Liparis loeselii

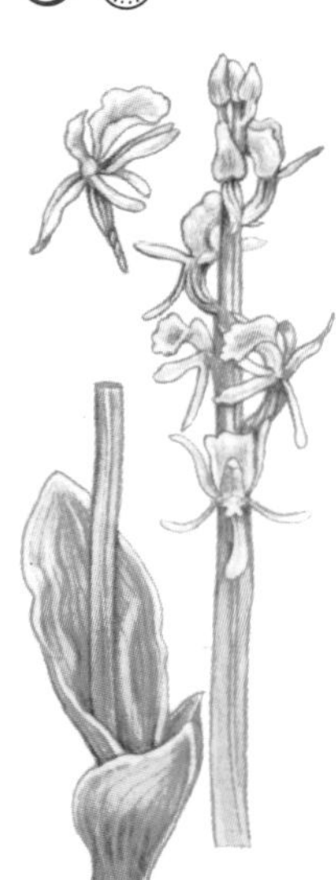

Bulbous, lvs v glossy; fls twisted, lip wavy, point upwards. *Ht:* 15 cm; *D:* C, E; *Fl:* 7

Calypso orchid

Calypso bulbosa

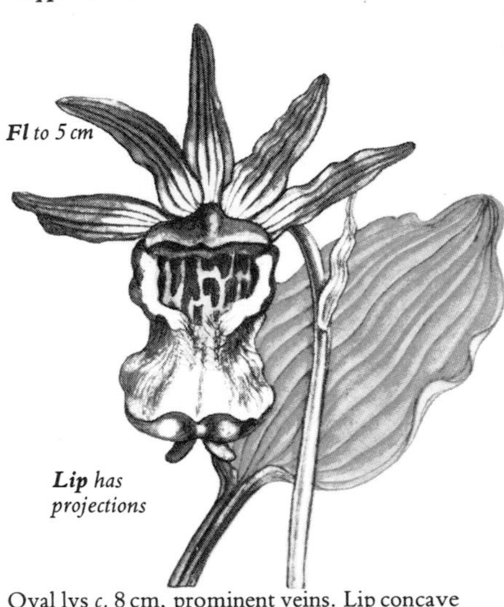

Oval lvs *c.* 8 cm, prominent veins. Lip concave forming a "shoe", other ptls and spls erect, lip hry. *Ht:* 15 cm; *D:* N; *Fl:* 5–7

Violet birdsnest orchid

Limodorum abortivum

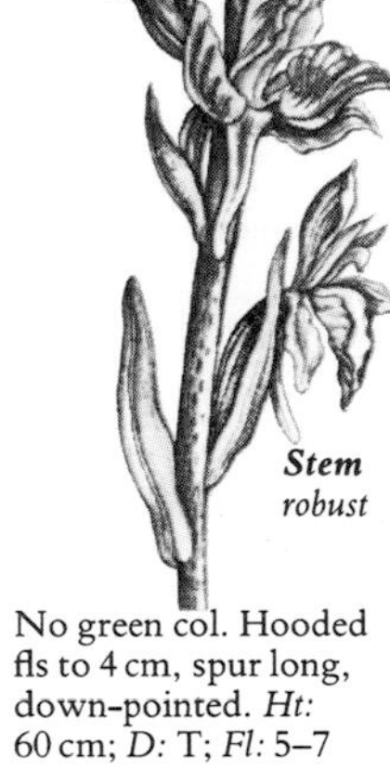

No green col. Hooded fls to 4 cm, spur long, down-pointed. *Ht:* 60 cm; *D:* T; *Fl:* 5–7

Birdsnest orchid

Neottia nidus-avis

No green pigment; lvs scale-like. Loose infl, lip large, 2-lobed at base. *Ht:* 35 cm; *D:* T (not N); *Fl:* 6–7

Creeping lady's tresses

Goodyera repens

Has stolons, lvs oval, stkd, net-veined in rosettes. Fls frag. *Ht:* 20 cm; *D:* N, mts in C, S; *Fl:* 7–8

Autumn lady's tresses

Spiranthes spiralis

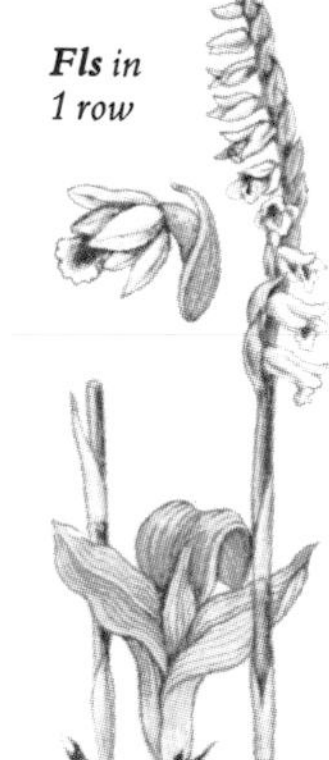

Leaves green, scale-like. Infl spirally twisted. *Ht:* 15 cm; *D:* T (not N); *Fl:* 8–9

Lesser twayblade

Listera cordata

Basal lvs to 3 cm

Basal lvs in 1 opp pr, narrow at base. Lip reddish, 2-lobed, under 5 mm. *Ht:* 10 cm; *D:* N, C; *Fl:* 7–9

Common twayblade

L. ovata

Lvs to 20 cm

Basal lvs in 1 opp pr. Lip yellow-green, 2-lobed to 1.5 cm. *Ht:* 45 cm; *D:* T; *Fl:* 6–7

Red helleborine

Cephalanthera rubra

Spls pointed

Lvs pointed

Stem stickily hry above; fl longer than bracts. *Ht:* 35 cm; *D:* T (not N, NW); *Fl:* 6–7

White helleborine

C. damasonium

Oval lvs. Fl parts much shorter than bracts, not spread, spls blunt. *Ht:* 35 cm; *D:* T (not N); *Fl:* 5–6

Narrow-leaved helleborine

C. longifolia

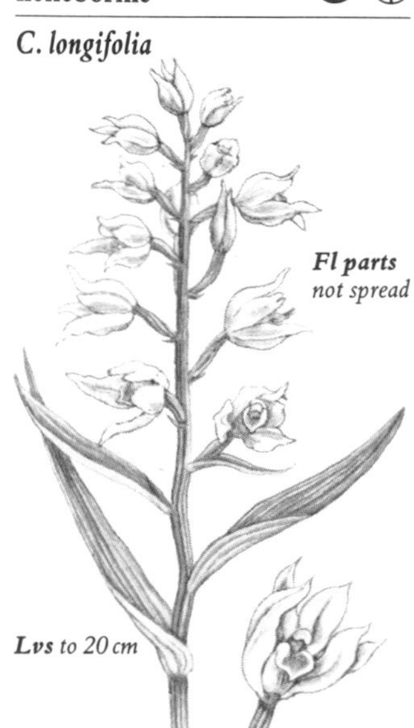

Pointed lance-shaped lvs. Most fls longer than bracts, pointed spls. *Ht:* 45 cm; *D:* C, E; *Fl:* 5–7

Marsh helleborine  

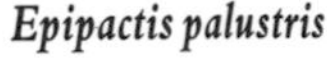
Epipactis palustris

Patch-forming with rhizome. Spls brown-purple, hry on outside. *Ht:* 30 cm; *D:* T (not N); *Fl:* 6–8

Broad-leaved helleborine  

E. helleborine

Leaves spirally arranged. Fls have large round appendage over stigma. *Ht:* 65 cm; *D:* T (not N); *Fl:* 7–10

Dark red helleborine

E. atrorubens

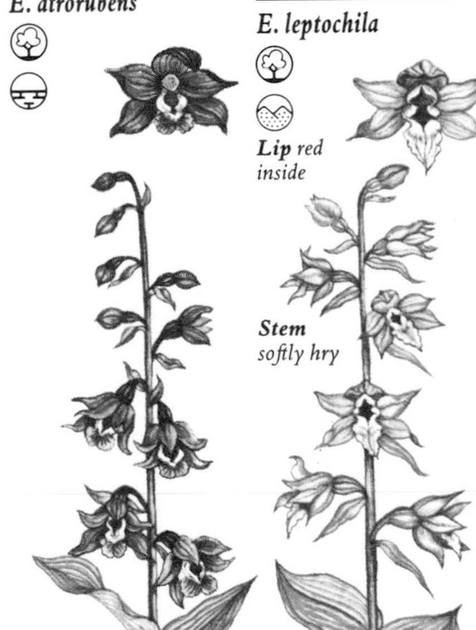

Stem to 30 cm, dense soft hrs. Pointed lvs in opp ranks; fls red-purple all over. *D:* T (local in W); *Fl:* 6–7

Narrow-lipped helleborine 

E. leptochila

Leaves in 2 opposite ranks; spread fl parts shorter than lowest bracts. *Ht:* 55 cm; *D:* C, W (local); *Fl:* 6–8

Green-flowered helleborine

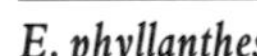
E. phyllanthes

Stem to 45 cm, usually hrlss. Fls droop vertically from hrlss fl stk. Lip cup white inside. *D:* W; *Fl:* 7–9

Arum family Araceae

Herbs with small flowers crowded on to a club-shaped spadix and surrounded by a bract or spathe. Male flowers are in the upper spadix, female below with 4–6 petals.

Lords and ladies, Cuckoo pint

Arum maculatum

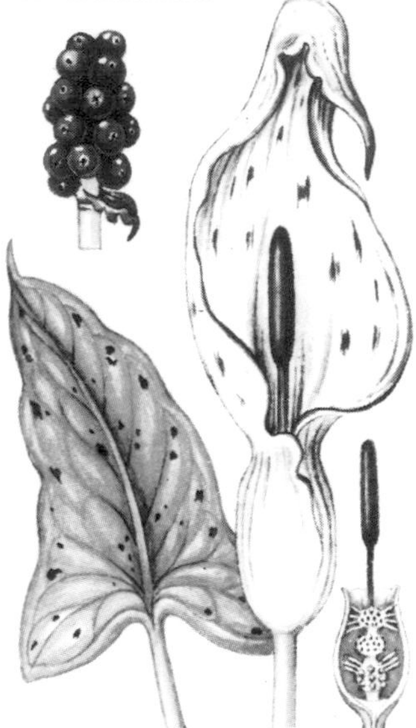

Hairless per to 25 cm. Lvs to 20 cm with dark green midrib arise in spring. Spadix to 12 cm, half spathe length. *D:* T (not N); *Fl:* 4–5

Large cuckoo pint

A. italicum

Hairless per. Lvs to 30 cm with pale midrib arise in winter (by Dec). Spadix ⅓ × spathe, yellow tip, spathe 35 cm. *D:* W; *Fl:* 4–5

Bog arum

Calla palustris

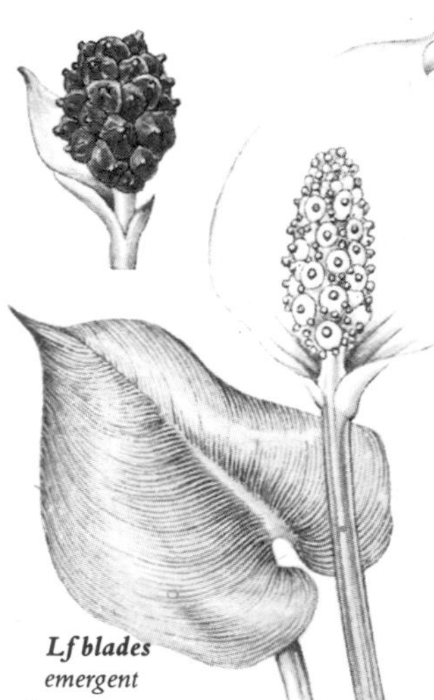

Lf blades *emergent*

Aquatic per to 30 cm. Lvs heart-shaped, spathe to 7 cm, flat, 2 × spadix. *D:* C, E; *Fl:* 6–8

Sweet flag

Acorus calamus

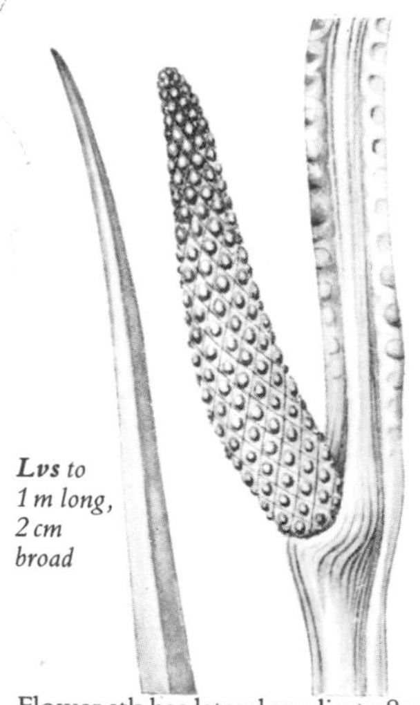

Lvs *to 1 m long, 2 cm broad*

Flower stk has lateral spadix to 8 cm and continues to lfy tip. *Ht:* 1 m; *D:* T (not far N); *Fl:* 5–7

Duckweed family Lemnaceae

Floating aquatics with leaf-like or disc-shaped stems from whose undersides roots and male and female flower buds arise.

Common duckweed 

Lemna minor

Floating disc to 4 mm diam, flat on both sides, 1 unbranched rt usually *c.* 4 cm. *D:* T; *Fl:* 6–7

Greater duckweed 

Spirodela polyrhiza

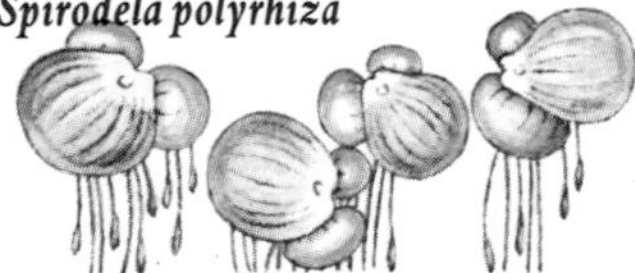

Disc to 8 mm, reddish below. Sev rts to 3 cm arise from underside centre. *D:* T (not N); *Fl:* 7

Ivy-leaved duckweed

L. trisulca

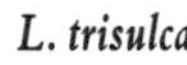

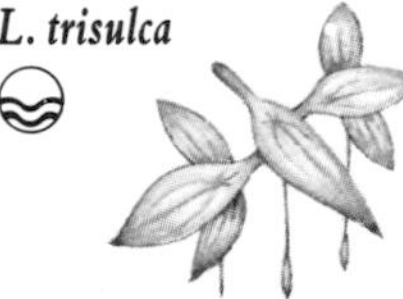

Submerged; 3 discs held together in lobed plate to 1.2 cm. *D:* T (not far N); *Fl:* 5–7

Gibbous duckweed

L. gibba

Discs swollen, convex above and below to 5 mm; 1 unbranched rt. *D:* T (not N); *Fl:* 6–7

Rootless duckweed

Wolffia arrhiza

Disc rtlss, egg-shaped to 1 mm, rarely fls. V much smaller than *Lemna* spp. *D:* C, S

Bur-reed family Sparganiaceae
Reedmace family Typhaceae

Perennial linear-leaved aquatics. Bur-reeds have globular inflorescences of single-sexed flowers. Reedmaces have a spadix with male flowers above, female flowers lower down.

Branched bur-reed

Sparganium erectum

Branched infl, ♂ heads at branch tips, ♀ at bases. *Ht:* 1 m; *D:* T (not far N); *Fl:* 6–8

Reedmace

Typha latifolia

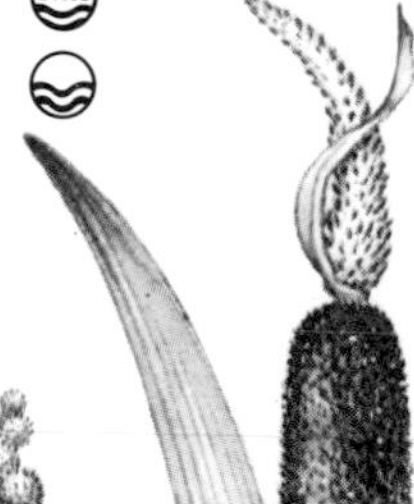

Broad lvs. ♂ part of infl immediately over ♀. *Ht:* 2 m; *D:* T (not far N); *Fl:* 6–7

Lesser reedmace

T. angustifolia

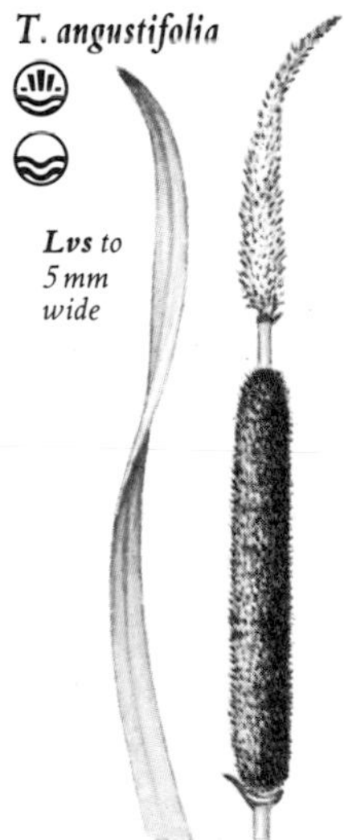

Narrow lvs; gap of 1–9 cm between ♂ and ♀ fls. *Ht:* 2.5 m; *D:* T (not far N); *Fl:* 6–7

Index

Entries in brackets are plants mentioned in the text but not described in full. English family names have been omitted but can be found by looking up the English names of the plants they cover. The entry 'pea', for example, will take you to the pea family.

Aceras anthropophorum 173
Achillea millefolium 154
ptarmica 154
Acinos arvensis 114
Aconite, Winter 32
Aconitum napellus 31
Acorus calamus 180
Actaea spicata 34
Adonis aestivalis 33
annua 33
vernalis 33
Adoxa moschatellina 131
Aegopodium podagraria 89
Aethusa cynapium 86
Agrimonia eupatoria 54
Agrimony 54
Hemp 152
Agrostemma githago 26
Ajuga chamaepitys 112
genevensis 112
reptans 112
Alchemilla alpina 54
vulgaris 54
Alexanders 90
Alisma plantago-aquatica 156
Alismataceae 156
Alison, Small 37
Alkanet, Green 106
Alliaria petiolata 43
Allium ampeloprasum 162
oleraceum 162
schoenoprasum 163
scordoprasum 162
scordoprasum subsp *rotundum* 163
senescens 163
sphaerocephalon 162
ursinum 162
vineale 162
Allseed 70
Four-leaved 22
Althaea hirsuta 75
officinalis 75
Alyssum alyssoides 37
Amaryllidaceae 167
Anacamptis pyramidalis 173
Anagallis arvensis 97
tenella 97
Anarrhinum bellidifolium 124
Anchusa arvensis 107
officinalis 107
Andromeda polifolia 95
Androsace lactea 97
maxima 97
Androsace, Large 97
White 97
Andryala, Common 141
Andryala integrifolia 141
Anemone apennina 30
narcissiflora 30
nemorosa 30
palmata 31
ranunculoides 30
sylvestris 31
Anemone, Blue 30
Narcissus-flowered 30
Palmate 31
Wood 30
Yellow 30
Angelica (archangelica) 87
sylvestris 87
Antennaria dioica 152
Anthemis arvensis 140
Anthericum liliago 160
Anthriscus caucalis 85
sylvestris 85
Anthyllis vulneraria 59
Antirrhinum majus 124
Aphanes arvensis 55
Apium graveolens 89
nodiflorum 89
Apocynaceae 102
Aquilegia vulgaris 31
Arabidopsis thaliana 40
Arabis alpina 40
hirsuta 40
turrita 40
Araceae 180
Araliaceae 84
Archangel, Yellow 116
Arctium lappa 147
minus 147
(tomentosa) 147
Arctostaphylos alpinus 94
uva-ursi 94
Arenaria ciliata 21
serpyllifolia 21
Aristolochia clematitis 14
Armeria alliaceae 99
maritima 99
Armoracia rusticana 42
Arnoseris minima 146
Arrowhead 156
Artemisia absinthium 155
campestris 155
maritima 155
vulgaris 155
Arum italicum 180
maculatum 180
Aruncus dioicus 55
Asarabacca 14
Asarum europaeum 14
Asclepiadaceae 102
Asparagus officinalis 166
Asperugo procumbens 108
Asperula arvensis 103
cynanchica 103
Asphodel, Bog 165
German 165
Scottish 165
Aster, Sea 137
Aster tripolium 137
Astragalus alpinus 60
cicer 60
danicus 60
frigidus 60
glycyphyllos 60
norvegicus 60
Astrantia major 91
Atriplex hastata 19
littoralis 19
patula 18
Atropa belladonna 117
Auricula 96
Avens, Alpine 54
Mountain 54
Water 54
Azalea, Wild 94

Baldellia ranunculoides 156
Ballota nigra 115
Balm, Bastard 116
Balsam, Himalayan 74
Orange 74
Small 74
Touch-me-not 74
Balsaminaceae 74
Baneberry 34
Barbarea vulgaris 41
Bartsia, Alpine 127
Red 125
Yellow 127
Bartsia alpina 127
Basil, Wild 114
Bearberry, Alpine 94
Black 94
Bedstraw, Heath 103
Hedge 103
Lady's 103
Marsh 104
Northern 104
Slender 104
Bellis perennis 137
Bellflower, Bearded 135
Clustered 134
Creeping 135
Giant 135
Ivy-leaved 135
Nettle-leaved 135
Spreading 134
Berula erecta 87
Beta maritima 19
Betony 116
Bidens cernua 154
tripartita 154
Bilberry 94
Bindweed, Field 105
Hedge 105
Sea 105
Birdsfoot 58
Birdsfoot trefoil 57
Marsh 57
Birdsnest, Yellow 92

Birthwort 14
Biscutella laevigata 43
Bistort 17
Alpine 17
Amphibious 17
Bittercress, Coralroot 41
Hairy 41
Large 41
Wavy 41
Bittersweet 117
Blackberry see Bramble
Blackstonia perfoliata 101
Bladderseed 91
Bladderwort, Greater 130
Lesser 130
Blinks 20
Bluebell 161
Blue-eyed grass 169
Bogbean 102
Bog myrtle see Sweet gale
Bombycilaena erecta 153
Borage 106
Boraginaceae 106–9
Borago officinalis 106
Bramble 53
Arctic 53
Stone 53
Brassica nigra 43
oleracea 43
Brooklime 121
Brookweed 98
Broom 66
Black 66
Clustered 66
Winged 66
Broomrape, Common 129
Greater 128
Knapweed 128
Purple 129
Thistle 128
Bryonia cretica 82
Bryony, Black 169
White 82
Buckwheat 17
Bugle 112
Blue 112
Buglossoides arvensis 107
purpurocaeruleum 107
Bugloss 107
Viper's 109
Bulrush see Reedmace
Bunium bulbocastanum 86
Bupleurum falcatum 90
rotundifolium 90
tenuissimum 90
Burdock, Greater 147
Lesser 147
Bur marigold, Nodding 154
Trifid 154
Burnet, Great 55
Salad 55
Bur-reed, Branched 181
Butcher's broom 166
Butomaceae 157
Butomus umbellatus 157
Butterbur 154
Buttercup, Bulbous 29
Celery-leaved 28
Corn 29
Creeping 29
Glacial 29
Goldilocks 28
Large white 28
Meadow 28
Butterwort, Alpine 129
Common 129
Hairy 130
Large-flowered 129
Pale 129

Cabbage, Wild 43
Cakile maritima 38
Calamintha sylvatica 113
Caldesia parnassifolia 156
Calla palustris 180
Callitrichaceae 109
Callitriche stagnalis 109
Calluna vulgaris 93
Caltha palustris 31
Calypso bulbosa 177
Calystegia sepium 105
soldanella 105
Campanulaceae 134–6
Campanula barbata 135
glomerata 134
latifolia 135
patula 134
rapunculoides 135
rotundifolia 134
tracehlium 135
Campion, Bladder 24
Moss 25
Red 24
Sea 25
White 24
Cannabaceae 13
Caprifoliaceae 132
Capsella bursa-pastoris 37
Caraway 86
Whorled 86
Cardamine amara 41
bulbifera 41
flexuosa 41
hirsuta 41
pratense 41
Cardaria draba 42
Carduus acanthoides 150
crispus 150
nutans 150
Carlina acaulis 148
vulgaris 148
Caryophyllaceae 20–27
Carrot family 84–90
Carrot, Moon 86
Wild 86
Carum carvi 86
verticillatum 86
Catchfly, Alpine 26
Forked 24
Northern 24
Nottingham 25
Catchfly *continued*
Rock 25
Sand 24
Spanish 25
Sticky 27
White sticky 24
Catmint 113
Catsear 141
Smooth 141
Spotted 141
Caucalis platycarpos 85
Celandine, Greater 36
Lesser 29
Celery, Wild 89
Centaurea aspera 151
calcitrapa 151
cyanus 151
(jacea) 151
montana 151
nigra 151
scabiosa 151
Centaurium erythraea 101
littorale 101
Centaury 101
Seaside 101
Yellow 101
Centranthus ruber 132
Cephalanthera damasonium 178
longifolia 178
rubra 178
Cerastium alpinum 21
arvense 20
diffusum 21
fontanum 20
glomeratum 20
Ceratophyllum demersum 28
Chamaedaphne calyculata 95
Chaemaespartium sagittale 66
Chaerophyllum temulentum 85
Chamaecytisus supinus 66
Chamomile, Corn 140
Chamomilla suaveolens 137
Chamorchis alpina 172
Charlock 42
Cheiranthus cheiri 36
Chelidonium majus 36
Chenopodiaceae 18–19
Chenopodium album 18
murale 18
polyspermum 18
rubrum 18
vulvaria 18
Chervil, Bur 85
Rough 85
Chickweed 23
Upright 23
Water 23
Chicory 146
Chimaphila umbellata 92
Chives 163
Christmas rose 33
Chrysanthemum segetum 140

Chrysosplenium
alternifolium 49
oppositifolium 49
Cicely, Sweet 87
Cicendia filiformis 101
Cicerbita alpina 150
Cichorium intybus 146
Cicuta virosa 87
Cinquefoil, Alpine 53
Creeping 52
Hairy 52
Marsh 52
Norwegian 52
Shrubby 52
Circaea alpina 81
lutetiana 81
Cirsium acaule 148
arvense 149
dissectum 149
eriophorum 149
helenioides 149
oleraceum 148
palustre 149
vulgare 148
Cistaceae 79
Clary, Meadow 114
Wild 114
Cleavers 104
False 104
Clematis vitalba 34
Clinopodium vulgare 114
Clover, Alsike 56
Haresfoot 56
Mountain 56
Red 56
Strawberry 57
Suffocated 57
Sulphur 57
White 56
Zig-zag 56
Cochlearia anglica 39
officinalis 39
pyrenaica 39
Coeloglossum viride 174
Colchicum autumnale
164
Columbine 31
Cottonweed 155
Coltsfoot 140
Purple 140
Colutea arborescens 64
Comfrey 106
Tuberous 106
Compositae 137–55
Conium maculatum 85
Conopodium majus 86
Consolida orientalis 31
regalis 31
Convallaria majalis 161
Convolvulaceae 105
Convolvulus arvensis 105
Conyza canadensis 138
Corallorhiza trifida 174
Coral necklace 22
Coriander 85
Coriandrum sativum 85
Cornaceae 83
Corn cockle 26
Cornel, Dwarf 83
Cornflower 151
Perennial 151
Cornmint 112
Cornsalad 133
Cornus suecica 83
Coronilla coronata 61
emerus 61
minima 61
vaginalis 61
varia 61
Coronopus squamatus 40
Corydalis claviculata 36
lutea 36
solida 36
Corydalis, Bulbous 36
Climbing 36
Yellow 36
Cowbane 87
Cowberry 94
Cowslip 96
Cow-wheat, Common
126
Crested 126
Field 126
Wood 126
Crambe maritima 38
Cranberry 94
Cranesbill, Bloody 68
Cut-leaved 69
Dove's foot 69
Hedgerow 68
Long-stalked 69
Marsh 69
Meadow 68
Shining 68
Wood 68
Crassulaceae 46–7
Crassula tillaea 47
Crepis capillaris 144
paludosa 144
vesicaria 144
Creeping Jenny 98
Cress, Hoary 42
Swine 40
Thale 40
Crithmum maritimum 88
Crocus vernus 169
Crocus, Sand 169
Spring 169
Crosswort 104
Crowberry 95
Crowfoot, Ivy-leaved
30
River water 30
Water 30
(*Cruciata laevipes*) 104
Cruciferae 36–44
Cuckoo flower 41
Cuckoo pint 180
Large 180
Cucurbitaceae 82
Cudweed, Common
152
Dwarf 153
Heath 153
Marsh 153
Small 153
Cuscuta epithymum 105
europaea 105
Cyclamen hederifolium
97
purpurascens 97
Cymbalaria muralis 123
Cynoglossum
germanicum 106
officinale 106
Cyphel, Mossy 22
Cypripedium calceolus
174
Cytisus scoparius 66

Daboecia cantabrica 94
Dactylorhiza fuchsii 175
incarnata 175
maculata 175
majalis subsp
praetermissa 175
majalis subsp
purpurella 175
Daffodil, Wild 167
Daisy 137
Ox-eye 140
Damasonium alisma 156
Dandelion 141
Daphne laureola 76
mezereum 76
Datura stramonium 117
Daucus carota 86
Dead nettle, Henbit
110
Red 110
Spotted 110
White 110
Delphinium elatum 31
Descurainia sophia 38
Dianthus armeria 26
carthusianorum 26
deltoides 26
gallicus 26
gratianopolitanus 26
superbus 26
Diapensiaceae 91
Diapensia lapponica 91
Digitalis grandiflora 122
purpurea 122
Dioscoreaceae 169
Diplotaxis muralis 37
Dipsacaceae 133–4
Dipsacus fullonum 134
pilosus 134
Dittander 38
Dock, Broad-leaved 15
Clustered 15
Curled 16
Fiddle 15
Golden 15
Marsh 16
Scottish 16
Shore 16
Water 16
Wood 15
Dodder, Common 105
Greater 105
Dogwood family 83
Doronicum pardalianches
139
Draba aizoides 39
alpina 39
incana 39
Dracocephalum
ruyschiana 115
Dragonhead, Northern
115
Dragon's teeth 58

Dropwort 55
Drosera anglica 45
intermedia 45
rotundifolia 45
Droseraceae 45
Dryas octopetala 54
Duckweed 181
Gibbous 181
Greater 181
Ivy-leaved 181
Rootless 181

Echinops sphaerocephalus 147
Echium vulgare 109
Eel grass 158
Elecampane 139
Elodea canadensis 157
Empetraceae 95
Empetrum nigrum 95
Enchanter's nightshade 81
Alpine 81
Epilobium adenocaulon 81
anagallidifolium 80
angustifolium 80
hirsutum 81
montanum 80
palustre 80
parviflorum 81
Epipactis atrorubens 179
helleborine 179
leptochila 179
palustris 179
phyllanthes 179
Epipogium aphyllum 176
Eranthis hyemalis 32
Erica ciliaris 93
cinerea 93
erigena 93
herbacea 93
tetralix 93
vagans 93
Ericaceae 93–5
Erigeron acer 138
Erinus alpinus 121
Erodium cicutarium 69
malacoides 69
maritimum 69
moschatum 69
Erophila verna 39
Erucastrum gallicum 37
Eryngium campestre 88
maritimum 88
Eryngo, Field 88
Erysimum cheiranthoides 43
Eupatorium cannabinum 152
Euphorbia amygdaloides 71
cyparissias 72
exigua 71
helioscopia 72
lathyrus 72
paralias 71
peplis 71
peplus 72
portlandica 71
Euphorbiaceae 71–2
Euphrasia spp 121
Evening primrose, Large-flowered 81
Eyebright 121

Fagopyrum esculentum 17
Fat hen 18
Felwort, Marsh 101
Fennel 90
Hog's 88
Fenugreek 57
Classical 65
Star-fruited 65
Figwort 122
Balm-leaved 123
French 123
Water 122
Yellow 122
Filaginella uliginosa 153
Filago vulgaris 152
Filipendula ulmaria 55
vulgaris 55
Flax, Pale 70
Perennial 70
Purging 70
Yellow 70
Fleabane 138
Blue 138
Canadian 138
Common 139
Small 139
Fleawort, Field 143
Marsh 143
Flixweed 38
Flower of Jove 27
Fluellen, Round-leaved 126
Sharp-leaved 126
Foeniculum vulgare 90
Forgetmenot, Bur 108
Creeping 108
Early 108
Field 108
Marsh 108
Tufted 108
Wood 108
Foxglove 122
Fairy 121
Large yellow 122
Fragaria moschata 53
vesca 53
Frankenia laevis 82
Frankeniaceae 82
Fritillaria meleagris 161
Frogbit 157
Fumana procumbens 79
Fumaria officinalis 36
Fumitory, Common 36

Gagea 164
Belgian 165
Least 165
Meadow 165
Gagea arvensis 164
lutea 164
minima 165
pratensis 165
spathacea 165
Galanthus nivalis 167
Galega officinalis 63
Galeopsis angustifolia 110
speciosa 111
tetrahit 110
Galinsoga parviflora 138
Galium aparine 104
boreale 104
mollugo 103
odoratum 103
palustre 104
pumilum 104
saxatile 103
spurium 104
verum 103
Gallant soldier 138
Garlic, Crow 162
Field 162
German 163
Genista anglica 66
germanica 66
tinctoria 66
Gentianaceae 99–101
Gentian, Alpine 100
Autumn 100
Cross 100
Field 101
Fringed 101
Great yellow 100
Marsh 99
Northern 101
Purple 100
Slender 100
Spring 100
Gentiana cruciata 100
lutea 100
nivalis 100
pneumonanthe 99
purpurea 100
verna 100
Gentianella amarella 100
aurea 101
campestris 101
ciliata 101
tenella 100
Geraniaceae 68–9
Geranium columbinum 69
dissectum 69
lucidum 68
molle 69
palustre 69
pratense 68
pyrenaicum 68
robertianum 68
sanguineum 68
sylvaticum 68
Germander, Cut-leaved 115
Mountain 114
Wall 115
Water 115
Geum montanum 54
rivale 54
urbanum 54
Gladiolus illyricus 169
Glasswort 19
Glaucium corniculatum 35
flavum 35
Glaux maritima 98
Glechoma hederacea 116

Globe flower 32
Globularia vulgaris 128
Gipsywort 112
Goatsbeard 143
Goat's rue 63
Golden rod 138
Goodyera repens 177
Goosefoot, Many-seeded 18
Nettle-leaved 18
Red 18
Stinking 18
Goosegrass see Cleavers
Gorse 67
Dwarf 67
Western dwarf 67
Grass of Parnassus 50
Grass poly 82
Gratiola officinalis 125
Greenweed, Dyer's 66
German 66
Groenlandia densa 158
Gromwell 107
Corn 107
Purple 107
Ground elder 89
Ground pine 112
Groundsel 142
Guttiferae 76–7
Gymnadenia conopsea 176
Gypsophila, Annual 25
Creeping 25
Gypsophila muralis 25
repens 25
Gypsywort 112

Halimione portulacoides 19
Haloragaceae 83
Hammarbya paludosa 176
Harebell 134
Hare's ear, Sickle 90
Smallest 90
Hawkbit, Rough 141
Hawksbeard, Beaked 144
Marsh 144
Smooth 144
Hawkweed, Alpine 144
Leafy 144
Mouse-ear 144
Orange 144
Heath, Cornish 93
Cross-leaved 93
Dorset 93
Irish 93
St Dabeoc's 94
Heather 93
Bell 93
Mountain 95
Spring 93
Hedera helix 84
Hedysarum hedysaroides 65
Helianthemum apenninum 79
canum 79
nummularium 79
Helichrysum arenarium 153
Hellebore, Green 33
Stinking 33
Helleborine, Broad-leaved 179
Dark red 179
Green-flowered 179
Marsh 179
Narrow-leaved 178
Narrow-lipped 179
Red 178
White 178
Helleborus foetidus 33
niger 33
viridis 33
Hemlock 85
Hemp nettle 110
Large-flowered 111
Red 110
Henbane 117
Hepatica nobilis 34
Heracleum sphondylium 84
Herb bennet 54
Herb Paris 166
Herb Robert 68
Herminium monorchis 174
Herniaria glabra 23
Hieracium alpinum 144
auranticum 144
pilosella 144
umbellatum 144
Himantoglossum hircinum 173
Hippocrepis comosa 61
Hippuridaceae 83
Hippuris vulgaris 83
Hogweed 84
Homogyne alpina 140
Honesty, (Annual) 44
Perennial 44
Honewort 86
Honeysuckle 132
Perfoliate 132
Honkenya peploides 21
Hop 13
Horehound, Black 115
White 116
Hornwort, Rigid 28
Hottonia palustris 98
Hound's tongue 106
Green 106
Houseleek, Hen-and-chickens 47
Humulus lupulus 13
Hyacinth, Grape 163
Small grape 163
Tassel 163
Hyacinthoides non-scripta 161
Hydrocharis morsus-ranae 157
Hydrocharitaceae 157
Hydrocotyle vulgaris 90
Hysocyamus niger 117
Hypericum androsaemum 77
elodes 77
hirsutum 77
Hypericum continued
humifusum 77
perforatum 76
pulchrum 77
tetrapterum 77
Hypochoeris glabra 141
maculata 141
radicata 141

Illecebrum verticillatum 22
Impatiens capensis 74
glandulifera 74
noli-tangere 74
parviflora 74
Inula britannica 138
conyza 138
crithmoides 139
helenium 139
Iridaceae 168–9
Iris, Butterfly 168
Siberian 168
Stinking 168
Wild 168
Yellow 168
Iris aphylla 168
foetidissima 168
pseudacorus 168
sibirica 168
spuria 168
Isatis tinctoria 44
Ivy 84
Ground 116

Jack-go-to-bed-at-noon see Goatsbeard
Jack-in-the-pulpit 180
Jacob's ladder 105
Jasione montana 136
Jovibarba sobolifera 47

Kale, Sea 38
Kickxia elantine 126
spuria 126
Kingcup see Marigold, marsh
Knapweed, Black 151
Greater 151
Knautia arvensis 133
dipsacifolia 133
Knotgrass 17

Labiateae 110–16
Lactuca perennis 146
saligna 146
serriola 146
Lady's mantle 54
Alpine 54
Lady's tresses, Autumn 177
Creeping 177
Lamiastrum galeobdolon 116
Lamium album 110
amplexicaule 110
maculatum 110
purpureum 110
Lamb's succory 146
Lappula squarrosa 108
Lapsana communis 146

Larkspur, Alpine 31
Eastern 31
Forking 31
Laserpitium latifolium 87
Lathraea squamaria 129
Lathyrus aphaca 62
japonicus 63
montanus 62
nissolia 62
palustris 63
pratensis 62
sylvestris 62
tuberosus 63
vernus 62
Leatherleaf 95
Ledum palustre 95
Leek, Round-headed 162
Sand 162
Wild 162, 163
Legousia hybrida 136
speculum-veneris 136
Leguminosae 56–67
Lembotropis nigricans 66
Lemna gibba 181
minor 181
trisulca 181
Lentibulariaceae 129–30
Lentil, Wild 60
Leonurus cardiaca 112
Leopardsbane 139
Leontodon (autumnalis) 141
hispidus 141
Lepidium campestre 38
latifolium 38
Lettuce, Blue 146
Least 146
Prickly 146
Purple 147
Wall 147
Leucanthemum vulgare 140
Leucojum aestivum 167
vernum 167
Ligusticum scoticum 90
Liliaceae 159–66
Lilium bulbiferum 159
martagon 159
Lily, Kerry 160
Martagon 159
May 160
Orange 159
St Bernard's 160
Snowdon 160
Lily of the valley 161
Limodorum abortivum 177
Limonium binervosum 99
vulgare 99
Limosella aquatica 125
Linaceae 70
Linaria alpina 123
repens 123
vulgaris 123
Linnaea borealis 132
Linum bienne 70
catharticum 70
flavum 70
perenne 70
Liparis loeselii 176
Liquorice, Wild 60
Listera cordata 178
ovata 178
Lithospermum officinale 107
Littorella uniflora 131
Lloydia serotina 160
Lobelia dortmanna 136
urens 136
Lobelia, Heath 136
Water 136
Logfia minima 153
Loiseleuria procumbens 94
Lonicera caprifolium 132
periclymenum 132
Loosestrife, Purple 82
Tufted 98
Yellow 98
Lords and ladies 180
Lousewort, Leafy 124
Marsh 124
Lotus corniculatus 57
uliginosus 57
Lovage, Scots 90
Love-in-a-mist 31
Ludwigia palustris 81
Lunaria (annua) 44
rediviva 44
Lungwort 107
Luronium natans 156
Lychnis alpina 26
flos-cuculi 26
flos-jovis 27
viscaria 27
Lycopus europaeus 112
Lysimachia nemorum 98
nummularia 98
thyrsiflora 98
vulgaris 98
Lythraceae 82
Lythrum hyssopifolia 82
salicaria 82

Madder, Field 104
Wild 103
Madwort 108
Maianthemum bifolium 160
Mallow, Common 75
Dwarf 75
Marsh 75
Musk 75
Rough 75
Malvaceae 75
Malva moschata 75
neglecta 75
sylvestris 75
Marestail 83
Marigold, Corn 140
Marsh 31
Marjoram 113
Marrubium vulgare 116
Matricaria maritima 137
matricarioides 137
(perforata) 137
Matthiola sinuata 38
Mayweed, Pineapple 137
Sea 137
Meadow rue, Alpine 34
Common 34
Lesser 34
Meadow saffron 164
Meadowsweet 55
Meconopsis cambrica 35
Medicago arabica 64
falcata 64
lupulina 64
Medick, Black 64
Sickle 64
Spotted 64
Melilot, Common 63
Tall 63
White 63
Melilotus alba 63
altissima 63
officinalis 63
Melittis melissophyllum 116
Melampyrum arvense 126
cristatum 126
nemorosum 127
pratense 126
sylvaticum 126
Mentha aquatica 112
arvensis 112
spicata 113
Menyanthaceae 102
Menyanthes trifoliata 102
Mercurialis annua 72
perennis 72
Mercury, Annual 72
Dog's 72
Mertensia maritima 109
Meum anthamanticum 87
Mezereon 76
Micropus 153
Mignonette, Rampion 45
Upright 44
Wild 44
Milfoil see Yarrow
Milk vetch, Alpine 60
Hairy 59
Mountain 59
Norwegian 60
Purple 60
Yellow 59
Yellow alpine 60
Milkweed 102
Milkwort, Chalk 73
Common 73
Sea 98
Shrubby 73
Thyme-leaved 73
Mimulus guttatus 127
Minuartia sedoides 22
verna 22
Mistletoe 14
Moehringia muscosa 21
trinervia 21
Moenchia erecta 23
Moneses uniflora 92
Moneywort, Cornish 127
Monkey flower 127
Monkshood 31
Monotropa hypopitys 92
Montia fontana 20

Moor king 124
Moschatel 131
Motherwort 112
Mouse-ear, Alpine 21
Common 20
Field 20
Sea 21
Sticky 20
Mousetail 34
Mountain everlasting 152
Mudwort 125
Mugwort 155
Mullein, Dark 118
Great 118
Hoary 118
Moth 118
Orange 118
White 119
Muscari botryoides 163
comosum 163
neglectum 163
Mustard, Ball 43
Black 43
Buckler 43
Garlic 43
Hedge 37
Treacle 43
White 43
Mycelis muralis 147
Myosotis arvensis 108
(discolor) 108
laxa 108
ramosissima 108
scorpioides 108
secunda 108
sylvatica 108
Myosoton aquaticum 23
Myosurus minimus 34
Myricaceae 12
Myrica gale 12
Myriophyllum alterniflorum 83
spicatum 83
verticillatum 83
Myrrhis odorata 87

Naiad, Holly-leaved 159
Slender 159
Najadaceae 159
Najas flexilis 159
marina 159
Narcissus pseudonarcissus 167
Narthecium ossifragum 165
Nasturtium officinale 41
Navelwort 47, 109
Neottia nidus-avis 177
Nepeta cataria 113
Neslia paniculata 43
Nettle, Annual 13
Stinging 13
Nigella damascena 31
Nightshade, Black 117
Deadly 117
Hairy 117
Woody 117
Nigritella nigra 173
Nipplewort 146
Nonea pulla 107
Nuphar lutea 27
Nymphaceae 27
Nymphaea alba 27
Nymphoides peltata 102

Odontites lutea 125
verna 125
Oenanthe aquatica 89
crocata 89
fistulosa 89
lachenalii 89
Oenothera erythrosepala 81
Old man's beard see Traveller's joy
Omalotheca supina 153
sylvatica 153
Omphalodes scorpioides 109
Onagraceae 80–1
Onobrychis viciifolia 65
Ononis natrix 65
pusilla 64
reclinata 64
repens 64
spinosa 65
Onopordum acanthium 150
Ophrys apifera 172
fuciflora 172
insectifera 172
sphegodes 173
Orache, Common 18
Grass-leaved 19
Spear-leaved 19
Orchidaceae 170–9
Orchid, Bee 172
Birdsnest 177
Black vanilla 173
Bog 172, 176
Bug 171
Burnt 171
Calypso 177
Common spotted 175
Coralroot 174
Early Marsh 175
Early purple 170
Early spider 173
False musk 172
Fen 176
Fly 172
Fragrant 176
Frog 174
Ghost 176
Greater butterfly 176
Green-winged 171
Heath spotted 175
Lady 170
Lady's slipper 174
Late spider 172
Lesser butterfly 176
Lizard 173
Loose-flowered 171
Man 173
Military 170
Monkey 171
Musk 174
Northern marsh 175
Pale-flowered 172
Orchid *continued*
Pyramidal 173
Southern marsh 175
Toothed 170
Violet birdsnest 177
White frog 174
Orchis coriophora 171
laxiflora 171
laxiflora subsp *palustris* 172
mascula 170
militaris 170
morio 171
pallens 172
purpurea 170
simia 171
tridentata 170
ustulata 171
Origanum vulgare 113
Ornithogallum nutans 164
pyrenaicum 164
umbellatum 164
Ornithopus perpusillus 58
(Orpine) 47
Orobanchaceae 128–9
Orobanche elatior 128
minor 129
rapum-genistae 128
reticulata 128
purpurea 129
Orthilia secunda 92
Otanthus maritimus 155
Oxalidaceae 67
Oxalis acetosella 67
corniculata 67
Oxlip 96
Ox-tongue, Bristly 143
Oxyria digyna 16
Oxytropis campestris 59
halleri 59
pilosa 59
Oyster plant 109

Paeonia officinalis 34
Pansy, Field 79
Wild 79
Papaver argemone 35
dubium 35
radicatum 35
rhoeas 35
Papaveraceae 35–6
Parentucellia viscosa 127
Parietaria diffusa 13
Paris quadrifolia 166
Parnassiaceae 50
Parnassia palustris 50
Parsley, Cambridge milk 85
Corn 88
Cow 85
Fool's 86
Greater bur 85
Knotted bur 84
Milk 88
Small bur 85
Spreading bur 84
Stone 85
Upright hedge 84

Parsley piert 55
Parsnip, Greater water 87
Lesser water 87
Wild 91
Pasque flower 32
Alpine 32
Pale 32
Small 32
Pastinaca sativa 91
Pea, Marsh 63
Narrow-leaved everlasting 62
Sea 63
Spring 62
Tuberous 63
Pearlwort, Knotted 22
Sea 22
Pedicularis foliosa 124
palustris 124
sceptrum-carolinum 124
sylvatica 124
Pellitory-of-the-wall 13
Pennycress, Field 42
Pennywort, Marsh 90
Wall see Navelwort
Pentaglottis sempervirens 106
Peony 34
Pepperwort, Field 38
Persicaria, Pale 17
Periwinkle, Greater 102
Lesser 102
Petasites hybridus 154
Petrorhagia saxifraga 26
Petroselinum segetum 88
Petty whin 66
Peucedanum officinale 88
palustre 88
Pheasant's eye 33
Summer 33
Yellow 33
Phyllodoce caerulea 95
Physospermum cornubiense 91
Phyteuma orbiculare 136
spicatum 136
Picris echioides 143
Pignut 86
Great 86
Pimpernel, Bog 97
Scarlet 97
Yellow 98
Pimpinella major 88
saxifraga 88
Pinguicula alpina 129
grandiflora 129
lusitanica 129
villosa 130
vulgaris 129
Pink, Carthusian 26
Cheddar 26
Deptford 26
Jersey 26
Large 26
Maiden 26
Sea see Thrift
Plantaginaceae 130–1
Plantago arenaria 131
coronopus 131
lanceolata 130
major 130
maritima 131
media 131
Plantain, Branched 131
Buckshorn 131
Greater 130
Hoary 131
Ribwort 130
Sea 131
Platanthera bifolia 176
chlorantha 176
Ploughman's spikenard 138
Plumbaginaceae 99
Polemoniaceae 105
Polemonium caeruleum 105
Polycarpon tetraphyllum 22
Polygala calcarea 73
chamaebuxus 73
serpyllifolia 73
vulgaris 73
Polygonaceae 15–17
Polygonatum multiflorum 166
verticillatum 166
Polygonum amphibium 17
aviculare 17
bistorta 17
hydropiper 17
lapathifolium 17
persicaria 17
viviparum 17
Pondweed, Bog 158
Broad-leaved 158
Canadian 157
Opposite-leaved 158
Shining 158
Poppy, Arctic 35
Common 35
Long-headed 35
Prickly 35
Red horned 35
Welsh 35
Yellow horned 35
Portulacaceae 20
Potamogetonaceae 158
Potamogeton lucens 158
natans 158
polygonifolius 158
Potentilla anserina 52
argentea 52
crantzii 53
erecta 52
fruticosa 52
norvegica 52
palustris 52
reptans 52
sterilis 52
Prenanthes purpurea 147
Primrose 96
Birdseye 96
Scandinavian 96
Scottish 96
Primula auricula 96
elatior 96
Primula continued
farinosa 96
scandinavica 96
scotica 96
veris 96
vulgaris 96
Primulaceae 96–8
Prunella laciniata 116
vulgaris 116
Pseudorchis albida 174
Pulicaria dysenterica 139
vulgaris 139
Pulmonaria officinalis 107
Pulsatilla alpina 32
pratensis 32
vernalis 32
vulgaris 32
Purslane, Hampshire 81
Sea 19
Pyrolaceae 92
Pyrola chlorantha 92
minor 92
rotundifolia 92

Radiola linoides 70
Radish, Horse 42
Sea 42
Wild 42
Ragged Robin 26
Ragwort 142
Alpine 142
Broad-leaved 142
Hoary 143
Marsh 143
Oxford 142
Rampion, Round-headed 136
Spiked 136
Ramsons 162
Ranunculaceae 28–34
Ranunculus acris 28
aquatilis 30
arvensis 29
auricomus 28
bulbosus 29
ficaria 29
flammula 29
fluitans 30
glacialis 29
hederaceus 30
lingua 29
platanifolius 28
repens 29
sceleratus 28
Raphanus maritimus 42
raphanistrum 42
Redshank 17
Reedmace 181
Reseda alba 44
lutea 44
luteola 45
phyteuma 45
Resedaceae 44–5
Rest harrow 64
Hairy 64
Large yellow 65
Small 64
Spiny 65
Rhinanthus minor 125

Rhodiola rosea 46
Rhododendron ponticum 95
Rock cress, Alpine 40
Hairy 40
Rocket, Hairy 37
London 37
Sea 38
Rock rose 79
Hoary 79
Spotted 79
White 79
Romulea columnea 169
Rorippa amphibia 40
islandica 40
Rosa arvensis 50
canina 50
gallica 51
pendulina 51
pimpinellifolia 51
rubiginosa 51
stylosa 51
tomentosa 51
Rosaceae 50–5
Rose, Alpine 51
Burnet 51
Dog 50
Downy 51
Field 50
Provence 51
Wild 51
Rosemary, Bog 95
Rose-root 46
Rubiaceae 103–4
Rubia peregrina 103
Rubus arcticus 53
(caesius) 53
(chamaemorus) 53
fruticosus 53
saxatilis 53
Rue 73
Rumex acetosa 15
acetosella 15
aquaticus 16
conglomeratus 15
crispus 16
hydrolapathum 16
maritimus 15
obtusifolius 15
palustris 16
pulcher 15
rupestris 16
sanguineus 15
Ruppia maritima 159
Rupturewort 23
Ruscus aculeatus 166
Rush, Flowering 157
Rutaceae 73
Ruta graveolens 73

Sage, Wild 114
Wood 114
Sagina maritima 22
nodosa 22
Sagittaria sagittifolia 156
Sainfoin 65
St John's wort, Hairy 77
Marsh 77
Perforate 76
Slender 77
St John's wort *continued*
Square-stemmed 77
Trailing 77
Salicaceae 12
Salicornia europea 19
Salix herbacea 12
repens 12
Salsola kali 19
Saltwort, Prickly 19
Salvia pratensis 114
nemorosa 114
verbenaca 114
Samolus valerandi 98
Samphire, Golden 139
Rock 88
Sandwort, Fringed 21
Mossy 21
Sea 21
Spring 22
Three-nerved 21
Thyme-leaved 21
Sanguisorba minor 55
officinalis 55
Sanicle 91
Sanicula europaea 91
Saponaria officinalis 26
Saussurea alpina 150
Saw wort 152
Alpine 150
Saxifraga aizoides 49
cernua 48
granulata 48
hypnoides 48
nivalis 48
oppositifolia 49
stellaris 49
tridactylites 48
Saxifragaceae 48–9
Saxifrage, Alternate-leaved golden 49
Arctic 48
Burnet 88
Drooping 48
Greater burnet 88
Meadow 48
Mossy 48
Opposite-leaved golden 49
Pepper 91
Purple 49
Rue-leaved 48
Starry 49
Yellow 49
Scabiosa columbaria 134
Scabious, Devilsbit 133
Field 133
Sheepsbit 136
Small 134
Wood 133
Scandix pecten-veneris 89
Scilla autumnalis 161
bifolia 161
verna 161
Scorpion senna 61
Scorpion vetch 61
Lesser 61
Small 61
Scorzonera laciniata 145
Scrophularia auriculata 122
canina 123
Scrophularia continued
nodosa 122
scorodonia 123
vernalis 122
Scrophulariaceae 118–27
Scurvy grass, Alpine 39
Common 39
English 39
Scutellaria galericulata 115
minor 115
Sea beet 19
Seablite, Annual 19
Sea heath 82
Sea holly 88
Sea lavender 99
Rock 99
Sedum acre 46
album 46
alpestre 46
anglicum 46
forsteranum 47
reflexum 47
(telephium) 47
Self-heal 116
Cut-leaved 116
Selinum carvifolia 85
Senecio aquaticus 143
congestus 143
erucifolius 143
fluviatilis 142
integrifolius 143
jacobaea 142
nemorensis 142
squalidus 142
(sylvaticus) 142
vulgaris 142
Senna, Bladder 64
Sermountain 87
Serratula tinctoria 152
Seseli libanotis 86
Shepherd's needle 89
Shepherd's purse 37
Sherardia arvensis 104
Shoreweed 131
Sibbaldia procumbens 53
Sibthorpia europaea 127
Silaum silaus 91
Silene acaulis 25
alba 24
conica 24
dichotoma 24
dioica 24
maritima 25
nutans 25
otites 25
rupestris 25
viscosa 24
vulgaris 24
wahlbergella 24
Silverweed 52
Silybum marianum 147
Simethis planifolia 160
Sinapis albe 43
arvensis 42
Sison amomum 85
Sisymbrium irio 37
officinale 37
Sisyrinchium bermudianum 169

Sium latifolium 87
Skullcap 115
Lesser 115
Smyrnium olusatrum 90
Snapdragon 124
Sneezewort 154
Snowbell, Alpine 97
Snowdrop 167
Snowdrop windflower 31
Snowflake, Spring 167
Summer 167
Soapwort 26
Solanceae 117
Solanum dulcamara 117
luteum 117
nigrum 117
Soldanella alpina 97
Solidago virgaurea 138
Solomon's seal 166
Whorled 166
Sonchus arvensis 145
asper 145
oleraceus 145
palustris 145
Sorrel, Common 15
Mountain 16
Sheep's 15
Sowbread 97
Sow thistle, Alpine 150
Marsh 145
Perennial 145
Prickly 145
Smooth 145
Sparganiceae 181
Sparganium erectum 181
Spearmint 113
Spearwort, Greater 29
Lesser 29
Speedwell, Common field 119
Germander 119
Heath 119
Ivy-leaved 119
Large 119
Marsh 121
Rock 120
Slender 121
Spiked 120
Spring 120
Thyme-leaved 120
Wall 120
Water 120
Wood 121
Spergula arvensis 22
Spergularia marina 22
Spignel 87
Spiraea, Goat's beard 55
Spiranthes spiralis 177
Spirodela polyrhiza 181
Spurge, Caper 72
Cypress 72
Dwarf 71
Petty 72
Portland 71
Purple 71
Sea 71
Sun 72
Wood 71
Spurge laurel 76
Spurrey, Corn 22
Lesser sea 22
Squill, Alpine 161
Autumn 161
Spring 161
Squinancywort 103
Stachys alpina 111
arvensis 111
germanica 111
officinalis 116
palustris 111
recta 111
sylvatica 111
Star-fruit 156
Star of Bethlehem, Common 164
Drooping 164
Spiked 164
Yellow 164
Stellaria graminea 23
holostea 23
media 23
palustris 23
Stitchwort, Greater 23
Lesser 23
Marsh 23
Stock, Sea 38
Stonecrop, Alpine 46
Biting 46
English 46
Mossy 47
Reflexed 47
Rock 47
White 46
Storksbill 69
Musk 69
Sea 69
Soft 69
Stratiotes aloides 157
Strawberry, Barren 52
Hautbois 53
Wild 53
Succisa pratensis 133
Sueda maritima 19
Sundew, Common 45
Great 45
Oblong-leaved 45
Sweet briar 51
Sweet flag 180
Sweet gale 12
Swertia perennis 101
Symphytum officinale 106
tuberosum 106

Tamus communis 169
Tanacetum vulgare 140
Tansy 140
Taraxacum officinale 141
Tare, Hairy 59
Tasselweed, Beaked 159
Teasel 134
Small 134
Tetragonolobus maritimus 58
Teucrium botrys 115
chamaedrys 115
montanum 114
scordium 115
scorodonia 114
Thalictrum alpinum 34
flavum 34
minus 34
Thistle, Cabbage 148
Carline 148
Cotton 150
Creeping 149
Globe 147
Marsh 149
Meadow 149
Melancholy 149
Milk 147
Musk 150
Red star 151
Rough star 151
Spear 148
Stemless 148
Stemless carline 148
Welted 150
Winged 150
Woolly 149
Thlaspi arvense 42
Thorn apple 117
Thorrow-wax 90
Thrift 99
Jersey 99
Thyme, Basil 114
Large wild 113
Wild 113
Thymelaea passerina 76
Thymelaeaceae 76
Thymus praecox (=*drucei*) 113
pulegioides 113
serpyllum 113
Toadflax, Alpine 123
Common 123
Daisy-leaved 124
Ivy-leaved 123
Pale 123
Tofieldia calyculata 165
pusilla 165
Toothwort 129
Torilis arvensis 84
japonica 84
nodosa 84
Tormentil 52
Tower cress 40
Tragopogon pratensis 143
Trapaceae 80
Trapa natans 80
Traveller's joy 34
Trefoil, Lesser yellow 57
Trientalis europaea 96
Trifolium arvense 56
dubium 57
fragiferum 57
hybridum 56
medium 56
montanum 56
ochroleucon 57
ornithopodioides 57
pratense 56
repens 56
suffocatum 57
Trigonella foenum-graecum 65
monspeliaca 65
Trinia glauca 86
Trollius europaeus 32

Tuberaria guttata 79
Tulipa sylvestris 160
Tunic flower 26
Turgenia latifolia 85
Tussilago farfara 140
Tutsan 77
Twayblade 178
Lesser 178
Twinflower 132
Typha angustifolia 181
latifolia 181
Typhaceae 181

Ulex europeaus 67
gallii 67
minor 67
Umbelliferae 84–91
Umbilicus rupestris 47
Urtica dioica 13
urens 13
Utricularia minor 130
vulgaris 130

Vaccinium myrtillus 94
oxycoccus 94
uliginosum 94
vitis-idaea 94
Valerian, Common 132
Marsh 133
Red 132
Valeriana dioica 133
officinalis 132
Valerianaceae 132–3
Valerianella locusta 133
Venus' looking glass 136
Verbascum blattaria 118
lychnites 119
nigrum 118
phlomoides 118
pulverulentum 118
thapsus 118
Verbenaceae 109
Verbena officinalis 109
Veronica anagallis-aquatica 120
arvensis 120
austriaca 119
beccabunga 121
(catenata) 120
chamaedrys 119
filiformis 121
fruticans 120
hederifolia 119
montana 121
officinalis 119
persica 119
scutellata 121
serpyllifolia 120
spicata 120
verna 120
Vervain 109
Vetch, Bush 58
Common 58
Crown 61
Horseshoe 61
Kidney 59
Tufted 58
Upright 58
Wood 58
Yellow 59
Vetchling, Bitter 62
Grass 62
Meadow 62
Yellow 62
Vicia cracca 58
hirsuta 59
lutea 59
orobus 58
sativa 58
sepium 58
sylvatica 58
Vinca major 102
minor 102
Vincetoxicum officinale 102
Viola arvensis 79
canina 78
hirta 78
odorata 78
palustris 78
persicifolia 78
reichenbachiana 78
riviniana 78
rupestris 78
tricolor 79
Violaceae 78–9
Violet, Bog 78
Common dog 78
Early dog 78
Hairy 78
Heath 78
Marsh 78
Sweet 78
Teesdale 78
Water 98
Viscum album 14

Wahlenbergia hederacea 135
Wallflower 36
Wall rocket, Annual 37
Water chestnut 80
Watercress 41
Fool's 89
Water dropwort 89
Fine-leaved 89
Hemlock 89
Parsley 89
Water lily, Fringed 102
White 27
Yellow 27
Water milfoil 83
Alternate-leaved 83
Spiked 83
Whorled 83
Watermint 112
Water pepper 17
Water plantain, Common 156
Floating 156
Lesser 156
Parnassus-leaved 156
Water soldier 157
Water starwort 109
Weld 45
Whitlow grass, Alpine 39
Common 39
Hoary 39
Yellow 39
Whortleberry, Bog 94
Willow, Creeping 12
Dwarf 12
Willowherb, Alpine 80
American 81
Broad-leaved 80
Great 81
Hoary 81
Marsh 80
Rosebay 80
Wintercress 41
Wintergreen 92
Chickweed 97
One-flowered 92
Round-leaved 92
Toothed 92
Umbellate 92
Yellow 92
Woad 44
Wolffia arrhiza 181
Woodruff 103
Blue 103
Wood sorrel 67
Wormwood 155
Field 155
Sea 155
Woundwort, Downy 111
Field 111
Hedge 111
Limestone 111
Marsh 111
Yellow 111

Yarrow 154
Yellowcress, Great 40
Marsh 40
Yellow rattle 125
Yellow wort 101

Zostera marina 158
(noltii) 158

Further reading

For more detailed descriptions consult:
Flora Europaea ed. T.G. Tutin and others (CUP)
Flora of the British Isles A.R. Clapham, T.G. Tutin and E.F. Warburg (CUP)
Flowers of Europe O. Polunin (OUP)
Wild Flowers of Britain and Northern Europe R.G. Fitter, A. Fitter and M. Blamey (Collins)